# ENJOY IT

## BUSINESS

THE 21 STEP GUIDE

## SUCCESSION &

TO YOUR SUCCESSION

## EXIT PLANNING

· · · · · · · · · · · · · · · · · · · ·

## Craig West

Published by:
Boolarong Press
38/1631 Wynnum Road
Tingalpa Qld 4173
Australia.
www.boolarongpress.com.au

First published 2018

A catalogue record for this book is available from the National Library of Australia

ISBN: 978 1 925522 92 1

Editor: Amelia Stuckey, Words Unstuck

Typeset in Museo Sans 10pt by Boolarong Press

Printed and bound in China by Everbest Printing Investment Limited

**Disclaimer**

# CONTENTS

**Craig West**

Succession Plus Pty Ltd
Level 3, 50 York St
Sydney NSW 2000
www.successionplus.com.au

# INTRODUCTION

As an accountant from a public practice background and a strategic business adviser, I've been helping businesses for over 20 years. As well as that, I have studied and worked on a Master's degree in taxation law, specifically around capital gains tax, and more specifically around the sale of businesses. So I've spent a lot of time advising accounting firms on the issue of capital gains tax, particularly around exit.

What I found as a result of doing that, is there are a lot of businesses who make really bad exits, either failing completely or exit with bad outcomes, wrong pricing, wrong structure, or paid too much tax etc. There are also a number of businesses that were badly prepared, or not prepared at all for their exit. That led me to realise my passion for finding out why that was the case and doing something about it.

My boutique advisory practice, Succession Plus, helps mid-market business owners design and implement a business succession and exit plan to maximise sale value on exit. Our practice is probably the largest consulting practice specifically focused on succession and exit planning around Australia.

I am one of a few accredited exit planning advisers in Australia. I have been focused on Business Succession and Exit planning since 2009, so I am well placed to help you realise the goals you set for your business sale or succession.

The baby boomer generation started to reach their 65th birthdays in 2011, and over 5,000 Australians per week will turn 65 in the next 17 years. The baby boomers are what is driving the number of business owners who are approaching retirement. The average age of small business owners in Australia is 58, and it is estimated that over 50,000 small business owners will be looking to 'exit' each year, that is to sell the business or pass it on to the next generation. Over 50%, unfortunately, will exit due to death, illness, divorce, dispute, financial distress, bankruptcy or other unforeseen events.

Many business owners expect the sale of their business to fund their retirement, with over 30% reliant on it as the primary source. Many are concerned about their level of superannuation following the GFC and the volatile markets of recent years. We know that since 2008, when the GFC occurred, almost half of the business owners have delayed their retirement.

With so many business owners in weak financial positions looking to sell, and a lack of cashed-up buyers in the market, it's more important than ever to plan your business exit to extract the highest possible value. You can't just start to think about it when you turn 64 — if you don't plan, you get a poor price. But a good succession plan is a win-win for everyone — you get the best price, the buyer gets a good business and your customers and staff are looked after. About 34% of retired business owners do not have an adequately funded retirement.

At Succession Plus we take a holistic view to succession planning, looking at your business and personal goals and putting processes and systems in place to help you reach the best outcome, offering expert advice in management, taxation, employee incentives and accounting issues.

We've identified a number of steps that you can take to dramatically improve the performance and preparedness of your business, and hence the value on exit. We take you through those steps over a number of years as you go through the gradual stages of transition.

If you have been working hard in your business for many years to create wealth for you and your family, this book will help you to realise the full potential of all your efforts and investment. These are the rewards you set out to achieve. I don't try to give you a one size fits all or a 'do it yourself' manual, but you'll get an understanding of the scope and processes involved in successful succession and exit planning. If you are close to retirement or need to exit quickly, you may not be able to go through all the steps. But I'll steer you towards some crucial quick fixes to help you get prepared.

**Craig West**

# PROLOGUE

"If you are looking to build your business and exit, maximising value and ensuring the business continues successfully then this 21 step guide should be your bible — it is a simple and practical process to work through to ensure you are able to 'begin with the end in mind'. It is not too early to start — follow the steps outlined in the book by our own mentored CEO and exit planning guru Craig West and you are far more likely to exit successfully."

**Mark Bouris AM — Entrepreneur, Innovator, Author and Academic**

"Exit planning should be part of every business owner's strategic business plan. We should always be prepared to get hit by that proverbial truck. A functional exit plan must take a three-pronged approach to maximise value, plan for tax, estate planning and financial planning, and create a blueprint for your business and personal life.

Don't put off establishing your exit plan till tomorrow. Start today to maximise the value of your life on this earth by reading this book."

**Peter G. Christman, CEPA — The Original Exit Planning Coach and Mentor; CEO, The Christman Group — Value Enhancement**

"As the current President and CEO of the Exit Planning Institute I am often asked "How do I know if this is the right year to sell my company?" Timing the market perfectly is almost impossible. Exiting is not the end; it's the beginning of your next life. Plan for what you are going to do after the exit and make sure you have discussed the plan with trusted advisers, family, and friends.

If you are prepared, this may be your year. If you are not prepared, choose to take the next year or two to get prepared or risk ending up in the category of those who regretted selling. Succession Plus will help you to choose your time and maximise your results on exit."

**Christopher M. Snider, CEPA — Founder/President of Aspire Management; CEO/President of the Exit Planning Institute**

# WHAT IS BUSINESS SUCCESSION AND EXIT PLANNING ALL ABOUT?

Most people go into business not only to earn an annual income but, more importantly, to ultimately extract the wealth created with a lump sum to fund their retirement or next venture. But many don't think about how to exit their business until it's nearly time to retire. Worse, many find they are forced to sell or leave their business suddenly due to illness, disability, debt, bankruptcy, legal disputes or divorce.

You can't just put up a 'for sale' price on your business and expect that someone will come along and pay you the price you want. And if you do just put an advertisement in the paper or online, don't think that the price you get represents the true value of your business.

For many Australians the family home is their greatest asset. For business owners, the business may be the largest asset with the family home second. Yet many business owners will spend more time and effort preparing the family home for sale than their business. Most of us wouldn't just do a quick tidy up two weeks before the auction of our home and hope for the best. Selling a business, just like starting a business, requires a strategic succession plan, whether you plan to sell to family, employees or complete strangers. Otherwise you risk losing the long-term value of the investment that you have worked hard to create.

Understanding the three key factors of Business Succession and Exit Planning is critical to developing a successful plan — the co-ordination and preparation of the three factors is what ultimately leads to a successful exit.

- **The Business** — most businesses are not exit or sale ready, they are owner dependent and often lack effective systems and processes, they are run like small business — even though they may be quite large.
- **The Owner/s** — most baby boomer business owners are very strongly "attached" to their business — they identify with the business in what is called role-identity fusion. They need time and space to get comfortable about what the exit actually looks like and importantly what does life after the business mean.

- **The Money** — the business, the owner/s and their finances are often complicated and interwoven and therefore hard to separate — The Exit Planning Institute estimates that up to 90% of an owner's wealth is tied up in and linked to the business — this needs to be resolved before an exit can take place, and to ensure the owner and their family are adequately funded for retirement.

A strategic succession plan is a vision of the future, broken into the steps you need to take to achieve that vision. To maximise the value of your business on exit, you have to plan your exit long before it happens. This will allow you time for a smooth transition, but it will also give you much better security should anything unexpected happen to you, the other shareholders or your family members.

Business Succession Planning is a holistic process to help you align your personal and financial goals with your business performance and value. We help you to identify the current position and value of your business, the price you need for your business sale to meet your personal objectives, and then develop a strategy to help you breach the gap. The process from planning to exit may need five to ten years. Our aim is to have your business adequately prepared, and at peak performance to ensure you get the best return. If you are passing the business on to family members, we help you to put processes in place to make sure the business doesn't crumble the minute you hang up your keys. We will explain to you that WHO buys your business is a key factor in the price that you achieve, and help you to position your business so that you can attract the best buyer.

The most successful business succession plans are those that have been carefully and slowly considered over a period of time, are implemented gradually, constantly monitored and reviewed, have realistic strategic outcomes and "Begin with the end in mind".

## 21-Step Process

We use and recommend a five-stage process, all focused around value — identity, protect, maximise, extract and manage value. All of these stages have a number of key steps, 21 in all, designed to effectively prepare the business, the owner and the financial position to maximise business value and achieve a successful exit.

This process has been developed over time — when I first published Enjoy It in 2006 our process had only 9 steps, mainly focused on preparing the business, but as we worked with clients and learned more about their needs and the issues that were stopping them from being successful the process was further developed into 11, then 15 and finally 21 steps — the process now covers all of the key issues — business, personal and financial to ensure maximum success.

The process allows time and space for owners to get very clear on what Business Succession and Exit Planning means to them — for many it is not about the money, but more about preserving their legacy, looking after staff, customers and suppliers, and the process needs to firstly identify the key drivers and aspirations of the founders and secondly, provide a mechanism for them to be successful in achieving those key goals and outcomes.

To fully implement the 21 steps, we typically work with clients over a 12 to 18 month period (and with some clients much longer) and we always work closely with the clients' key advisers — accountant, financial planner, lawyers, bankers etc. This will help speed up the process and ensure the best possible result. This is very much a trusted adviser relationship and we work closely with the owners, family members, key employees and other stakeholders to balance interest and ensure all business succession and exit planning needs are met.

This book takes you through 21 steps to exiting your business over five stages:
- Stage One: Identify Value
- Stage Two: Protect Value
- Stage Three: Maximise Value

- Stage Four: Extract Value
- Stage Five: Manage Value

Each stage may take months or years depending on your personal goals, your situation, your business readiness and your industry.

| Stage One:<br>Identify Value | STEP 1: Goals and Outcomes |
| | STEP 2: Fact Find |
| | STEP 3: Stage One Report — INSIGHTS |
| Stage Two:<br>Protect Value | STEP 4: Financial Planning |
| | STEP 5: Unplanned Events |
| | STEP 6: De-Risking |
| Stage Three:<br>Maximise Value | STEP 7: Exit Options |
| | STEP 8: Strategic Planning Business Model |
| | STEP 9: Strategic Financials |
| | STEP 10: Systems and Procedures |
| | STEP 11: Marketing and Sales |
| | STEP 12: Corporate Governance |
| | STEP 13: Ownership Mindset |
| | STEP 14: Peak Performance Trust |
| | STEP 15: Management Succession |
| Stage Four:<br>Extract Value | STEP 16: Tax Planning |
| | STEP 17: Documentation |
| | STEP 18: Liquidity Event |
| Stage Five:<br>Manage Value | STEP 19: Ongoing Investment Planning |
| | STEP 20: Asset Protection |
| | STEP 21: Estate Planning |

## The M3 Framework

At Succession Plus we use the 21-Step Process, however it is interesting to have a look at some new research around the M3 Framework that has recently come out of the United States. We will compare it to the 21-Steps. You will see an overlap with our 21-step process, and you'll see that there are some steps in our process that are purely business, or purely money, or about oneself, but most of them have some sort of overlap and interconnectedness between the various parts of the M3 Framework.

M3 Framework was published in 2016 by a group called Orange Kiwi, who are the experts in the psychology of entrepreneurs at significant points of transition and exit.

If you look at our first step, it's about goals and outcomes. This is about legacy, vision, and mission. What is it that you really want to achieve from entering into a succession plan? Then we examine the business, perform some fact finding (Step 2) and we do a stage one report (Step 3), which analyses the business and assesses the risks, and opportunities, the growth strategies etc. It also overlaps into money as we look at the assets, liabilities, and insurances, and make sure that they are managed together properly. We then move into financial planning (step 4), which is purely about your money and wealth situation, and then into unplanned events (Step 5), which is a combination of business and money. Stage 3 (Steps 7 − 15) examines the business. At that point we will know what the outcome is, what the goal is, what your exit strategy looks like and what you are actually trying to achieve.

The next issue to think about is the actual transaction, which occurs at step 18 after performing some planning. Firstly, tax planning, which affects both money and self, maybe sometimes the business as well. Documentation must be addressed, which is mainly a business and money issue in the M3 Framework. We move towards post-exit stage 5 (Steps 19-21), what do we do about our money, where do we invest it, how do we protect our assets and estate planning?

## Underlying principles of the M3 Framework

There are some underlying principles that we need to understand. Firstly, business owners are hardwired to build and run a business. A business owner's life, business, and wealth are interwoven, and they are not easily separated. Significant transitions expose owners and their businesses to both internal and external threats and challenges.

Exploiting opportunities and successfully exiting requires a substantial change for owners, for their families, and for the business.

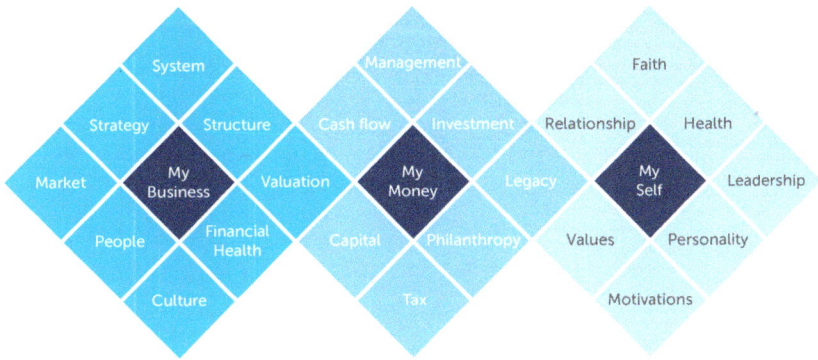

The M3 Framework has three headings, as you can see in the illustration — My Business, My Money and My Self — with eight boxes surrounding them. These are the issues that build the business.

## My Business

The issues in the My Business box are straight forward in terms of the types of things that we talk to business owners about all the time, such as:
- improve your systems
- document and build your strategy
- look at your structure overall

- look at the market that your business operates in
- assess the market environment — is it growing, shrinking, or likely to be disrupted?
- valuation — what's the business worth? how do we know how much it's worth?
- how are your people managed?
- have we got your culture and engagement piece in place?
- what does the financial health of the business actually look like?

## My Money

The next section is My Money. The individual's money and the management of finances, cash flow, both business and personal are examined. You will see from the illustration that there is some overlap.

Investments will also be assessed. Are there investments outside the business? Once this is established we can start to think about what sort of legacy you might leave. There is an overlap with legacy to the next section. What about capital? How is it managed? Where is it invested? Philanthropy is becoming more common for Australian business owners, such as setting up a philanthropic trust to contribute money towards the grandchildren's education, or to a local charity, or community group, etc.

Taxation is another big issue in terms of money and personal finance. The step between My Business and My Money is the valuation. What is the business worth? Once we know that, we can use it or take advantage of it when we are starting to think about transitioning from the business to the money.

## My Self

The last step, and the important part around the psychology of succession, is My Self. You will see from the illustration that legacy links My Money and My Self. What can you do with the money that you have generated out of the business? What sort of legacy can I leave? But in terms of My Self, some more serious topics for the individual are assessed, such as relationships, health, leadership, values, personality, and motivations.

## Legacy

Legacy is about what the owner can hand on to another generation. Sometimes these can be tangible things like money or maybe the business. Business owners who care about their legacy have an opportunity to craft the type of legacy that they want to leave as part of their exit. The most obvious example of that is passing the business on to the next generation. But sometimes, it's not about that, sometimes it's about the brand and reputation.

The succession and exit plan can be designed to match that legacy. Once you discuss what it actually looks like to build a legacy, we can map that into a succession and exit strategy as part of an overall plan.

## Values

Values are the owner's beliefs that shape how they live and work. They relate directly to the owner's success. In exit planning you often see behaviours like self-sabotage, or an inability to make decisions. A simple stalling or pausing of the process because the owner simply cannot make a decision to go one way or the other is not uncommon. These behaviours link to the owners' value systems.

## Motivation

Motivation is also important. Everybody is driven by certain motivational desires which must be satisfied in order to have psychological health. What we need to think about, as we transition owners through, is that motivations complicate the process by leading to clashes and pitfalls that can actually sabotage our exit strategy altogether, which obviously creates some problems.

## Relationships

Succession can shift relationships away from those that the owners used to work with, to other kinds of relationships. As advisers we need to be aware of these changes.

## Personality

Business owners are complicated and unique individuals. They have developed many different skill sets and behaviours to grow and manage their business. But most owners are wired a certain way, to build the business. Whilst that's a big strength when you're building your business, it actually also has a downside, most critically at significant points of change or transition during succession.

We need to get an understanding of the owner's natural tendencies and their natural incarnations, because that will allow us to then leverage those strengths and manage the weaknesses through the transition.

## Leadership

There are three different types of leadership that owners operate within. They operate in the business as a CEO or the Founder or the Managing Director. They operate in their family relationships — they may be the father, mother, grandfather, daughter, or the sister and themselves. There are different leadership tensions, that come into play when you start to look at all of those together.

The following diagram shows where our 21-Step process overlaps with the M3 Framework.

| | 21 STEPS | M3 | |
|---|---|---|---|
| **Stage One:** Identify Value | **STEP 1:** Goals and Outcomes | My Self | My Money |
| | **STEP 2:** Fact Find | My Business | My Money |
| | **STEP 3:** Stage One Report — INSIGHTS | My Business | |
| **Stage Two:** Protect Value | **STEP 4:** Financial Planning | My Money | |
| | **STEP 5:** Unplanned Events | My Business | My Money |
| | **STEP 6:** De-Risking | My Business | |
| **Stage Three:** Maximise Value | **STEP 7:** Exit Options | My Business | |
| | **STEP 8:** Strategic Planning Business Model | My Business | |
| | **STEP 9:** Strategic Financials | My Business | |
| | **STEP 10:** Systems and Procedures | My Business | |
| | **STEP 11:** Marketing and Sales | My Business | |
| | **STEP 12:** Corporate Governance | My Business | |
| | **STEP 13:** Ownership Mindset | My Business | |
| | **STEP 14:** Peak Performance Trust | My Business | |
| | **STEP 15:** Management Succession | My Business | |
| **Stage Four:** Extract Value | **STEP 16:** Tax Planning | My Money | My Self |
| | **STEP 17:** Documentation | My Business | My Money |
| | **STEP 18:** Liquidity Event | My Business | My Money |
| **Stage Five:** Manage Value | **STEP 19:** Ongoing Investment Planning | My Money | My Self |
| | **STEP 20:** Asset Protection | My Money | My Self |
| | **STEP 21:** Estate Planning | My Money | My Self |

## Why is now a good time to think about business succession and exit planning?

As any financial planner will tell you, the average amount needed to fund retirement in Australia is at least $1 million. We are living longer than ever before, and life expectancy is constantly improving, so we need more money to fund retirement — unless of course we wish to rely on a government pension. An Australian male who is 50 years old in 2018 can expect to live until 82 years old and females to 85 years. That's potentially around 20 years to fund in retirement.

According to the KPMG and Family Business Australia and Private Business Survey 2015 (RMIT University), the average age of family business owners is 58 years. Almost half of business owners surveyed see themselves working in the business beyond 65 years of age, with over 30% saying they will be relying solely on the sale of their business to fund their retirement.

The baby boomer generation began turning 65 in 2011, and from now until 2030 over 5,000 Australians will hit retirement age each week. It is estimated that over the next decade the retirement of family business owners will see the transfer of approximately $1.6 trillion in wealth, which surely must make succession planning one of the most significant issues facing small to medium enterprise (SME) owners. Yet incredibly, despite 61% of business owners surveyed admitting their businesses are not sale or succession ready, 52.2% do not intend to do anything about it over the next twelve months.

The Global Financial Crisis and the more recent European crisis has had a negative impact on market sentiment around the globe. Cash is harder to access, and potential buyers drive a harder bargain, putting pressure on valuation multiples (more about this later). Many baby boomers are delaying retirement because the value of their nest egg has diminished, whether that is in the share market, superannuation, real estate or the value of their business. With estimates of 50,000 businesses for sale each year for the foreseeable future, the small

### Australian Population Turning 65 Years of Age - Weekly

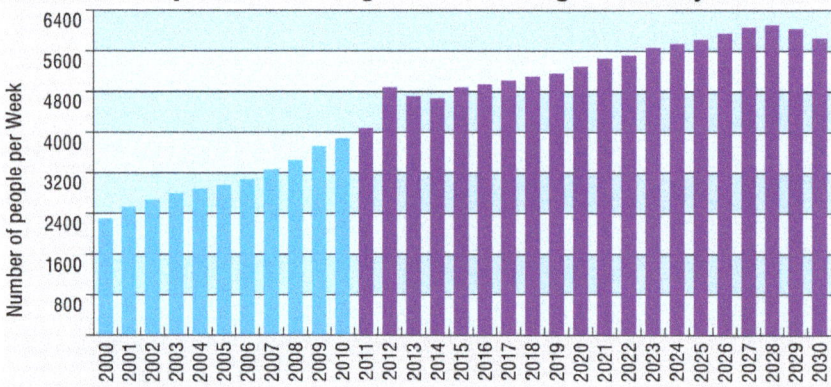

business market may become flooded, which will put further pressure on business values. Many business owners will simply close the door.

At Succession Plus we are finding that there are some cashed up buyers and companies out there, with Australian listed companies having the highest cash to assets ratio in nearly 30 years. So, they are using that cash to fund growth through acquisition, making acquisitions of much smaller businesses than they might have ten years ago. But the competition in the market can mean that buyers are a little more particular about the businesses they buy, so the businesses need to be better prepared if they are to find the right buyer and the right price.

According to an article in May 2016 in the Sydney Morning Herald, Australian companies are among the world's biggest cash hoarders. Domestic corporations are more inclined than most to keep cash on deposit or in government bonds as a buffer against deteriorating conditions or a stash for opportunities as they arise.

The RBA has also noted a broad-based secular rise in corporate cash at Australian companies over the past 25 years. Using Australian Bureau of Statistics data, it found that the aggregate cash-to-assets ratio had climbed from 9.5 per cent in 1990 to 13.5 per cent in 2015.

The ratio is different to the OECD comparison because the ABS data excludes non-listed companies and is asset-weighted, meaning smaller companies that tend to hold more cash as a ratio of total assets are given less weight in the final figure.

"The trend increase in the cash holdings of publicly listed companies can be largely explained by changes in observable company characteristics," the RBA says.

"In particular, relative to their counterparts of 25 years ago, publicly listed companies today have better growth opportunities and are more likely to operate in 'risky' industries, and these characteristics are correlated with higher levels of corporate cash."

The authors also found a dispersion in the concentration of cash among Australian companies, meaning the trend applies across all company sizes.

## Sale of Businesses

The following graph shows that the volume of listed businesses for sale continued to grow marginally to the quarter ending December 2017.

**Figure 1**    Volume trend % of listed businesses

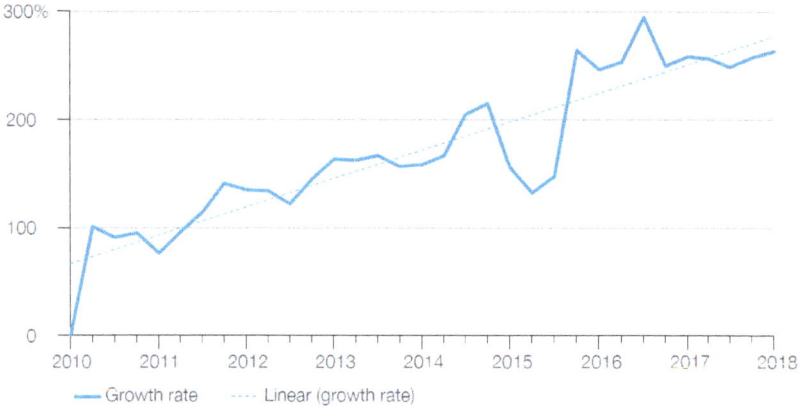

Despite a marginal gain in the proportion of listed businesses for sale in the December 2017 quarter, the following graph shows a marginal decline in the average VMB-RMIT Index values across the four business sectors and the whole sample.

**Figure 2**    Mean VMB-RMIT Index by size of businesses

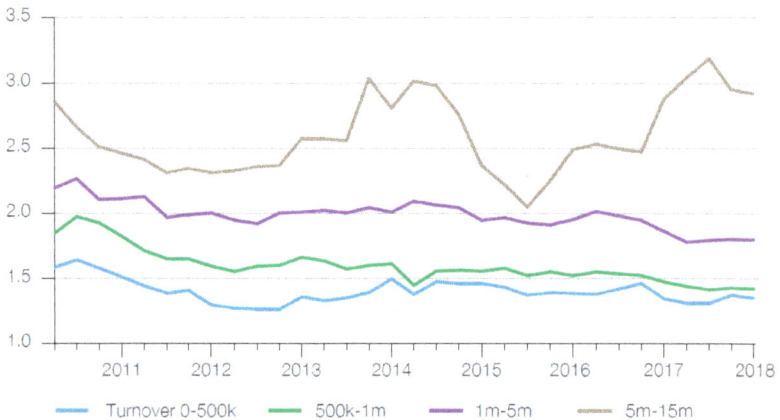

SUCCESSION

As a responsible business owner, it makes sense to start your exit strategy when you are 'at your peak' — ideally when the business is doing well and you have the energy and enthusiasm to make the appropriate changes. Many business owners are finding it hard to keep up with technology and the new competitive environment that brings. If you feel defeated and lose market share your business value will diminish, so start the process when you still have some fight and passion for your business. You may need to grow your business to make it more attractive to a buyer, or you may need to transition client relationships gradually to a general manager.

In the current market the best chance of success is to be prepared and plan ahead. If you always "Begin with the end in mind", you are much better prepared for making the right decisions along the way, following the steps towards your long-term vision. If you start preparation early, you will get a deeper understanding of the potential value of your business and have the time to make positive changes to increase your chances of a good sale.

On a financial level, a well-planned business exit will not only enable you to attract a higher sell price, it will also let you minimise tax on the proceeds, using staged payments, superannuation contributions and taking full advantage of tax concessions. If you put your business up for sale suddenly, you may be met with a tax bill just when you don't need it.

According to the Australian Bureau of Statistics (ABS, 2017), there are 2.238 million active businesses in Australia as at December 2017. Approximately 868,250 (38.8%) of these businesses are small to medium sized businesses (SMEs). This is shown in the following pie chart. The following bar graphs highlight the number of businesses based on turnover as well as by the number of employees.

About 70% of privately owned businesses in Australia are owned by families, and baby boomers own the majority. Baby-boomers are those people born following World War 2 between 1946 and 1964.

Finally, if you do have to exit from your business unexpectedly due to poor health or other issues, the further you are down your exit plan, the better the outcome is likely to be for you and your loved ones.

A poorly planned or poorly executed succession will often lead to dispute, poor customer experiences, business decline and financial pressure. Is that what you have worked all these years for?

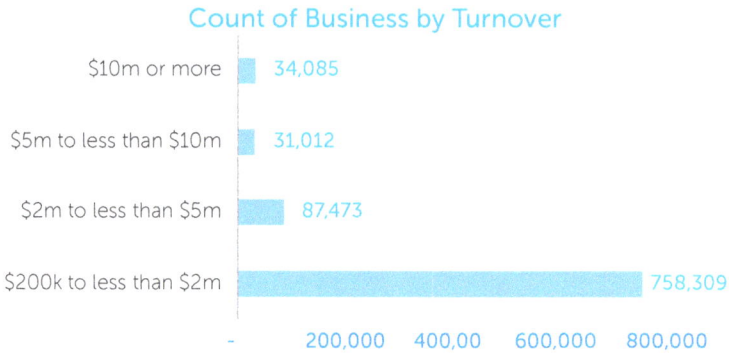

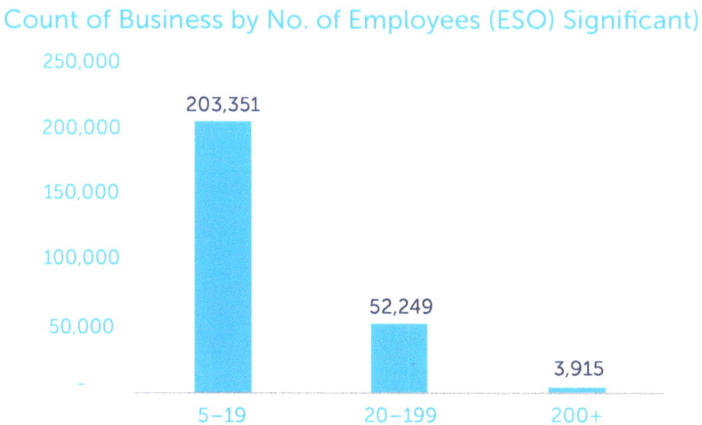

## Businesses by Employment Size

Out of **2.238** million businesses in Australia:

**38.8**% Employing businesses

**61.2**% Non-employing businesses

## Count of Business by Turnover

| Turnover | Count |
|---|---|
| $10m or more | 34,085 |
| $5m to less than $10m | 31,012 |
| $2m to less than $5m | 87,473 |
| $200k to less than $2m | 758,309 |

-   200,000   400,00   600,000   800,000

## Count of Business by No. of Employees (ESO) Significant)

| No. of Employees | Count |
|---|---|
| 5–19 | 203,351 |
| 20–199 | 52,249 |
| 200+ | 3,915 |

Source: Australian Bureau of Statistics, 2017

As business owners approach retirement, most will cease to own their businesses, however, up to 83% have no defined or documented business succession or exit plan. The KPMG report on family business states that 76% of family businesses intend to appoint a new CEO in the next five years and further that 72% expect to have some transfer of ownership in the next five years. This represents a large number of transitions over the next ten years and a large amount of wealth to be "transferred". The transfer of ownership represents a significant stage in entrepreneurial activity. It is through this transition that the founders remove themselves from the business they own. This relates to ownership, decision making and generating a capital surplus for their efforts.

## Identifying Value

I am going to take you through our unique 21 step process that will help you to reach a successful business exit. This is not a do it yourself process; you will need to get some help and advice along the way. But the better you understand the process, the more you can get involved, take on the tasks that you can do, and have clear expectations of the people who advise you on the rest. In the introduction I've focused on why planning is important, and consistent with that, I'll go through the initial steps, in the Identifying Value stage in more detail. Once you are clear about where you are trying to head and why, getting there is a whole lot easier.

## Case Study

The following case study will take you through each step to exit your business through the five stages. The material includes the intellectual property of Succession Plus Australia Pty Limited who claims copyright ownership, including the detailed explanation of the 21-Step Business Succession and Exit Planning methodology, tools and templates used to deliver that process with business owners. This material must not be reproduced or distributed without the express written permission of the owner.

## Background

Mr & Mrs Smith (both baby boomers in their late 60s) run a light manufacturing business in suburban Sydney. The business was "inherited" from Mrs Smith's father in 2000, who started the business from scratch after World War II, originally operating from his garage.

About 18 years ago they also sold 30% of the business to Rod Jones — the Sales Manager — a brilliant young salesman who has been a great employee and director and added considerable value to the business over time.

### Existing Structure

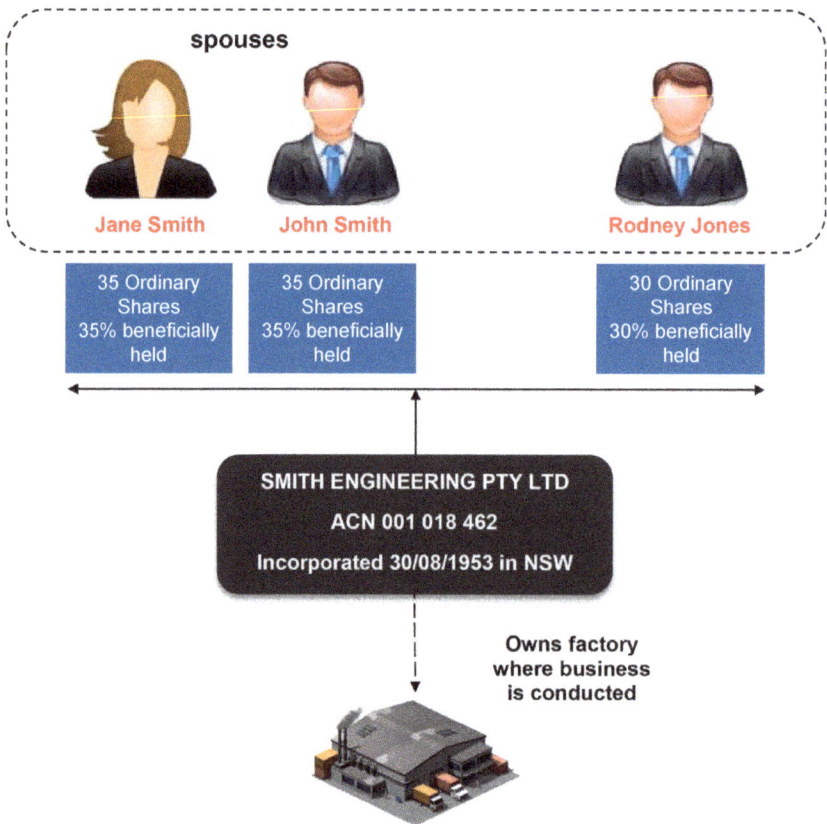

| spouses | | |
| --- | --- | --- |
| Jane Smith | John Smith | Rodney Jones |
| 35 Ordinary Shares 35% beneficially held | 35 Ordinary Shares 35% beneficially held | 30 Ordinary Shares 30% beneficially held |

**SMITH ENGINEERING PTY LTD**

**ACN 001 018 462**

**Incorporated 30/08/1953 in NSW**

**Owns factory where business is conducted**

The company makes aluminium display stands for retail stores and has been stable and profitable for many years with several long-term and loyal customers. Several years ago (August 2006), the Smiths purchased the factory from the landlord. The company owns several large machines used in the factory acquired over several years and the premises has been modified and customised to suit production.

## Business Succession

The Smiths' son, Gary, is the Production/Manufacturing Manager but they both know that he cannot run the business without help and expertise — he is very good practically but less so managing finance. During 2015, he was appointed company General Manager and took over the day to day management of the business. Following this move, gross profit dropped nearly 10% and net profits were down by $300,000 and several key staff left as a result of his management style.

Both Mr and Mrs Smith are currently in good physical and mental health but they are getting older and "slowing down."

## Financial Summary

The company has been slowly but consistently growing and currently has a turnover of approximately $8 million and is quite profitable with the 2016 Financial Year producing a NOPAT of $958,000.

**SMITH ENGINEERING**

|  | 2013 | 2014 | 2015 | 2016 |
|---|---|---|---|---|
| Sales Revenue | $5,771,884 | $6,561,310 | $7,481,200 | $8,093,000 |
| Cost of Goods Sold | $3,173,500 | $3,377,800 | $4,501,740 | $4,101,720 |
| Gross Profit | $2,598,384 | $3,183,510 | $2,979,460 | $3,991,280 |
| Gross Margin (%) | 45.02% | 48.52% | 39.83% | 49.32% |
| Overheads | $1,770,102 | $1,883,319 | $2,109,344 | $2,504,826 |
| EBIT | $828,282 | $1,300,191 | $870,116 | $1,486,454 |
| Interest Cost | $117,937 | $135,717 | $121,536 | $117,691 |
| Net Profit Before Tax | $710,345 | $1,164,474 | $748,580 | $1,368,763 |
| Tax | $213,104 | $349,342 | $224,574 | $410,629 |
| NOPAT | $497,242 | $815,132 | $524,006 | $958,134 |
|  | 8.6% | 12.4% | 7.0% | 11.8% |

In order to finalise a Business Succession and Exit Plan, they approached their financial adviser and accountants (who work in the same firm and have been advising the family for many years). Whilst the family knows they need to do something, they really are unsure what options are available.

## Solution

The owners agree to start the process with a Stage One Insights report giving them a comprehensive review and analysis of the various issues/value drivers before launching into a Strategic Succession Plan based on Succession Plus's 21-step process.

# STEP 1
# GOALS & OUTCOMES

The first step is deciding what outcome you want for your retirement from the business. It'll differ for everyone in terms of your financial and lifestyle goals, but there are a number of key factors to consider and discuss with your business advisers and financial planner. As we work through the steps in the book you'll get a better understanding of what is realistically achievable from your business, but we'll start by identifying the main drivers and influencers in your exit plan.

## 1.1 Initial Interview

Ask yourself the following questions. It might be useful to jot down your responses to discuss with your adviser.

1    Do you have a valuation/sales price in mind for your business?
2    Do you have personal/financial goals that your business sale needs to fund or make time for?
3    When do you want to leave the business?
4    Are you happy to stage your exit over several years?
5    Do you want a lump sum to retire with, or could you work with several payments over time?
6    Do you want to retain any ownership in the business?
7    Do you want to transition the business to a family member?
8    Do you have any key members of staff that would be keen to take on the business?
9    Do you have a potential/interested buyer in mind?
10   Do you have a view of what the business will look like after you retire?
11   Are you interested in leaving a legacy?
12   What is your vision for the business in 10 years' time?
13   What do you plan to do post retirement?

Answering those questions honestly may make you feel quite ready and comfortable, or you may realise you have never really thought about these things before, let alone know how to make them happen. Some of these questions will prompt you to consider whether you have a strong preference for one form of action versus another. Going through the succession planning process will help you to aim for your preferred action, whilst also preparing you and making your business better able to adapt to alternative routes if needed. Now that you have a big picture view of where you'd like to be, let's look a bit deeper into where you actually are.

## 1.2 Case Study

### *Welcome Pack*

Upon acceptance of the proposal, the immediate step is to issue a welcome letter, which provides an overview of the Stage One process, as well as lists down all the information required for the analysis. The welcome letter is sent through along with softcopies of the forms/tools in fillable PDF formats.

### Step 1 — Goals and Outcomes

As an initial step, the owners are asked to provide information around long-term goals to ensure the business strategy meets their preferred/chosen outcomes and also to ensure that their goals are compatible. The personal profile analysis is discussed in detail in section 13.4.

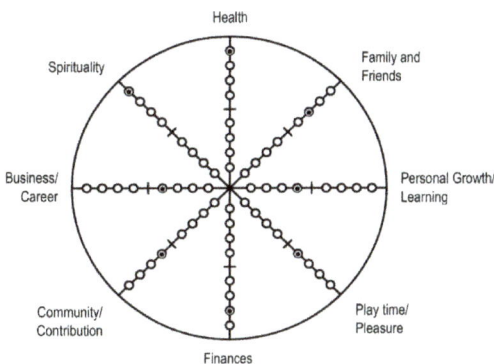

The "Wheel of Life" is one way to discover what Jane, Bob and Rodney value most in their lives and how satisfied they are with all areas of their life.

## Goal Setting Workbook — Jane Smith

Jane has identified that she values her:

1. faith
2. family
3. health.

If she won the lottery, she would make large donations to several charities and semi-retire.

Another question asked is what you would do if you found out you only had 6 months to live. Jane would retire immediately, volunteer to help out at her church, spend as much time as possible with her family and write a memoir. She would also have a living funeral.

Jane is then asked how satisfied she is in each area of the "Wheel of Life" and what she would need to do, to be completely satisfied.

These are summaried below:

- Financial — she is nearly completely satisfied
- Relationships with family and friends — Jane would like to spend more time with them, such as on a house boat on the Hawesbury River.
- Health — she feels good for an old lady
- Spare Time — she feels like she doesn't have any spare time
- Contributions to others — she would voluntary work like she used to
- Spiritual development — starting talk to God again
- Personal Growth/Learning — Jane might start reading one book a month
- Business/Career — Jane feels like she has achieved these goals.

## Goal Setting Workbook — John Smith

The three things John values most in life are his grandchildren, business and his boat. He would buy a holiday home up the coast if he won the lottery. If he only had 6 months to live, he would fish every day and see as much of the grandchildren as he could.

John was also asked to identify his level of satisfaction for all areas on the "Wheel of Life" diagram.

He was concerned about his health, particularly his cholesterol and his family history of diabetes.

He is most concerned with his Business/Career. To feel completely satisfied he needs help with a proper handover to Rodney.

The things that give him the greatest feeling of self-worth is building up his business when his father passed it onto him, as well as having a family.

## Goal Setting Workbook — Rodney Jones

Rodney values his family, good times and memories and a Royal Enfield motorcycle the most in life. If he won the lottery, Rodney would retire as soon as he could transition out without hurting the business. He would also go on a trip around the world with his family.

To feel completely satisfied with each section in the "Wheel of Life", he would need to achieve the following:

- Financial — have a lot more money in liquid assets
- Family/Friends — ensure his wife Pat is well.
- Health — exercise more
- Play time/Pleasure — spend more time playing golf and rugby, working too much
- Business/Career — he is happy.

# • STEP 2
# FACT FIND

We'll start with looking at your business to determine the value and identifying any issues, strengths and opportunities.

## 2.1 Discovering what your business is all about

With your exit planning adviser, you'll go through the following questions:

- What does the business currently look like?
- What would it be worth in its current state?
- What are some of the risks in the business?
- What are the opportunities in the future?
- What profit is the business currently making, and are your financials up to date?
- What do you need to do to prepare for due diligence?

## 2.2 A business versus a job

An important part of this process is establishing what you have to sell — do you have a business, or are you self-employed?

In some cases business owners who have started or bought a business have simply bought themselves a job. They may have bought a database or a few customer contracts (common in trades such as plumbing, mechanics), but the income is essentially derived from the business owner directly servicing clients. Robert Kiyosaki's definition of a job is 'Just Over Broke' because there's no equity value. The day you stop working, the money stops.

This type of business has little or no resale value, unless you can find a way to replace yourself in the business with at least the same results. A good way to determine whether or not you have 'a business' is to consider how long you could be removed from it without affecting operations. If you could take weeks off and the business would continue to survive and produce income, you have a business. If you've got a position where you have to be there all the time, you've got a job. The income stops when you stop.

It is important at this point to identify whether you have a 'job' so that you can spend time in your succession planning building a business, or making the most of what you have. An adviser will help determine the best path for you.

## 2.3 Case Study

The owners are asked to provide further business and background information when a welcome letter is issued.

### Benchmarking

The next step is to conduct a benchmarking analysis on your business as part of the Insights Report. You need to identify the roles each employee performs, how many staff perform that role and how many hours per annum that they carry out that particular role. The salary and superannuation amounts need to be allocated to each of these roles. This also needs to be done for all of the owners of your business.

### Addbacks

Further information is to be provided by the owners to "normalise" the earnings of the business. The following items are some examples of income and expenses to add back or adjust to the business earnings:

- Director's non-market salaries
- Superannuation above the minimum of 9.5%
- Unusual repair or maintenance cost
- Consultant's fees not in the ordinary course of business
- Once off purchase/expenses
- Profit/loss on sale of a fixed asset
- Rent of facilities at above or below market value
- Rent expense — where rent is not paid
- Donations/sponsorships
- Lawsuits and other legal fees
- Prepaid sales
- Future or past sale.

The table below lists the information required for our fact find:

| ITEM | INFORMATION / DOCUMENTATION REQUIRED | Check if supplied |
|---|---|---|
| | **Company Information** | |
| 1 | Benchmarking Questionnaire - attached | |
| 2 | "Mud map" of company structures (show all companies involved in report and how they connect plus ownership of each, if applicable). | |
| | | |
| | **Financial Information** | |
| 3 | Management Accounts 2017 (for *all* relevant entities) | |
| 4 | Financial Statements and Tax Returns – Last 5 Years | |
| 4.1 | Financial Statements and Tax Returns – year ended 30 June 2017 (for *all* relevant entities) | |
| 4.2 | Financial Statements and Tax Returns – year ended 30 June 2016 (for *all* relevant entities) | |
| 4.3 | Financial Statements and Tax Returns – year ended 30 June 2015 (for *all* relevant entities) | |
| 4.4 | Financial Statements and Tax Returns – year ended 30 June 2014 (for *all* relevant entities) | |
| 4.5 | Financial Statements and Tax Returns – year ended 30 June 2013 (for *all* relevant entities) | |
| 5 | Add backs Schedule – used to normalize income & expense - attached | |
| | | |
| | **Staffing Information** | |
| 6 | Staff listing by position/duties & salary summary (year ended 30 June 2017) | |
| | | |
| | **ASIC Information** | |
| 7 | Breakdown of ASIC Detail on Shareholding: Ownership Detail - attached) | |
| | | |
| | **Stakeholders Information** | |
| 8 | Completed Goal Setting Questionnaires (for every person who holds a current ownership stake in *any* of the relevant entities) – attached | |
| 9 | Completed Structuring Profile Questionnaires (for every person who holds a current ownership stake in *any* of the relevant entities) – attached | |
| 10 | Company Profile and Brochures | |
| 11 | Business Names Listing | |
| 12 | Income breakdown by type/area | |
| | | |
| | **Staffing Information** | |
| 13 | Organisational Chart | |
| | | |
| | **ASIC Information** | |
| 14 | ASIC Company Statement (most recent within past 12 months) | |
| 15 | Certificate of Company Registration | |
| 16 | Memorandum & Articles (or Company Constitution) | |
| 17 | Shareholders Agreements (if applicable) | |
| 18 | Buy/Sell Agreements & Funding Agreements (if applicable) | |

SUCCESSION

## • STEP 3

# STAGE ONE REPORT — INSIGHTS

The next step is comprehensive analysis and diagnosis — getting into the detail of your business, assessing it as it currently stands and identifying ways to increase the value. Then we'll prioritise the areas that need action.

## 3.1 Structural Review

First, we look at how your business has been set up and structured, for example whether you operate as a sole trader or have set up a limited company, partnership or family trust. We see many businesses that started 10 or more years ago that were set up as a shelf company, with husband and wife the only two shareholders. Husband and wife are probably also directors, which is fine when you first start out because it's quick, easy and cheap.

But over time the business grows, you purchase other assets such as equipment or real estate. Some companies buy the premises they operate out of, and the real estate is held in the trading entity, along with say a stake in another business or a significant piece of equipment, with no separation of risk and assets. Part of our job is to minimise the risks with the right ownership structure. To many people asset protection means, being able to control assets or have access to assets which they do not actually own, so that if they are sued the assets are not at risk. Common examples are assets being owned by a family company or trust, or being placed in the spouse's name.

The key is separation — wherever possible, quarantine the assets from the risk, especially capital appreciating assets like property, by creating completely separate structures. And where husband and wife are both directors, they are both at risk **individually**. So we need to find a way to protect them too. It's not that the wrong structure

has been set up, but that the business has changed over the years, has increased in value and taken on assets and risks, and that the original structure is no longer appropriate.

Another aspect of asset protection is having adequate insurance cover, and good systems in place to prevent faulty goods, negligence or injury. We also look at where we want those assets to end up. Perhaps you want to keep the business premises and rent it to the new owners to create an ongoing income stream. If so, you won't want it sitting in a trading entity, but more likely in a self-managed superannuation fund, trust or other structure.

Here we'll work closely with your financial planner to get the most benefit from your assets.

## 3.2 Financial Analysis

As an accountant I tend to focus on the financial analysis next, but I'd also argue that it's actually not the most important area in determining value. But we do need to get a good understanding of how the business is performing. We use a financial analysis tool to show the business owners a snapshot of the financial performance and the areas for improvement.

The following diagram shows a typical overview of the financial position of a small business. It assesses the business's profitability, cashflow, debt levels, efficiency, and highlights the good and bad with green ticks or red crosses. The tool focuses on measurements that are relevant to your business — in this example eleven measures were deemed not applicable, and eight were favourable, so the business owner can see clearly that they need to focus attention on improving the three unfavourable measures — net profit margin, debt levels and collecting cash from customers more quickly. This business scored a B+, which is above average for a small to medium business (refer to section 3.7).

It is important to know the key financial drivers and performance indicators at any stage of your business so that you can step in and make improvements (refer also to section 9.3 and 9.4). This is of

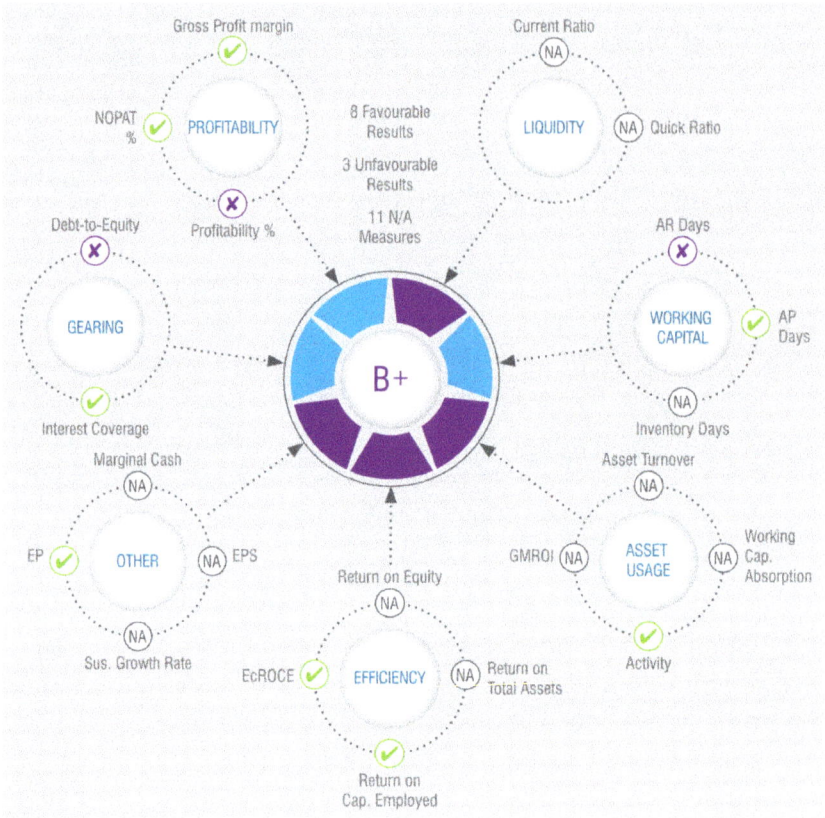

course crucial when you are preparing your business for sale. The potential buyer will look at the financial performance of your business, but also how well you manage the financial data, and how quickly you act on key financial indicators to improve performance.

## 3.3 Benchmarking and Profit Gap

Benchmarking is a process of comparing your business metrics with other similar businesses. Not many business owners think of benchmarking their business, and most do not have access to data to be able to do this. At Succession Plus we identify the key performance indicators in your business and benchmark them against industry averages to identify areas of improvement, or 'the profit gap' between where you are and where you could be.

Benchmarking uses largely financial data but also uses statistics such as the number of employees, floor space utilised, total equipment or assets. Some of these measures of efficiency don't stand out from your management accounts. But a buyer will want to understand how you are positioned in the market to assess your relative value.

If, for example, you operate an accounting firm, where your profit depends on billing time for services, benchmarking would look at billable hours, total fees earned per full time employee (or equivalent) and overheads. The graphs below show benchmark reporting for a professional services firm versus industry averages.

This firm's debt collection is slower than the industry average, which may lead to cashflow issues.

## Average debtor days

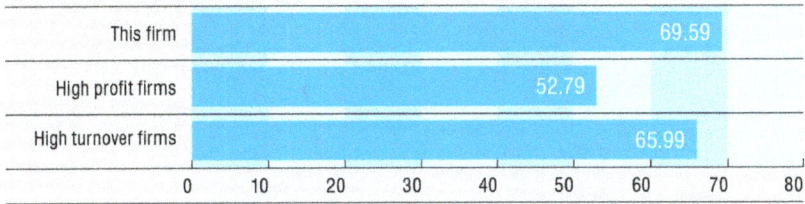

| | |
|---|---|
| This firm | 69.59 |
| High profit firms | 52.79 |
| High turnover firms | 65.99 |

0  10  20  30  40  50  60  70  80

This firm's average net profit after tax (NPAT) per principal is much lower than the industry average. While this may be largely driven by

## Average NPAT per principal

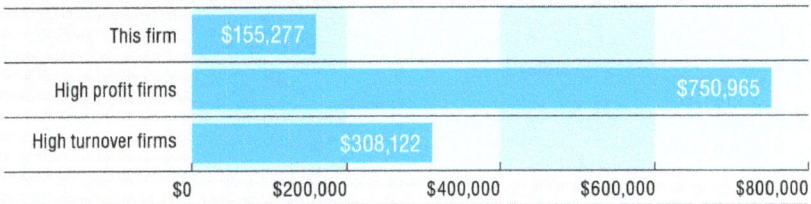

| | |
|---|---|
| This firm | $155,277 |
| High profit firms | $750,965 |
| High turnover firms | $308,122 |

$0  $200,000  $400,000  $600,000  $800,000

the size and profile of the firm, it prompts additional analysis into pricing, volume of work, utilisation of staff and costs.

This firm spends more of its total income on minor overheads than the industry average, which will put pressure on NPAT.

## Minor overheads as % total income

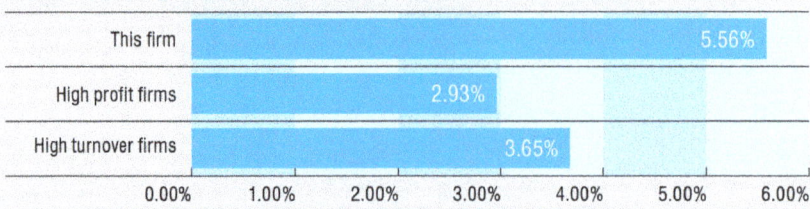

| | |
|---|---|
| This firm | 5.56% |
| High profit firms | 2.93% |
| High turnover firms | 3.65% |

0.00%  1.00%  2.00%  3.00%  4.00%  5.00%  6.00%

While the firm may be too small to reach the industry averages, benchmarking gives us a good starting point that highlights where we need to look deeper to improve the future performance of the business.

When we benchmarked one of our Sydney clients, a professional services firm, we found the IT costs were significantly higher than its industry competitors. Digging deeper, we saw that all of the firm's computers and systems were 15 years old, which meant the maintenance contractor was coming in almost every day to fix something. On the other hand, depreciation was much lower than the competitors as the assets were all fully written down long ago.

A buyer considering this business will need to factor in significant capital outlay to replace the IT assets, but can expect to spend less in maintenance costs as a result, therefore increasing profit.

When we benchmark a business we calculate the potential profit gap — the profit you could achieve if you were operating at industry average levels. On a simple level, if you produce a product at $1 and sell it at $2 you are making $1 or 50% margin. If your competitor is selling the same thing for $2 but it costs $0.75 to produce, he is making $1.25 or 62.5% margin. The profit gap is 12.5% or 25 cents. Benchmarking assumes that you should be able to operate at roughly the same level as industry averages.

Sometimes there is a significant gap between the current profitability and profitability that could be achieved at maximum efficiency. Once we work out where the business is over or underperforming or overspending, we focus on resolving individual issues to close the gap, improving profitability and value.

| Your Profit Gaps relative to the Most Profitable firms: | This Business | High Profit Firms Average | Profit Gap Relative to High Proft Firms |
|---|---|---|---|
| If you could achieve the average level of fees per person | | $245,000 | |
| then your firm's present fees of | $3,800,000 | | |
| would need a total personnel of | 15.51 | | |
| but you presently have total personnel of | 19 | | |
| so you are overstaffed by | | | 3.49 |
| and at your average salary cost per employee of | $65,000 | | |
| your salary-related Profit Gap is: | | | $226,837 |
| If you could achieve the average level of non-salary overheads | 25.80% | 24.00% | |
| you should reduce your overheads by | | | 1.8% |
| then on your present turnover of | $3,800,000 | | |
| you are over spending by | | | $68,400 |
| You asset turnover is presently | 1.90 | 2 | |
| but your current revenue of | $3,800,000 | | |
| suggests you should have assets of | | | $1,900,000 |
| Currently you have assets (net of any loans to owners) of | $2,100,000 | | |
| So you could look to reduce total assets by | | | $200,000 |
| If this could save you interest at, say, | 9.00% | | |
| Then you'd close a Profit Gap of: | | | $18,000 |

| Your total Profit Gap: | Relative to high profit firms |
|---|---|
| 1. Bringing your personnel numbers back could yield | $226,837 |
| 2. Reducing non-salary overheads could yield | $68,400 |
| 3. Reducing your investment in the firm could yield | $18,000 |
| So your total Profit Gap is | $313,237 |
| Which is ... of your current profit level | 43% |

## 3.4 Non-financial Analysis

Our non-financial evaluation is basically an interview process where we look at the operations of the business and determine where there is risk. We use a similar tool to score various areas of the business. It will be these areas that ultimately affect the multiple you can achieve on sale. But these are also the areas that are largely in your control, and some can be improved relatively easily.

Some of the interview questions are as follows:

1    Do you have an up to date company profile and website?
2    Do you have all of your intellectual property registered and up to date? For example business name registrations, trademarks, patents.
3    Are your financial statements, BAS, payroll and tax returns in order?
4    Do you have monthly or quarterly management accounts?
5    Do you have an annual budget for the current year?
6    Do you have monthly management meetings, and do you have minutes of those meetings?
7    Do you have robust accounting systems that allow you to run reports on top customers, top suppliers, debtors, creditors, KPIs?
8    Do you have employee agreements in place for all your employees?
9    Are you meeting your obligations re employees — leave balances, superannuation contribution, award rates, payroll tax, workers compensation?
10   Are all your vehicles registered, insured and lease payments up to date?
11   Do you have the lease agreements for your premises?
12   Are your company registration documents up to date? eg Articles of association, shareholder agreements etc.
13   Have you documented key processes, job descriptions and procedures (such as a safety manual, induction manual) in your business?

14 Do you have a board of directors or advisory board and do you communicate regularly?

15 Has your IT system been reviewed lately to ensure it meets your needs?

16 Do you have back-up facilities in place and a disaster recovery plan?

A prospective buyer will see the non-financial measures of your business as a reflection of how you manage your business — your attention to detail and compliance, your ability to plan and execute, how easily the business can operate without you, the quality of your staff, and whether they are locked into the business. They will also look not just at your financial performance, but how well you manage and use financial information.

The diagram below shows an architecture business with a C- rating. In the top left we have governance and compliance, and this

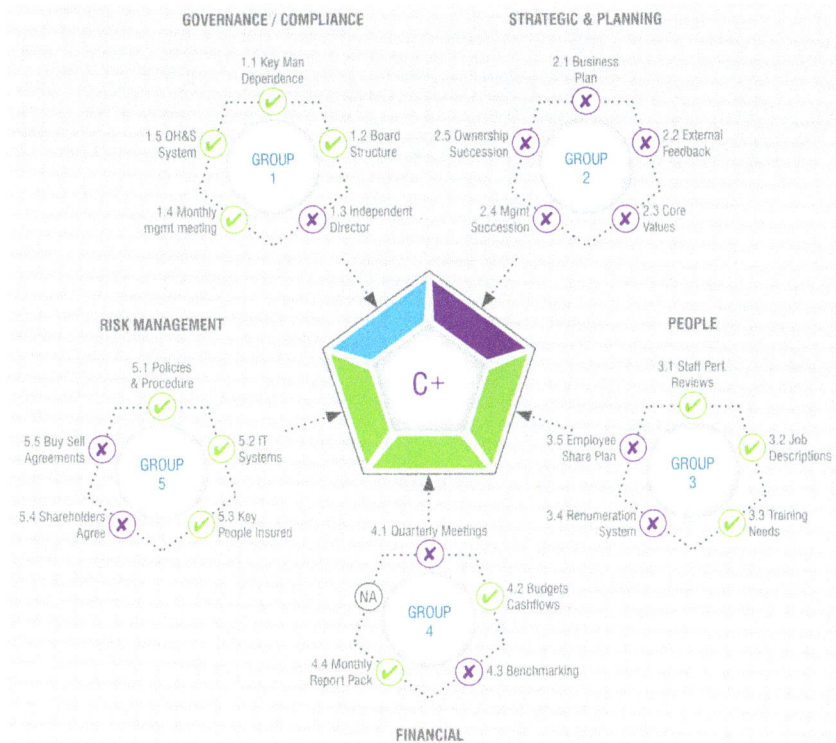

GOVERNANCE / COMPLIANCE

STRATEGIC & PLANNING

1.1 Key Man Dependence
1.5 OH&S System
1.2 Board Structure
GROUP 1
1.4 Monthly mgmt meeting
1.3 Independent Director

2.1 Business Plan
2.5 Ownership Succession
2.2 External Feedback
GROUP 2
2.4 Mgmt Succession
2.3 Core Values

RISK MANAGEMENT

PEOPLE

5.1 Policies & Procedure
5.5 Buy Sell Agreements
5.2 IT Systems
GROUP 5
5.4 Shareholders Agree
5.3 Key People Insured

C+

3.1 Staff Perf. Reviews
3.5 Employee Share Plan
3.2 Job Descriptions
GROUP 3
3.4 Renumeration System
3.3 Training Needs

4.1 Quarterly Meetings
NA
4.2 Budgets Cashflows
GROUP 4
4.4 Monthly Report Pack
4.3 Benchmarking

FINANCIAL

business has a tick for key man dependence. This is quite unusual in small to medium businesses, which are usually very dependent on the founders. In this business there are four architects, which means the business could continue to operate if one left.

This company is doing well in all areas of compliance except that it doesn't have an independent director, which would be an advantage to have further down the track to reduce perceived risk.

The company is performing less well in risk management and strategy. They have no shareholders or buy/sell agreement, which could cause quite significant issues if one partner leaves the business, gets sick or is hit by the proverbial bus.

Like many small companies this business has no business plan and no succession plan and they haven't had the business benchmarked. So, they don't really have a strong direction to determine the future value of the business. They also don't have a clear remuneration strategy or an employee share plan, which does expose some risk of staff turnover despite some good HR practices.

This diagram clearly shows the risks in the business and helps us to prioritise action — for example we would certainly recommend having a shareholders' agreement and buy/sell agreement prepared above appointing an independent director.

## 3.5 Valuation

Once we've gone through all of this analysis we arrive at a valuation figure, and we'll hit the pause button to protect the wealth that's already been created before we think about growing that value in order to reach your retirement goals. A major part of that protection involves decreasing business risk. But first a look at the mechanics behind valuations and some of the jargon that comes with it.

### Financial Valuations

There are several ways to value a business in a largely mathematical way, arriving at a financial valuation. No matter which method is used (with the exception of liquidation), and who prepares the valuation (be it an accountant, potential buyer, adviser or valuation expert), the various outcomes of a financial valuation will be largely consistent. The financial value should reflect the market value of the business, and what it would be worth to someone who takes it on and continues to run it in much the same way, capitalising on the potential identified.

A strategic valuation on the other hand, does not necessarily represent the market value of the business, but what that business is worth to the acquirer for strategic reasons. A strategic buyer is likely to pay well above the financial valuation of the business.

The following are examples of financial valuations.

## EBIT Multiple

An EBIT multiple valuation is derived by multiplying the annual ongoing profit of a business by a multiple. For example, a business that generates $500,000 per year and is valued at a multiple of 2 should achieve a sales price of $1 million. Despite being a mathematical calculation, many non-financial drivers impact the multiple, while the main financial driver is the profit figure.

The main drivers affecting the multiple are risk and potential. A business with low risk and high potential can achieve a high multiple, while a business with high risk and limited potential will achieve a low multiple.

Small businesses in Australia generally sell for multiples of around 2, but in recent times many businesses have been sold for multiples of less than 1; that is the business owner takes less than a year's profit to have the business taken off their hands.

In collaboration with RMIT University, the Value My Business — RMIT Index (VMB-RMIT Index) counters one of the major impediments to private business sales in Australia, namely the hidden nature of the market.

For the quarter ending 30 September 2017, domestic spending on food, clothing and household furnishings was a key contributor to growth, driven by a 0.7% rise in household consumption, which accounted for half of the overall increase in GDP. Despite the growth in the full-time employment rate, the increase in average hourly earnings has been the slowest since at least the mid-1960s.

There was a dramatic decline in the household savings to a nine-year low in the June 2017 quarter. Households had less money to spend from their current incomes, due to high levels of household debt. This situation would be compounded if housing prices continue to rise and other housing-related market conditions were to weaken.

However, the RBA warned that its forecasts for growth and inflation depend on the exchange rate remaining around current levels. The Australian dollar has been at levels not seen since 2014, having broken through US$0.80.

In contrast to the June 2017 Quarter, the September Quarter reveals a marginal drop in the average Middle Market VMB-RMIT Index values but slight growth in the average values of the other three categories as shown in the following graph.

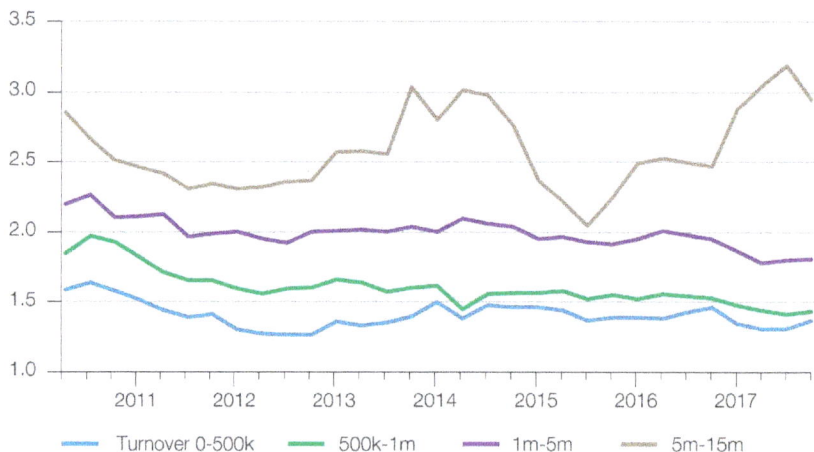

An overall increase in the number of businesses for sale over the September 2017 Quarter is reflected by a rebound in the VMB-RMIT Index values (i.e., Low, Median, Mean, and High multiple values). According to the Australian Bureau of Statistics, almost 60% of actively trading businesses have an annual turnover of less-than-200k and business exit rates are highest for businesses with an annual turnover of less-than-50k (19.4%). This sector is also associated with low VMB-

RMIT Index values. Average VMB-RMIT Index values of the Micro Business sector (Turnover less than 500,000) have shown a steady growth over the recent three quarters across four industry categories: wholesale trade (from 1.24 to 1.73); retail trade (from 1.28 to 1.38); accommodation and food services (from 1.15 to 1.28); and rental, hiring and real estate services (from 3.10 to 3.90).

A further sign of what appears to be a positive trend in the Micro Business Market, given the increase in the number of listings for sale this quarter, is a 2% decrease in the proportion of listings with a VMB-RMIT Index value that falls within the range of 'less-than-one'. A possible explanation is that the increasing value of the Micro market has bumped some into the higher values range of between 1 and 3. The proportion of listings within this range has risen accordingly.

For the first time in two years, despite the slight increase in the number of businesses for sale, the September 2017 Quarter reveals a marginal drop of average VMB-RMIT Index values in the Middle Market sector (Turnover 5-to-15-Million). However, this finding should be interpreted with caution given the fact that the sample size of this sector remains relatively small.

Risk and potential — key indicators
- Industry in which the business operates — some industries, such as hospitality and retail, attract a low multiple while professional services firms and medical practices can demand higher multiple (this is due to the relative predictability of future income
- Quality of governance, compliance and reporting
- Quality of the management team and staff
- Extent to which future revenue and costs are secured by contracts
- Levels of debts and management of cash
- Quality of customers and cash collection history
- Past track record in achieving goals set
- Quality of business assets, in particular intellectual property
- Barriers to entry for competitors and relative competitor strength
- Quality of the product or service and relative price points
- Ability to expand — reaching more customers with the same product, or the same customers with additional products
- Profitability, cash flow and financial position of the business
- Multiples achieved for other similar businesses

## Liquidation or Net Realisable Value

The liquidation value, sometimes referred to as a 'fire sale' reflects the price that could be achieved if the individual assets of the business were sold. This method is generally only used for a business that is in distress.

If the business will continue to operate, this method provides an indication of 'minimum value' since it does not take into account actual or potential earnings. This can be a helpful benchmark to assess valuations by other methods, or offers you might receive.

## Discounted Cash Flow

A discounted cash flow calculation, or DCF, models the present day value of the business's projected future net cash flows. It is a relatively complex calculation analysing future cash flows, capital structure and the costs of capital. Future cash flows are derived using past performance and future assumptions, many of which may be beyond the control of the management team (for example purchases in US$ at a forecast exchange rate).

This method is not popular due to the risk and uncertainty in the assumptions, but it is often used to estimate the value of start-up businesses, which are built on assumptions about the future.

## Capitalisation of Future Maintainable Earnings

Similar to the DCF, this method determines a valuation range using future expected earnings divided by a capitalisation rate (usually determined by reference to similar risk profile investments). It is appropriate for businesses that:

- are a going concern
- have been in existence for a number of years
- are not undergoing any significant transformation
- have historically stable profitability
- are not likely to experience significant growth or decline
- have products that do not face technological obsolescence.

More about this in the Maximising Value stage.

## 3.6 Reverse Due Diligence

An important step in the preparation process is reverse due diligence, a process that is very similar to the due diligence a buyer or an investor would undertake when looking at your business, so it will help you to start to get prepared. We give you a comprehensive list of all the things that we need to get together in terms of documentation, to identify any areas where we've got gaps, where we've got information that's out of date or where we can't find original documents.

It's surprising how many business owners come to us asking us to sell their business quickly, yet when we give them a list of the information we need it will take them six to eight weeks to collect it all. The information we ask for are management accounts — balance sheets, profit and loss statements, and a breakdown of clients, leases, contracts and agreements. They often don't have it, can't get it or have to wait for their accountant to prepare it. Once we do get it, it can sometimes prove impossible to reconcile with the BAS statements which have already been submitted.

It is important to be on top of this early on — it will make your business look much more professional and much less risky once you are asked to provide information.

Focus on getting the following up to date and ready for inspection:

- Financial statements and management accounts
- Trend analysis for the last 12 months
- Top 10 customers — spend, margins, terms
- Legal documentation — shareholders certificates up to date, all licences and IP current
- Employee contracts up to date and entitlements properly accounted for.

For an expanded list, please refer to the Succession Plus website: www.successionplus. com.au

## 3.7 Case Study

In reviewing the financials, a few key points were highlighted by the accountants:

1    The business is performing well financially but performance could be improved
2    the downturn in 2015 would raise concern with potential buyers/investors and needs to be explained
3    the financial statements are recast to allow further and more detailed analysis, and
4    the accountants referred the client directly to the Succession Plus accredited adviser for specialised advice to design and implement a Business Succession and Exit Plan.

Keep in mind the material in the case study is intellectual property of Succession Plus Australia Pty Limited who claims copyright ownership, including the detailed explanation of the 21-Step Business Succession and Exit Planning methodology, tools and templates used to deliver that process with business owners. This material must not be reproduced or distributed without the express written permission of the owner.

Financial Analysis

# Statement of Financial Performance

Profit and Loss Statement :     SMITH ENGINEERING PTY LTD

| | 2013 | 2014 | 2015 | 2016 |
|---|---|---|---|---|
| REVENUE | | | | |
| Sales | $5,771,884 | $6,561,310 | $7,481,200 | $8,093,000 |
| COST OF SALES | | | | |
| COS Goods | $3,173,500 | $3,377,800 | $4,501,740 | $4,101,720 |
| COS Other | - | - | - | - |
| COS Fixed | - | - | - | - |
| Non-Cash | - | - | - | - |
| GROSS PROFIT | $2,598,384 | $3,183,510 | $2,979,460 | $3,991,280 |
| | | | | |
| EXPENSES | | | | |
| Fixed | $240,000 | $256,000 | $245,000 | $287,734 |
| Variable | $1,623,940 | $1,707,746 | $1,954,863 | $2,276,995 |
| Non-Cash | $42,189 | $49,810 | $72,286 | $104,400 |
| TOTAL EXPENSES | $1,906,129 | $2,013,556 | $2,272,149 | $2,669,128 |
| OPERATING INCOME | $692,255 | $1,169,954 | $707,311 | $1,322,152 |
| Other Income | - | - | - | - |
| EARNINGS BEFORE INTEREST & TAX | $692,255 | $1,169,954 | $707,311 | $1,322,152 |
| | | | | |
| INTEREST | | | | |
| Interest | $117,937 | $135,717 | $121,536 | $117,691 |
| Other Loan Interest | - | - | - | - |
| Received (Excess Cash) | - | - | - | - |
| NET INTEREST | $117,937 | $135,717 | $121,536 | $117,691 |
| Tax | $172,295 | $310,271 | $175,733 | $361,338 |
| NET PROFIT AFTER TAX | $402,023 | $723,966 | $410,042 | $843,123 |
| | | | | |
| Adjustments | -$95,220 | -$91,167 | -$113,990 | -$114,381 |
| Abnormals | - | - | - | - |
| Minorities | - | - | - | - |
| NET INCOME | $497,243 | $815,133 | $524,032 | $957,504 |
| Dividends | $416,220 | $670,340 | $441,990 | $788,880 |
| RETAINED INCOME | $81,023 | $144,793 | $82,042 | $168,624 |
| Adjustments to Retained Income | - | - | - | - |

# Statement of Financial Position

Balance Sheet Statement :  SMITH ENGINEERING PTY LTD

FINANCE

| | 2013 | 2014 | 2015 | 2016 |
|---|---|---|---|---|
| Share Capital | $1,000 | $1,000 | $1,000 | $1,000 |
| Retained Income | $1,281,023 | $1,425,816 | $1,507,858 | $1,676,482 |
| Reserves | - | - | - | - |
| Other Equity | - | - | - | - |
| Minorities | - | - | - | - |
| TOTAL EQUITY | $1,282,023 | $1,426,816 | $1,508,858 | $1,677,482 |
| | | | | |
| OTHER FUNDING | | | | |
| Deferred Tax | - | - | - | - |
| Dividends | - | - | - | - |
| Other | - | - | - | $40,811 |
| TOTAL OTHER FUNDING | - | - | - | $40,811 |
| | | | | |
| DEBT | | | | |
| Short term debt | $105,000 | $107,000 | $108,000 | $107,000 |
| Long Term Debt | $1,949,580 | $1,895,778 | $1,833,423 | $1,777,130 |
| Other Loans | - | - | - | - |
| Excess Cash | - | - | - | - |
| TOTAL DEBT | $2,054,580 | $2,002,778 | $1,941,423 | $1,884,130 |
| TOTAL FINANCE | $3,336,603 | $3,429,594 | $3,450,281 | $3,602,423 |

# Statement of Financial Position

Balance Sheet Statement :      SMITH ENGINEERING PTY LTD

OPERATIONS

| | 2013 | 2014 | 2015 | 2016 |
|---|---|---|---|---|
| Accounts Receivable | $474,401 | $539,286 | $922,340 | $665,178 |
| Inventory | $264,458 | $281,483 | $346,651 | $341,810 |
| Other Current Assets | $711,602 | $808,929 | $332,621 | $665,029 |
| TOTAL CURRENT ASSETS | $1,450,461 | $1,629,698 | $1,601,612 | $1,672,017 |
| | | | | |
| Accounts Payable | $391,253 | $416,441 | $555,009 | $505,692 |
| Tax Liability | $23,818 | $29,182 | $27,311 | $36,587 |
| Accruals | $57,719 | $65,613 | $74,812 | $80,930 |
| Other Current Liabilities | $11,543 | $13,123 | $14,962 | $16,186 |
| TOTAL CURRENT LIABILITIES | $484,333 | $524,359 | $672,094 | $639,395 |
| WORKING CAPITAL | $966,128 | $1,105,339 | $929,518 | $1,032,623 |
| | | | | |
| NON-CURRENT ASSETS | | | | |
| Fixed Assets | $2,252,811 | $2,300,190 | $2,447,714 | $2,545,600 |
| Other Non-current Assets | $54,865 | $24,065 | $23,050 | $24,200 |
| Investments | $62,799 | - | $50,000 | - |
| TOTAL NON-CURRENT ASSETS | $2,370,475 | $2,324,255 | $2,520,764 | $2,569,800 |
| TOTAL OPERATIONS | $3,336,603 | $3,429,594 | $3,450,282 | $3,602,423 |

SMITH ENGINEERING PTY LTD (2013 - 2016)

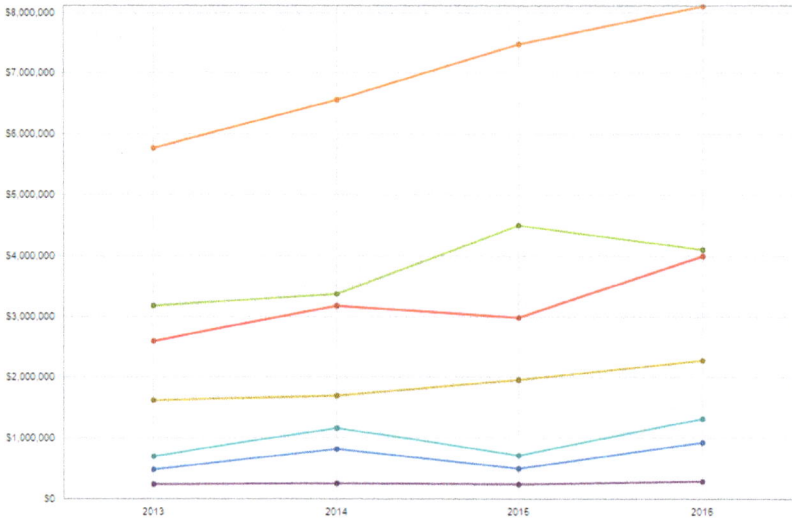

| | 2013 | 2014 | 2015 | 2016 |
|---|---|---|---|---|
| NOPAT | $484,579 | $818,968 | $495,118 | $925,507 |
| Sales | $5,771,884 | $6,561,310 | $7,481,200 | $8,093,000 |
| COS Other | $3,173,500 | $3,377,800 | $4,501,740 | $4,101,720 |
| Gross Profit | $2,598,384 | $3,183,510 | $2,979,460 | $3,991,280 |
| Fixed Expenses | $240,000 | $256,000 | $245,000 | $287,734 |
| Variable Expenses | $1,623,940 | $1,707,746 | $1,954,863 | $2,276,995 |
| EBIT | $692,255 | $1,169,954 | $707,312 | $1,322,152 |

## Addbacks and Adjustments

In most small businesses, there are items in the accounts which are not typical of "normal" business trading and which need to be adjusted to provide a more accurate picture of the business and its financial performance. In order to do this, we create a table of adjustments and addbacks.

Typically, these relate to owners' salary/wages (which are rarely at market value), superannuation for owners and family members, non-market expenses for related parties and other "one-off" or non-recurring expenses — for example a large legal case.

For Smith Engineering, the following addbacks have been identified:

**Adjustment and Add backs**

| | | | | |
|---|---|---|---|---|
| Imputed tax adjustment | ($40,808) | ($39,071) | ($48,814) | ($49,921) |
| Market rent adjustment | $60,028 | $68,238 | $77,804 | $113,302 |
| Market salary adjustment - John Smith | $120,000 | $122,000 | $125,000 | $130,000 |
| Dontaions | ($5,000) | ($8,000) | $0 | ($10,000) |
| Private expenses | ($24,000) | ($30,000) | ($25,000) | ($45,000) |
| Entertainment | ($15,000) | ($22,000) | ($15,000) | ($24,000) |
| | | | | |
| Total | $95,220 | $91,167 | $113,990 | $114,381 |

## Normalised Financials

**After Add backs and Adjustments**

| | | | | |
|---|---|---|---|---|
| **Sales Revenue** | $5,771,884 | $6,561,310 | $7,481,200 | $8,093,000 |
| | | | | |
| **Cost of Goods Sold** | $3,173,500 | $3,377,800 | $4,501,740 | $4,101,720 |
| **Gross Profit** | $2,598,384 | $3,183,510 | $2,979,460 | $3,991,280 |
| **Gross Margin (%)** | 45.0% | 48.5% | 39.8% | 49.3% |
| | | | | |
| **Overheads** | $1,906,129 | $2,013,556 | $2,272,148 | $2,669,128 |
| **EBIT** | $692,255 | $1,169,954 | $707,312 | $1,322,152 |
| **Interest Cost** | $117,937 | $135,717 | $121,536 | $117,691 |
| **Net Profit Before Tax** | $574,318 | $1,034,237 | $585,776 | $1,204,461 |
| | | | | |
| **Tax** | $172,295 | $310,271 | $175,733 | $361,338 |
| **NOPAT** | $402,022 | $723,966 | $410,043 | $843,123 |
| | 7.0% | 11.0% | 5.5% | 10.4% |

## Financial Scorecard

A full review of adjusted financial statements allows the financial information to be scored and areas of under-performance highlighted — a score of B++ is generally quite good for an SME.

FINANCIAL SCORECARD
SMITH ENGINEERING PTY LTD

For the Period 2016

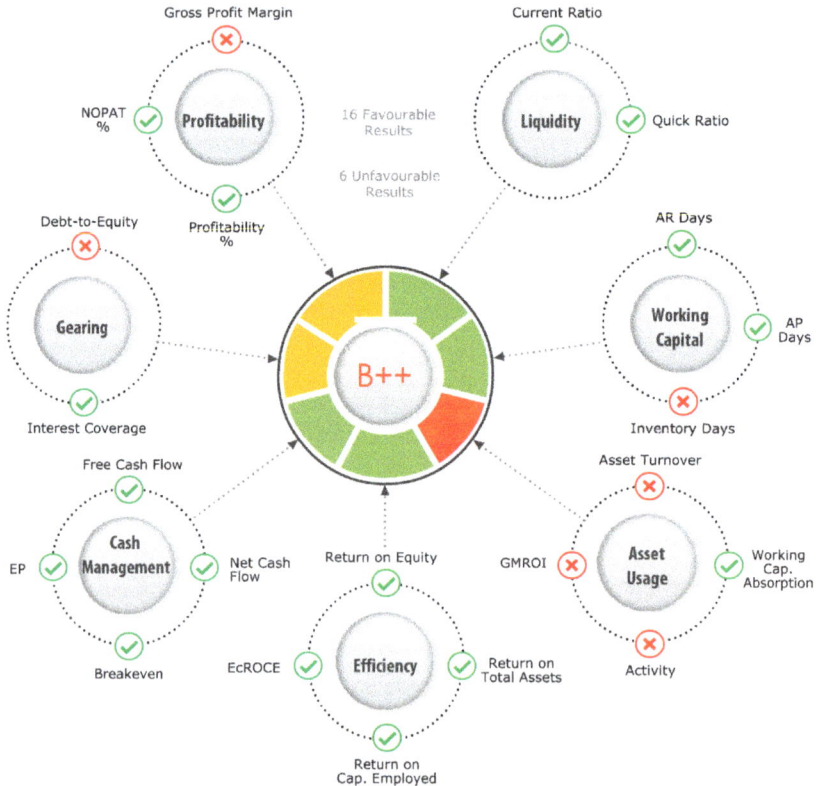

# Financial Ratios

FINANCIAL RATIOS
SMITH ENGINEERING PTY LTD
For the Period 2016

| | Result | Target | Target Type | Result | Weighting | Trend | Previous Period |
|---|---|---|---|---|---|---|---|
| **Liquidity Ratios** | | | | | | | |
| ▸ Current Ratio | 2.62:1 | 2 | A | ✓ | H | ▲ | (2.38:1) |
| ▸ Quick Ratio | 1.04:1 | 1 | A | ✓ | H | ▼ | (1.37:1) |
| **Working Capital** | | | | | | | |
| ▸ Accounts Receivable Days | 30 days | 45 | B | ✓ | H | ▼ | (45 days) |
| ▸ Accounts Payable Days | 45 days | 45 | B | ✓ | H | ◦ | (45 days) |
| ▸ Inventory Days | 30.42 days | 30 | B | ✗ | M | ▲ | (28.11 days) |
| **Profitability Ratios** | | | | | | | |
| ▸ Gross Profit Margin | 49.32% | 50 | A | ✗ | H | ▲ | (39.83%) |
| ▸ Profitability % | 16.34% | 15 | A | ✓ | H | ▲ | (9.45%) |
| ▸ NOPAT % | 11.44% | 10 | A | ✓ | H | ▲ | (6.62%) |
| **Efficiency Ratios** | | | | | | | |
| ▸ Return on Equity | 63.46% | 35 | A | ✓ | H | ▲ | (36.73%) |
| ▸ Return on Total Assets | 31.17% | 30 | A | ✓ | H | ▲ | (17.16%) |
| ▸ Return on Cap. Employed | 36.7% | 35 | A | ✓ | M | ▲ | (20.5%) |
| ▸ EcROCE | 25.69% | 25 | A | ✓ | M | ▲ | (14.35%) |
| **Asset Usage** | | | | | | | |
| ▸ Activity Ratio | 2.25 times | 3 | A | ✗ | M | ▲ | (2.17 times) |
| ▸ Asset Turnover Ratio | 1.91 times | 2.5 | A | ✗ | H | ▲ | (1.81 times) |
| ▸ GM return on Inventory | 1159.48% | 1200 | A | ✗ | M | ▲ | (948.67%) |
| ▸ Working Capital Absorption | 6.19% | 30 | B | ✓ | H | ▼ | (9.54%) |
| **Gearing** | | | | | | | |
| ▸ Interest Coverage Ratio | 11.23 times | 3 | A | ✓ | M | ▲ | (5.82 times |
| ▸ Debt-to-Equity Ratio | 1.12:1 | 1 | B | ✗ | M | ▼ | (1.29:1) |
| **Other** | | | | | | | |
| ▸ Breakeven | $1,851,227 | 0 | A | ✓ | H | ▼ | ($1,851,228) |
| ▸ Free Cash Flow | $773,366 | 0 | A | ✓ | H | ▼ | ($773,366) |
| ▸ Net Cash Flow | $57,294 | 0 | A | ✓ | H | ▲ | ($-171,467) |
| ▸ Economic Profit | $188,451 | 0 | A | ✓ | H | ▲ | ($-210,810) |

overall score = B++

* Target type: A = 'A'; B = 'B'
* Weighting: H = 'high'; M = 'medium'; L = 'low'; NA = 'not applicable';

## Breakeven Analysis

**BREAKEVEN ANALYSIS**

SMITH ENGINEERING PTY LTD

Sales Volume Breakeven for the Period 2016

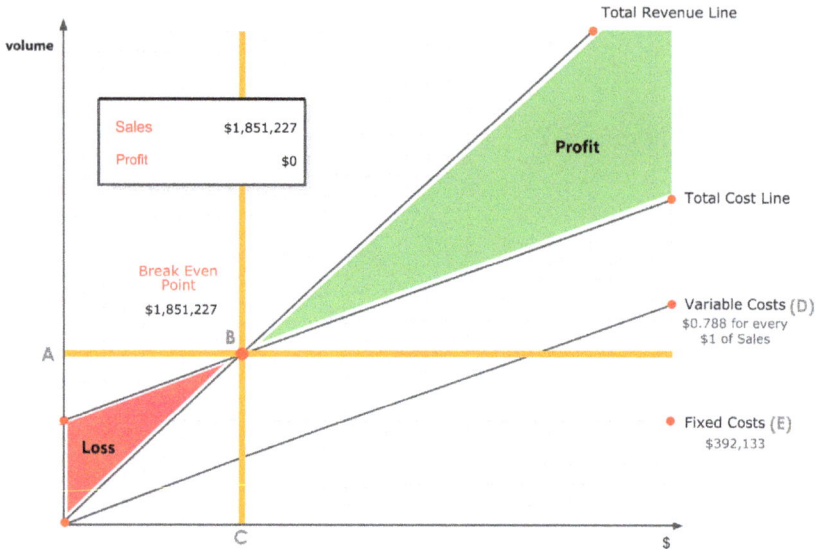

| VARIABLE COSTS | | FIXED COSTS | |
|---|---|---|---|
| COS Goods | $4,101,720 | COS Fixed | $0 |
| COS Other | $0 | COS NonCash | $0 |
| EXP Variable | $2,276,994 | EXP Fixed | $287,733 |
| | | Non-Cash | $104,399 |
| TOTAL VARIABLE COSTS (D) | $6,378,715 | TOTAL FIXED COSTS (E) | $392,133 |

| | |
|---|---|
| TOTAL  Sales | $8,093,000 |
| VARIABLE COST % | $0.788 for every $1 of Sales |
| BREAKEVEN (B) | $1,851,227 |
| SAFETY MARGIN<br>% Change to Revenue to<br>achieve breakeven | -77.1% |

The breakeven analysis shows a strong focus on variable costs and a very strong safety margin which shows the business could drop sales by 77% and still be 'OK'.

# Revenue to Cash Analysis

REVENUE-TO-CASH

SMITH ENGINEERING PTY LTD

Revenue-to-Cash Analysis for the Period 2016

| | | | | | | |
|---|---|---|---|---|---|---|
| ► Revenue | | $8,093,000 | | ► Interest | less | $117,691 |
| ► Change in Receivables | add | $257,162 | | ► Dividends Paid | less | $788,880 |
| CASH FROM SALES | | $8,350,161 | | ► Abnormal Items | less | $-114,381 |
| ► Cost of Sales | | $4,101,720 | | NET CASH PROFIT | | $494,985 |
| ► Changes in Inventory | less | $4,841 | | | | |
| ► Change in Payables | add | $49,317 | | ► Change in Other CA/CL | add | $-325,066 |
| CASH COST OF PRODUCTION | | $4,146,196 | | ► Change in NCAs (ex Depn & Amort) | add | $-153,436 |
| CASH GROSS PROFIT | | $4,203,965 | | ► Changes in Minorities | add | $0 |
| ► Variable Expenses | less | $2,276,995 | | ► Changes to Equity (ex Ret Inc) | less | $0 |
| ► Fixed Expenses | less | $287,733 | | ► Changes to Other Funding | less | $-40,811 |
| ► Other Income | add | $0 | | NET CASH FLOW | | $57,294 |
| OPERATING CASH PROFIT BEFORE TAX | | $1,639,237 | | | | |
| ► Cash Tax Paid | less | $352,062 | | Total Debt beginning of Period | | $1,941,423 |
| OPERATING CASH PROFIT AFTER TAX | | $1,287,175 | | Total Debt end of Period | | $1,884,130 |
| | | | | ► Net Cash Flow | | $57,293 |

# Free Cash Flow

**FREE CASH FLOW**

SMITH ENGINEERING PTY LTD

Free Cash Flow for the Period 2016

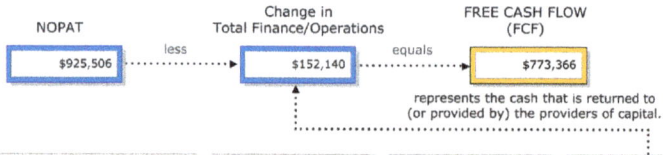

| | NOPAT | | Change in Total Finance/Operations | | FREE CASH FLOW (FCF) |
|---|---|---|---|---|---|
| | $925,506 | less | $152,140 | equals | $773,366 |

represents the cash that is returned to (or provided by) the providers of capital.

| CHANGE IN TOTAL OPERATIONS | Opening | Closing | | Change |
|---|---|---|---|---|
| ▶ Accounts Receivable | $922,339 | $665,178 | ▼ | $-257,161 |
| ▶ Inventory | $346,651 | $341,810 | ▼ | $-4,841 |
| ▶ Other Current Assets | $332,620 | $665,029 | ▲ | $332,408 |
| ▶ Accounts Payable | $555,009 | $505,691 | ▼ | $-49,317 |
| ▶ Tax Liability | $27,311 | $36,587 | ▲ | $9,276 |
| ▶ Accruals | $74,812 | $80,930 | ▲ | $6,118 |
| ▶ Other Current Liabilities | $14,962 | $16,186 | ▲ | $1,224 |
| ▶ Fixed Assets | $2,447,714 | $2,545,600 | ▲ | $97,886 |
| ▶ Other non-current assets | $23,050 | $24,200 | ▲ | $1,150 |
| ▶ Investments | $50,000 | $0 | ▼ | $-50,000 |
| ▶ Total Operations | $3,450,281 | $3,602,422 | ▲ | $152,140 |

▲▼ Positive Effect on Free Cash Flow
▲▼ Negative Effect on Free Cash Flow

▲▲ Increase Closing vs Opening Period
▼▼ Decrease Closing vs Opening Period

## Cash Flow Split

**CASH FLOW SPLIT**

SMITH ENGINEERING PTY LTD

Cash Flow Split for the Period 2016

▸▸ **CASH IN** ▸▸

| | |
|---|---|
| Sales | $8,093,000 |
| Change in Receivables | $257,162 |
| Abnormal Items | $114,381 |
| Changes to Other Funding | $40,811 |
| Changes in Inventory | $4,841 |

**CASH FLOW**

| | |
|---|---|
| $-49,317 | Change in Payables |
| $-117,691 | Interest |
| $-153,436 | Change in NCAs |
| $-287,733 | Fixed Expenses |
| $-325,066 | Change in Other CA/CL |
| $-352,062 | Cash Tax Paid |
| $-788,880 | Dividends |
| $-2,276,995 | Variable Expenses |
| $-4,101,720 | Cost of Sales |

▸▸ **CASH OUT** ▸▸

| TOTAL CASH IN | ▸▸ | NET CASH FLOW | ◂◂ | TOTAL CASH OUT |
|---|---|---|---|---|
| $8,510,195 | | $57,294 | | $8,452,900 |

## Sustainable Growth

The sustainable growth rate shows ability to grow the business at approximately 11% which is a strong result. This is used to highlight the growth factors which exist and the ability for the business to fund this growth.

**SUSTAINABLE GROWTH ANALYSIS**
SMITH ENGINEERING PTY LTD

Sustainable Growth for the Period 2016

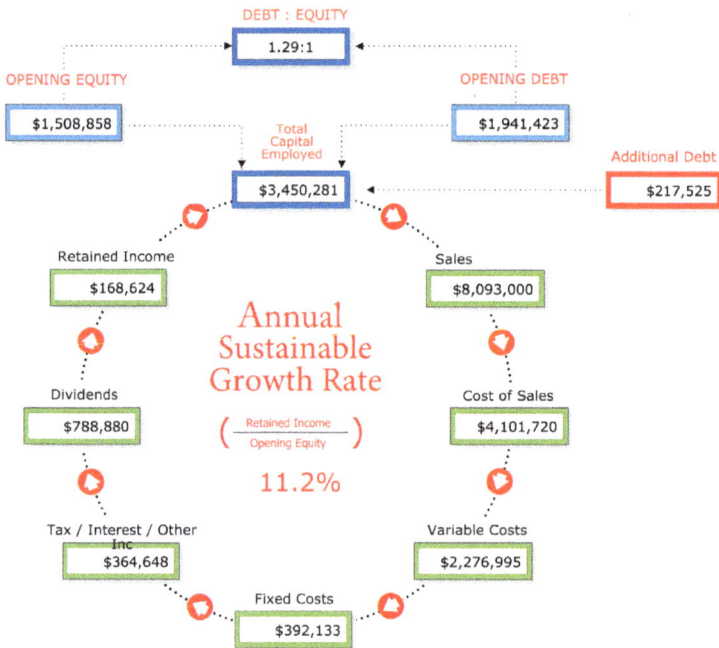

The sustainable growth model identifies how much a business can grow without changing the way it does business and without changing the debt : equity ratio.  This business can grow its Sales at an annual rate of no more than 11.2% without changing the way it does business or changing its financial structure.  Growth at a greater rate than 11.2% will require a combination of the following:

- the raising of more equity;
- the retention of more dividends;
- an increase in profitability;
- additional debt;

The sustainable growth rate is a good tool to establish funding position moving forward, especially if a part of the strategy is to grow the business.

## Credit Risk Scorecard

**CREDIT RISK SCORECARD**

SMITH ENGINEERING PTY LTD

For the Period 2016

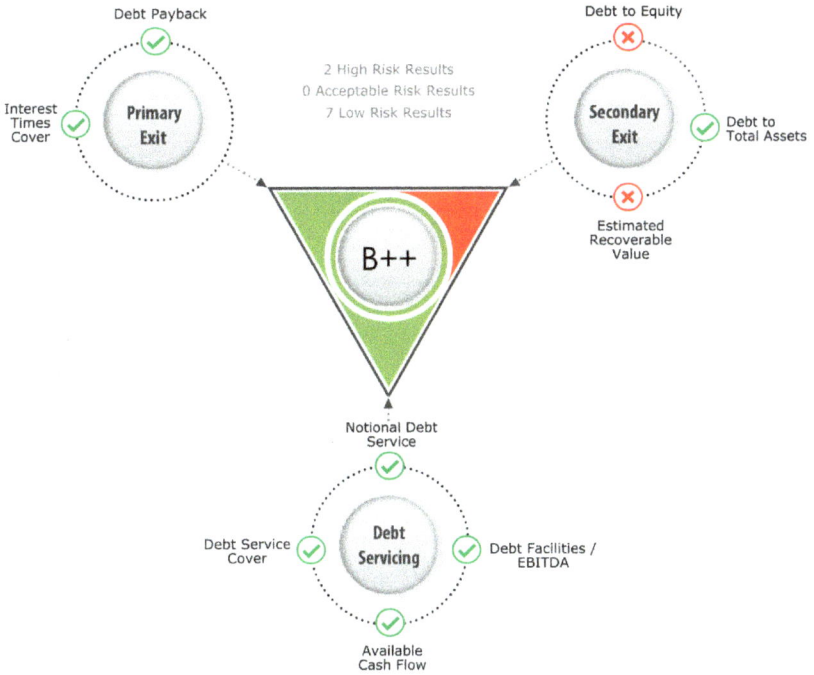

## Benchmarking Analysis

The benchmarking highlights over and under performance of the business against industry peers and similar industries/businesses.

| | Your Business: 2016 | Net Profit as % of Assets (AONS): Top 20% | Net Profit per Owner: $200,000 or more | Turnover: $3,200,000 or more |
|---|---|---|---|---|
| **Income** | | | | |
| Total Income | $8,093,000 | $3,300,099 | $4,426,416 | $7,660,820 |
| Less Cost of Goods Sold inc Sub Contractors | 50.68% | 41.14% | 44.44% | 53.70% |
| Equals Gross Profit | 49.32% | 58.86% | 55.56% | 46.30% |
| **Less Overheads as %'s of Total Income:** | | | | |
| Advertising & Promotion | 0.21% | 0.42% | 0.43% | 0.40% |
| Accounting & Legal Fees | 0.27% | 0.53% | 0.45% | 0.50% |
| All Insurance | 0.66% | 1.31% | 1.22% | 0.93% |
| Interest, Bank Charges etc | 1.45% | 0.40% | 0.62% | 0.50% |
| Rent of Premises | 1.40% | 2.64% | 2.87% | 2.84% |
| Other Occupancy Costs | 0.23% | 0.68% | 0.81% | 0.69% |
| Other Depreciation, Lease and HP | 1.29% | 1.29% | 1.35% | 1.47% |
| Repairs, Maint, Hire of Plant, Tool Replacem't | 1.01% | 1.06% | 1.35% | 1.22% |
| Staff On Costs | 1.25% | 1.70% | 1.86% | 2.42% |
| Telephone & Fax | 0.45% | 0.45% | 0.37% | 0.24% |
| Employees' Wages & Salaries | 21.13% | 18.77% | 20.08% | 18.49% |
| Vehicle Operating Costs | 0.89% | 2.13% | 2.02% | 1.83% |
| All Other Expenses | 0.00% | 3.24% | 3.09% | 4.28% |
| Total Overheads | 30.23% | 34.63% | 36.53% | 35.81% |
| Net Profit (bos*) | 19.08% | 24.23% | 19.03% | 10.49% |
| **Net Profit (bos*) per....** | | | | |
| Working Owner | $514,820 | $477,302 | $476,172 | $517,612 |
| Owner Workhour | $308.89 | $225.51 | $209.37 | $238.70 |
| **Total Income per...** | | | | |
| Person | $299,741 | $236,973 | $261,207 | $299,984 |
| $ of Wages # & Sub Contractor Payments | $4.24 | $3.40 | $3.63 | $4.34 |
| Sq Mtr Total Area | $4,496 | $4,288 | $4,147 | $3,950 |

(bos*) — Before Owner Salary

Wages in Smith Engineering are 21.13% of turnover and the average for similar sized businesses, is 18.49%. This represents a profit gap.

| | Your Business: 2016 | Net Profit as % of Assets (AONS): Top 20% | Net Profit per Owner: $200,000 or more | Turnover: $3,200,000 or more |
|---|---|---|---|---|
| **Gross Profit (Income less Materials and Payments to Independent Sub Contractors) per....** | | | | |
| Person | $147,825 | $138,235 | $141,240 | $139,004 |
| $ of Wages # & Sub Contractor Payments | $2.09 | $1.97 | $1.99 | $1.86 |
| Sq Mtr Total Area | $2,217 | $2,590 | $2,279 | $1,820 |
| **Non Personnel-Related Overheads per....** | | | | |
| Person | $23,549 | $33,134 | $37,796 | $44,895 |
| $ of Wages # & Sub Contractor Payments | $0.33 | $0.47 | $0.53 | $0.61 |
| Sq Mtr Total Area | $353 | $541 | $565 | $553 |
| **Personnel (fte personnel numbers)** | | | | |
| Working Owners | 3.00 | 1.40 | 1.48 | 1.13 |
| Direct/Production Staff | 20.00 | 8.55 | 12.93 | 16.16 |
| Any Other Staff | 4.00 | 1.76 | 2.33 | 2.92 |
| Total Personnel | 27.00 | 11.72 | 16.74 | 20.21 |
| Hours Worked per Owner per Year | 1,667 | 2,071 | 2,073 | 2,368 |

## Key Performance Indicator Graphs

### Income per Person

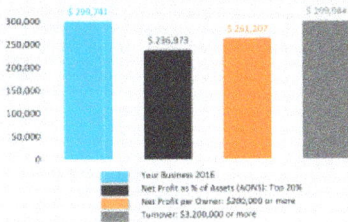

### Gross Profit per Person

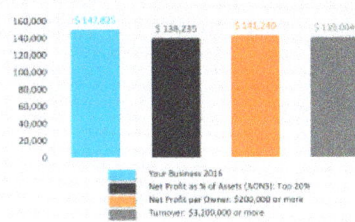

### Net Profit per Owner

### Non Personnel Overheads per Person

65

The profit gap analysis shows several areas of real cost savings in both wages and salaries and asset turnover. Combining these improves profitability by over $250,000.

| Your Profit Gaps relative to the Most Profitable firms: | Your Business | Benchmark Firms | Profit Gap Relative to Benchmark Firms |
|---|---|---|---|
| If you could achieve the average benchmark wages & salaries % of | | 19.10% | |
| then your business's present Revenue of | $ 8,093,000 | | |
| would require a wages & salaries cost of | | $ 1,545,763 | |
| But your wages and salaries cost is | $ 1,710,051 | | |
| Which is, as a % of your firm's revenue | 21.13% | | |
| and your W&S Profit Gap is: | | | $ 164,288 |
| If you could achieve the average level of non-salary | | | |
| expenses | 9.10% | 15.50% | |
| you should reduce your overheads by | | | No Profit Gap |
| then on your present turnover of | $ 8,093,000 | | |
| There is no profit gap | | | |
| Your asset turnover is presently | 1.91 | 2.50 | |
| Your current revenue of | $ 8,093,000 | | |
| suggests you should have assets of | | $ 3,237,200 | |
| Currently you have total assets (net of any loans to owners) of | $ 4,241,617 | | $ 90,397 |
| So you could look to reduce total assets by | | | |
| If so, this could save you interest at, say, | 9.00% | | |
| Then you'd close a Profit Gap of: | | | |

| Your total Profit Gap: | Relative to Benchmark firms |
|---|---|
| 1. Bringing your personnel numbers back could yield | $ 164,288 |
| 2. Reducing non-wages & salary overheads could yield | $ - |
| 3. Reducing your investment in the firm could yield | $ 90,398 |
| So your total Profit Gap is | $ 254,686 |
| Which is ... times your current profit level! | 0.47 |

## Non-financial Aspects of the Business and Weighted Average Cost of Capital (WACC)

It is quite common to see businesses which perform well financially score "badly" in the non-financial and "exit readiness" aspects of its business.

The quality of the non-financial aspects of the business and "exit readiness" impact on the risk in the business and ultimately the weighted average cost of capital (WACC) and in turn, the valuation itself. Many business owners are not aware of this impact and simply focus on profit only.

SUCCESSION

# Non-financial KPI Scorecard

**KPI SCORECARD**

SMITH  ENGINEERING  NON FINANCIAL

For the Period 2016

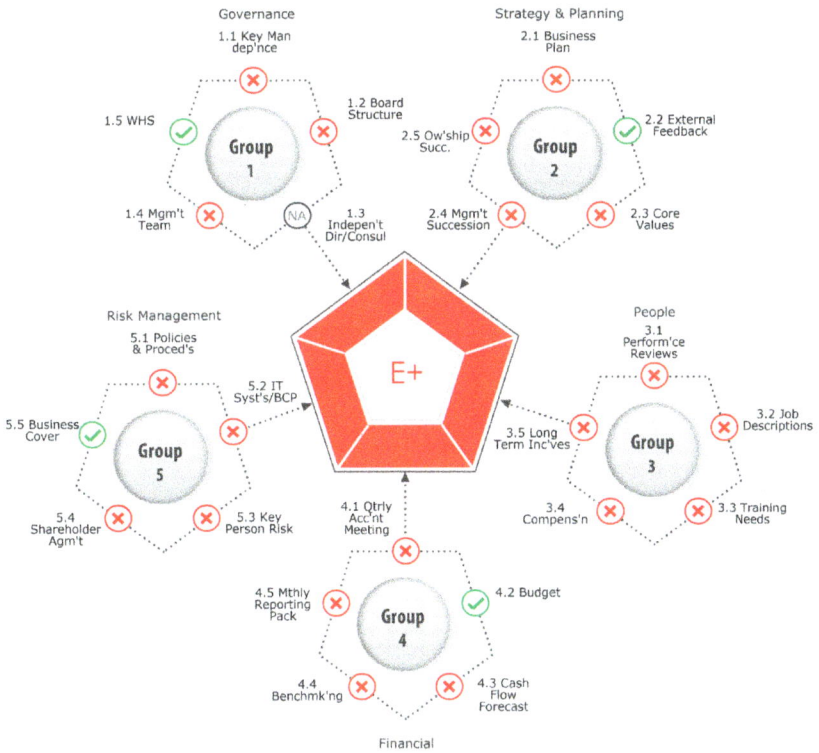

Governance

1.1 Key Man dep'nce

1.2 Board Structure

1.5 WHS

**Group 1**

1.4 Mgm't Team

NA

1.3 Indepen't Dir/Consul

Strategy & Planning

2.1 Business Plan

2.2 External Feedback

2.5 Ow'ship Succ.

**Group 2**

2.3 Core Values

2.4 Mgm't Succession

Risk Management

5.1 Policies & Proced's

5.2 IT Syst's/BCP

5.5 Business Cover

**Group 5**

5.4 Shareholder Agm't

5.3 Key Person Risk

People

3.1 Perform'ce Reviews

3.2 Job Descriptions

3.5 Long Term Inc'ves

**Group 3**

3.4 Compens'n

3.3 Training Needs

E+

4.1 Qtrly Acc'nt Meeting

4.5 Mthly Reporting Pack

**Group 4**

4.2 Budget

4.4 Benchmk'ng

4.3 Cash Flow Forecast

Financial

▶ 25 Total Metrics    ◀ Favourable Results    ▶ 20 Unfavourable    ▶ 1 N/A Measures

## Exit Readiness and Attractiveness KPI Scorecard

Not only the non-financial risks /operations need to be assessed but we need to review the business through the "lens" of a potential buyer:

1   Will they find it attractive?
2   What are the key features they are looking for?
3   Is the business sale or exit ready?

**KPI SCORECARD**
SMITH  ENGINEERING  EXIT READINESS
For the Period 2016

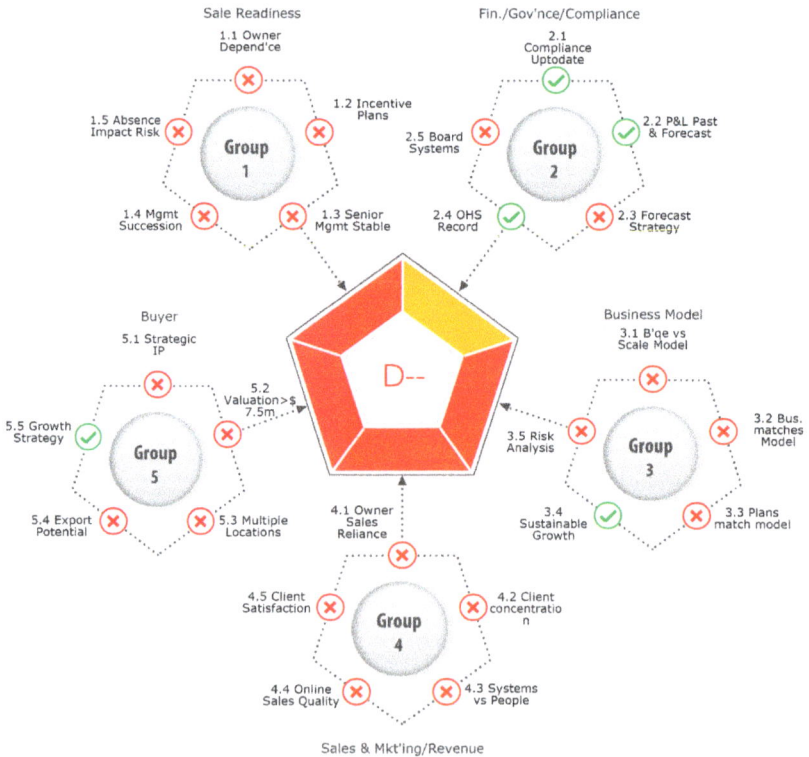

Sale Readiness
1.1 Owner Depend'ce
1.2 Incentive Plans
1.5 Absence Impact Risk
**Group 1**
1.4 Mgmt Succession
1.3 Senior Mgmt Stable

Fin./Gov'nce/Compliance
2.1 Compliance Uptodate
2.2 P&L Past & Forecast
2.5 Board Systems
**Group 2**
2.4 OHS Record
2.3 Forecast Strategy

Buyer
5.1 Strategic IP
5.2 Valuation>$ 7.5m
5.5 Growth Strategy
**Group 5**
5.4 Export Potential
5.3 Multiple Locations

**D--**

Business Model
3.1 B'qe vs Scale Model
3.2 Bus. matches Model
3.5 Risk Analysis
**Group 3**
3.4 Sustainable Growth
3.3 Plans match model

4.1 Owner Sales Reliance
4.5 Client Satisfaction
4.2 Client concentration
**Group 4**
4.4 Online Sales Quality
4.3 Systems vs People

Sales & Mkt'ing/Revenue

▸ 25 Total Metrics   ▸ 6 Favourable Results   ▸ 20 Unfavourable   ▸ 0 N/A Measures

# Non-financial KPI Results Commentary

## Governance/Compliance

### Key Person Dependence

Key person dependence will generally negatively affect a business's value, because a high level of key person dependence makes a successful transfer more difficult. Ideally, absence of the owners would be only minimally disruptive to the business also.

### Board structure

The main function of a Board of Directors is to guide the strategy of the business. The board also monitors business performance and contemplates how well it is likely to perform in the future, ensures the business is adequately resourced, sets policy, manages the GM/CEO and importantly, keeps shareholders informed.

To be effective, every appropriately-sized business should have a Board with diverse skills and experience, as well as reliable and useful systems in place to ensure the effectiveness of the board.

### Independent directors

Independent directors (or non-executive directors) are an excellent way to improve the breadth and depth of the board's knowledge and experiences. Ideally, those non-executive directors or board advisers invited will add significant value in terms of industry or business expertise, experience or contacts and strengthen strategic planning, decision making and corporate governance.

### Management team

Leadership is doing the right things, management is doing things right. If your managers work together effectively, through role clarity and productive meetings, your business has a much greater chance at success.

## Health & Safety System

If your workplace is unsafe, none of its other qualities will be relevant because it is at risk of government action. Having a robust health & safety system helps to ensure your workplace is safe. Ideally, your workplace's health & safety system is fully compliant with the law at all times.

## Strategy & Planning

## Business Plan

If you fail to plan, you plan to fail, as the old adage goes. The purpose of the Strategic Business Plan is to illustrate feasibility of your business idea, but also as a communicative document to your key stakeholders, mainly investors and employees.

## External feedback

External advisers are a great source of fresh ideas. Like an independent director, they can supply an outsider's perspective on issues that may be difficult to solve internally.

## Core values

If your business is clear on what it values, customers, employees and suppliers alike are much more likely to be aligned with those values. Alignment is critical to business success.

## Ownership/Management succession

Ownership succession and management succession are distinct concepts, but similar in spirit. Planning ahead and documenting the planning process, makes the transition more predictable and therefore less disruptive.

Adding people to and moving people around within the management team is a natural consequence of business development but can be disruptive. To alleviate the disruptive effects, having a clear and documented plan on how to achieve a transition from the managers' point of view makes the transition process more predictable, and therefore less disruptive.

Moreover, having a valid and up-to-date will, Powers of Attorney and Guardianship, and Family Wealth Plans should form central parts of your generational planning strategy.

## Marketing & Sales

Businesses with the highest and most resilient value tend to rely on sales machinery, rather than sales people (in particular owners), have a high degree of predictability and brand consistency. They are also capable of accessing reliable data about leads and customers from your CRM Google and social media.

## People

## Performance reviews

Performance reviews are an opportunity to align your staff's interest with the goals and objectives of the business. Many businesses miss an opportunity to use formal performance reviews and informal performance feedback as devices to stimulate employee engagement.

## Position descriptions

A position description is a useful tool in communicating to staff their objectives and roles. Great position descriptions stimulate employee engagement.

## Training needs

Your staff are a finite resource. If you have good procedures that enable a clear picture of what they are capable of, you are in a much better position to allocate training resources in a way that moves the business closer to achieving its objectives.

## Compensation

The calibre of staff that you attract and retain will be influenced by how you communicate with them through the compensation framework.

## Long-term Incentives / Employee Share Ownership Plan

An employee share plan can be useful as a way of rewarding committed employees, but also a means of increasing employee attraction and retention. This is because owning shares in a company tends to encourage employees to think and act like owners.

## Financial

## Budget/cash flow

Without adequate tools in place to illustrate the financial position of the business and where it expects and aims to be in the future, business direction is likely to suffer.

## Benchmarking

Benchmarking can be a useful exercise in determining the business' competitiveness, and can be used to inform or support the objectives set out in the Strategic Business Plan.

## Proactive Accountant

Proactive accountants can play a direct and influential role in business change and performance turnaround. Skillsets required to make a difference do not always come naturally to many accountants and, therefore, lack of proactive involvement needs addressing.

## Reporting

A monthly reporting pack should contain what the board or leadership team need to see to allow for informed decision making. Ideally, it would include an executive business summary with summaries of turnover, debtor analysis, headcount, Capex and KPI achievement along with cash flow, profit and loss and balance sheet trend information and schedules.

## Risk Management

### Policies & procedures

Policies and procedures are especially useful as risk alleviation tools. For example, if a key person with unique knowledge leaves your business, you may have difficulty continuing operations until that person is replaced. Appropriately documented however, knowledge can be transferred to others and other options become available, including training another member of staff.

### IT systems/BCP

Emergencies and natural disasters can cripple a business. With appropriate forethought though, the risk can be alleviated.

### Key person risk

Reducing key person risk is essential to increasing the value of a business. Insurance can alleviate the risk, but only if it is thought about and acted upon before a key person becomes unavailable, and not after.

### Shareholder agreement

Some businesses are thrown into chaos by the death or incapacity of an owner. While reducing dependence on owners is an excellent start, there should also be a plan in place for ownership transfer, to reduce disruption.

### Business cover

Insurance is top of mind for most people when they think about risk management. Each business has unique insurance needs which change over time as the business changes. Involving knowledgeable advisers who know your business in regular review processes is great practice in managing risk.

## Beta Factor Assessment

The following tool simply allows us to accurately assess various risks that impact the business and its value — risk is a significant aspect of the valuation equation. A risk assessment is discussed further in section 6.5.

### BETA FACTOR ASSESSMENT
SMITH ENGINEERING PTY LTD

Business Risk Assessment for the Period 2016

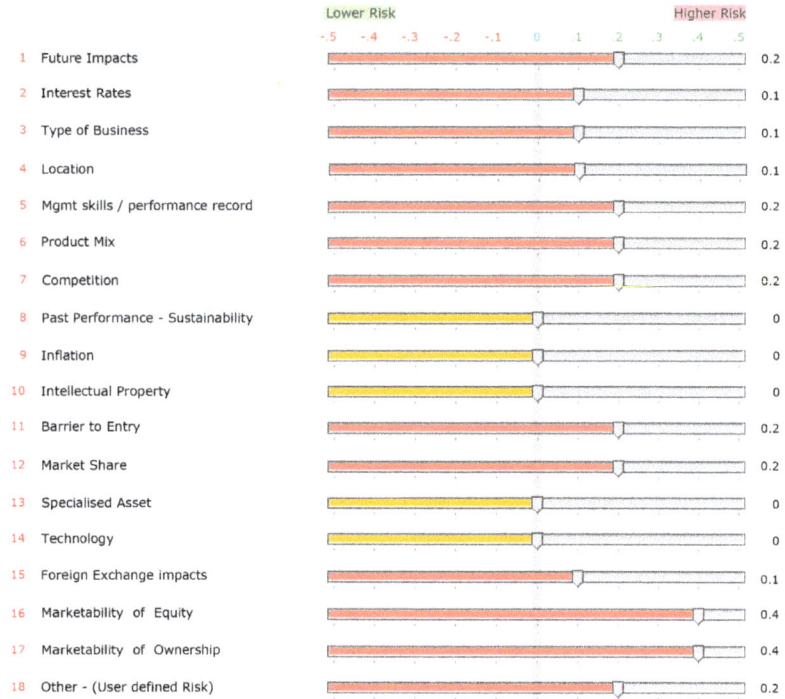

| | | Lower Risk | Higher Risk | Value |
|---|---|---|---|---|
| 1 | Future Impacts | | | 0.2 |
| 2 | Interest Rates | | | 0.1 |
| 3 | Type of Business | | | 0.1 |
| 4 | Location | | | 0.1 |
| 5 | Mgmt skills / performance record | | | 0.2 |
| 6 | Product Mix | | | 0.2 |
| 7 | Competition | | | 0.2 |
| 8 | Past Performance - Sustainability | | | 0 |
| 9 | Inflation | | | 0 |
| 10 | Intellectual Property | | | 0 |
| 11 | Barrier to Entry | | | 0.2 |
| 12 | Market Share | | | 0.2 |
| 13 | Specialised Asset | | | 0 |
| 14 | Technology | | | 0 |
| 15 | Foreign Exchange impacts | | | 0.1 |
| 16 | Marketability  of  Equity | | | 0.4 |
| 17 | Marketability  of  Ownership | | | 0.4 |
| 18 | Other - (User defined Risk) | | | 0.2 |

| Average market leveraging: | Market Asset Beta: | Net Adjustment: | Asset Beta: |
|---|---|---|---|
| 40 % | 0.7 | 2.6 | 3.3 |

(Leveraged Beta for the market is equal to '1')

| Risk factor | What this risk factor is about | Suggested improvement strategies |
|---|---|---|
| Future impacts | Whether the business is more or less vulnerable than the market average when exposed to future business impact. | Our view is that Smith Engineering is less vulnerable than the market average to future business impact, however, we apply a general level of risk to all service businesses owing to a pattern of disruption. |
| Interest rates | Whether changes in interest rates impact on volume of business carried out? (non-financing costs) | Businesses that are vulnerable to this risk tend to have enduring or growing levels of debt. Smith Engineering is showing a track record of debt reduction and is therefore rated at an average level of risk. No strategic recommendations to make beyond continued debt reduction where commercially astute. |
| Type of Business | Whether the type of business makes it more or less risky than the market. | Our view is that Smith Engineering does not have an abnormal level of risk here. While environmental consulting services and associated services are often legally mandatory, they are tied to the general level of confidence and overall economic output of the market. It is also our understanding that a program of industry / sectoral diversification has been undertaken in recent years, which we believe to be a sound approach to management of risk in this area. No further recommendations. |
| Location | Relative risk to physical location (distance from key suppliers, ports, customers, etc.) | We believe Smith Engineering has a somewhat higher level of risk than other businesses of its size (in other service industries) in that revenue is concentrated in NSW and resourcing in particular in Newcastle. Other offices are being developed, and we encourage this to continue to lower this risk. The possibility of Joint Ventures elsewhere might also be explored. |

| Risk factor | What this risk factor is about | Suggested improvement strategies |
|---|---|---|
| Management skills/performance record | The extent to which past performance of the business compares to the industry average. | Smith Engineering sustains a culture of deep commitment to corporate governance. To strengthen, we recommend increased formality and structure of the Board, increased involvement of the Associates in planning and strategy, increased involvement of senior management in Board meetings (e.g. to include Jonathan, Stephanie, John and Tim.) |
| Product Mix | Range and scope of product and the likelihood it will satisfy market demand and the customer's value proposition. | Our understanding is that Smith Engineering's service offering is under expansion, and has a normal level of risk exposure with respect to the broader industry sector. No further recommendations here. |
| Competition | How powerful the competition is. | Our understanding is that Smith Engineering's competitors pose a normal level of risk compared to other consulting businesses of its size. |
| Past performance — sustainability | How volatile has the past operational and financial performance relative to the market average. | Compounded annual rate of revenue growth 2012 — 2016 was (8.1%). We recommend increasing the robustness of the financial and non-financial reporting rigour — with a special emphasis on dashboard familiarity throughout the business. Moreover, we recommend investing in a new ERP system to make the necessary information flows more reliable and to reduce risk of information opacity among key decision makers. |
| Inflation | The extent to which the business is more or less vulnerable to changes in the rate of inflation. | Businesses most exposed to inflation risk are businesses with low elasticity of demand and low margins. Smith Engineering is neither. We therefore rate it as risk neutral and make no further recommendations around this. |

| Risk factor | What this risk factor is about | Suggested improvement strategies |
|---|---|---|
| Intellectual Property | The extent to which the business is dependent on IP and its ability to protect IP, such as patents etc. | Our understanding is that Smith Engineering is not reliant on proprietary Intellectual Property. We therefore rate it as risk neutral and make no further recommendations in this area. |
| Barrier to Entry | The relative ease for additional competition to enter the market. | Our understanding is that to conduct environmental consulting services there are no special legal requirements. While Smith Engineering has a very high concentration of talent and an enduring brand, there aren't major monetary obstacles, such as purchase of equipment or trade licenses to prevent competition from entering the market. This is an intrinsic risk to this business. |
| Market Share | This relates to the business' market share and concentration of individual market revenue to the business' total revenue. | Our understanding is that Smith Engineering has a significant portion of the market, but competitive risk does remain from both larger and smaller industry players with more flexible cost structures. |
| Specialised Asset | Refers to the extent to which there are a significant level of physical assets that are difficult to remove or relocate. | Our understanding is that there are no physical assets of this nature in the business. We therefore rate it as risk neutral and make no further recommendations around this. To counter, we recommend diversifying revenues away from the traditionally targeted mining sector toward other sectors where Smith Engineering has a natural advantage such as infrastructure and defense. |
| Technology | Refers to the extent to which the business is more or less vulnerable to technology developments. | Our understanding is that the business has a normal level of vulnerability to technology developments consistent with service businesses generally. |
| Foreign Exchange | The extent to which changes in FX rates impact on business volume. | Our understanding is that this business does not conduct international trade and this risk is of less concern. We rate it as risk neutral and make no further recommendations in this area. |

| Risk factor | What this risk factor is about | Suggested improvement strategies |
| --- | --- | --- |
| Marketability of Equity | How readily marketable is the equity in the business relative to the average. Actively traded listed companies are the most liquid, unlisted companies are the least liquid and thinly traded listed companies are somewhere in between. | Smith Engineering is an unlisted company, and therefore by definition, subject to a high risk marking in this category. Our understanding is that listing in any fashion is not in Smith Engineering's strategic future, and therefore this remains a systemic risk. |
| Marketability of Ownership | Compared to the marginal investor in a listed public company, the holders of the equity in Smith Engineering Australia are undiversified, with substantially significant wealth exposed to this business. Consequently, shareholders are exposed to both undiversifiable and diversifiable risk which returns a high-risk rating. Reductions in this risk component are linked to shareholder's increase in relative worth across a wide portfolio of assets outside of this business. | This is related to matters of personal financial planning and recommendations must be within strict compliance guidelines under Australian law. Specific strategic recommendations of this nature are therefore beyond the scope of this report. |
| User defined risk | We normally apply a standard rating of 0.5 here. Our recommendation is to have a practical succession and exit plan and conduct frequent reviews. | Smith Engineering is already implementing an employee share plan to create a perpetual succession vehicle, which is why it comes in under a typical client's score. However, until complete, this risk remains. |

## Cost of Funding (Weighted Average Cost of Capital)

This calculation is also important to the overall result. It allows us to determine the cost of capital and importantly what return we should be generating given the risk/s involved.

COST OF FUNDING (WEIGHTED AVERAGE COST OF CAPITAL)
SMITH ENGINEERING PTY LTD

**Weighted Average Cost of Capital for the Period 2016**

**Cost of Debt** (kd)

$kd = kmd (1-t)\%$

- Marginal interest rate (kmd)    7.41 %

     5.19 %

- Marginal corporate tax rate (t)    30 %

Cost of borrowing funds

**Cost of Equity** (ke)

- Risk free rate of return (Rf)    2 %

- Market Risk Premium (MRP)    6 %

**Beta** (β)

- Asset Beta    3.3

Leveraged Beta (β)    $ke = Rf + B (MRP)\%$

- Market Value of Debt / Market Value of Total Capital (wd)    48.7 %    5.49    34.96 %
  (for this organisation)

Cost of equity funds

**Weighted Average Cost of Capital**

$k / (1-t)$          $k = (wd \times kd) + ((1-wd) \times ke)$

**Before Tax WACC**    29.23 %      **After Tax WACC**    20.46 %

## Profitability Analysis

**PROFITABILITY ANALYSIS**
SMITH ENGINEERING PTY LTD (COPY)
Economic Profit Analysis for the Period 2016

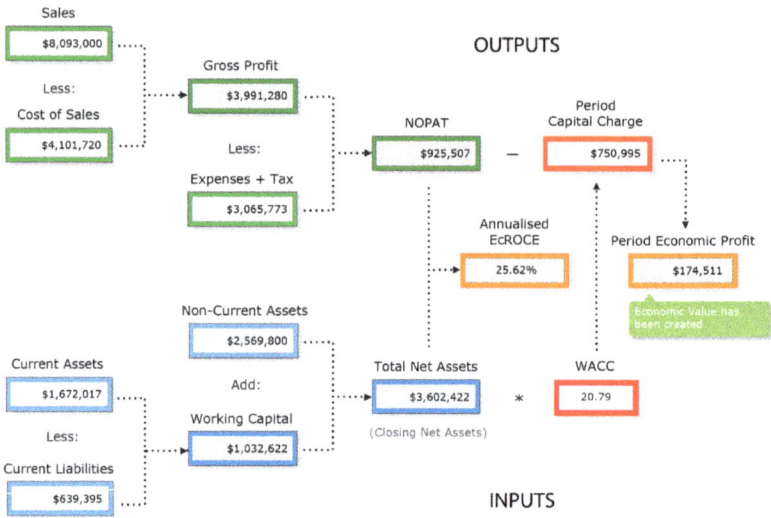

Sales
**$8,093,000**

Less:
Cost of Sales
**$4,101,720**

Gross Profit
**$3,991,280**

Less:
Expenses + Tax
**$3,065,773**

**OUTPUTS**

NOPAT
**$925,507**

Period
Capital Charge
**$750,995**

Annualised
EcROCE
**25.62%**

Period Economic Profit
**$174,511**

Economic Value has been created

Non-Current Assets
**$2,569,800**

Current Assets
**$1,672,017**

Add:
Working Capital
**$1,032,622**

Less:
Current Liabilities
**$639,395**

Total Net Assets
**$3,602,422**
(Closing Net Assets)

WACC
**20.79**

**INPUTS**

---

OPENING, CLOSING & AVERAGE ECONOMIC PROFIT

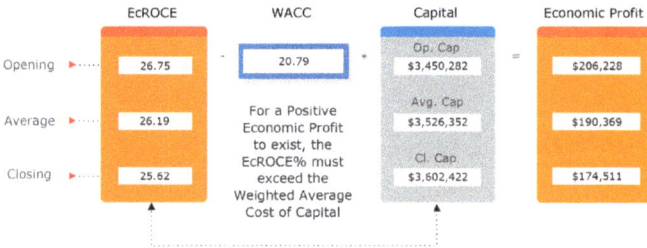

| | EcROCE | WACC | Capital | Economic Profit |
|---|---|---|---|---|
| Opening | 26.75 | 20.79 | Op. Cap $3,450,282 | $206,228 |
| Average | 26.19 | For a Positive Economic Profit to exist, the EcROCE% must exceed the Weighted Average Cost of Capital | Avg. Cap $3,526,352 | $190,369 |
| Closing | 25.62 | | Cl. Cap $3,602,422 | $174,511 |

### ECONOMIC PROFIT TRENDS
SMITH ENGINEERING PTY LTD (COPY)

Economic Profit Analysis for the Period 2016

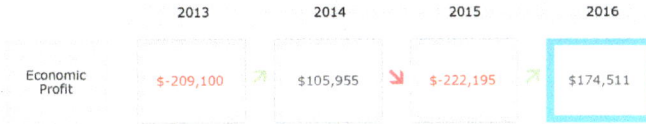

| | 2013 | 2014 | 2015 | 2016 |
|---|---|---|---|---|
| Economic Profit | $-209,100 ↗ | $105,955 ↘ | $-222,195 ↗ | $174,511 |

## Business Valuation — Future Maintainable Profits

### BUSINESS VALUATION - FUTURE MAINTAINABLE PROFITS (FMP) VALUATION
SMITH ENGINEERING PTY LTD (COPY)

Business Valuation at the Base Year 2016

Source Data

| | Base Year (2016) | Forecast Yr 1 | Forecast Yr 2 | Forecast Yr 3 | Forecast Yr 4 | Beyond |
|---|---|---|---|---|---|---|
| Revenue | $8,093,000 | - | - | - | - | |
| EBIT | $1,322,152 | - | - | - | - | |
| Op. Tax | $396,645 | - | - | - | - | |
| NOPAT | $922,977 | $973,741 | $1,027,297 | $1,083,798 | $1,143,407 | $1,143,407 |

NOPAT Growth Rates

| | | | | | | |
|---|---|---|---|---|---|---|
| NOPAT Growth Rate | | 5.5% | 5.5% | 5.5% | 5.5% | 0% |

Future Maintainable Profits Valuation

| | | | | | | |
|---|---|---|---|---|---|---|
| Cost of Capital | | 20.79% | 20.79% | 20.79% | 20.79% | 20.79% |
| NPV of NOPAT | | $806,144 | $704,099 | $614,972 | $537,127 | $2,583,585 |
| Cumulative NPV | | $806,144 | $1,510,244 | $2,125,216 | $2,662,344 | $5,245,929 |
| Business Value at Base Year | | | | | | $5,245,929 |
| Less: Debt at Base Year | | | | | | $1,884,130 |
| FMP Valuation - Equity Value at Base Year | | | | | | $3,361,799 |
| Owner's Value per Share | | (Avg. Share Price = $0 & No. of Shares = 0) | | | | N/A |

The above illustrates the effect of improving sales by 5%, cost of sales by 5%, and expenses by 5%. The result is an increase in EBIT of $434,983. That takes Smith Engineering Pty Ltd to best in class. That would take Smith Engineering Pty Ltd to $1,618,600 EBIT, and over 21% return on sales.

## Forecast Profit and Value Potential

| | Smith Engineering Pty Ltd | Smith Engineering Pty Ltd | Smith Engineering Pty Ltd | Smith Engineering Pty Ltd | Smith Engineering Pty Ltd |
|---|---|---|---|---|---|
| | as of today | after closing the profit gap | after achieving best in class (EBIT of 20%) | if attractiveness is improved | if sold to a listed company or a strategic exit |
| Revenue | $8,093,000 | $8,093,000 | $8,093,000 | $8,093,000 | $8,093,000 |
| EBIT | $1,322,152 | $1,576,837 | $1,618,600 | $1,618,600 | $1,618,600 |
| Multiple | 3.97 | 3.97 | 3.97 | 5.00 | 6.00 |
| Valuation | **$5.25M** | **$6.26M** | **$6.43M** | **$8.09M** | **$9.71M** |

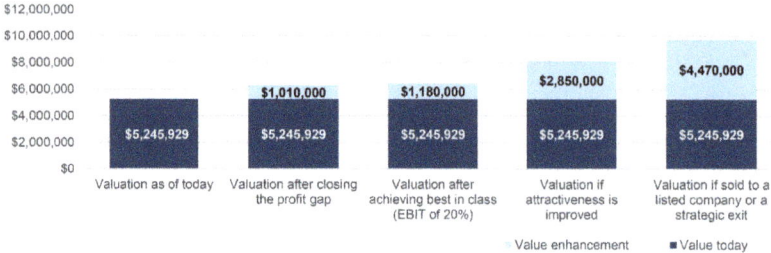

Value based on average of Future Maintainable Profits and Free Cash Flow Methods.

Many businesses owners erroneously believe that financial performance improvement is the only means of increasing the value of the business.

In fact, closing the profit gap and achieving best in class will lead to increased financial performance and therefore increase the value of the business.

However, at the right-hand side of diagram, we observe areas of substantial potential value improvement also include the boosting of attractiveness to external buyers and careful selection of a strategic acquirer, which have only an indirect relationship with profitability.

We can see the potential value uplift for Smith Engineering Pty Ltd, could be in the order of $4,470,000 over today's value, if recommendations in this report are carried out successfully.

19% of that improvement would come from closing the profit gap and a further 20% from reaching best practice EBIT margins. 26% of value improvement would be due to improving attractiveness and strategic acquirer selection.

## 21-Step Implementation Plan

After a detailed review of the report, the goal setting analysis and discussion of the proposed implementation plan, the owners agreed to proceed with a strategic advisory engagement as outlined by the implementation plan.

**Smith ENGINEERING**

**Implementation Plan for Smith Engineering**

| Stage | Step | Project | Status | FY 2017 | | | | | | | | | FY 2018 | | | | | | | | FY2019 | | | |
|---|---|---|---|---|---|---|---|---|---|---|---|---|---|---|---|---|---|---|---|---|---|---|---|---|
| | | | | Apr-17 | May-17 | Jun-17 | Jul-17 | Aug-17 | Sep-17 | Oct-17 | Nov-17 | Dec-17 | Jan-18 | Feb-18 | Mar-18 | Apr-18 | May-18 | Jun-18 | Jul-18 | Aug-18 | Sep-18 | Oct-18 | Nov-18 | Dec-18 | Jan-19 |
| One - Identify Value | 1. Goals & Outcomes | | | | | | | | | | | | | | | | | | | | | | | |
| | 2. Fact Find | | | | | | | | | | | | | | | | | | | | | | | |
| | 3. Stage One Report | 3a. Structural review | complete | | | | | | | | | | | | | | | | | | | | | | |
| | | 3b. Financial analysis | complete | | | | | | | | | | | | | | | | | | | | | | |
| | | 3c. Benchmarking and profit gap | complete | | | | | | | | | | | | | | | | | | | | | | |
| | | 3d. Non-financial Analysis | complete | | | | | | | | | | | | | | | | | | | | | | |
| | | 3e. Valuation | complete | | | | | | | | | | | | | | | | | | | | | | |
| Two - Protect Value | 4. Financial Planning | | | | | | | | | | | | | | | | | | | | | | | |
| | 5. Unplanned Events | | | | | | | | | | | | | | | | | | | | | | | |
| | 6. De-risking | 6a. Owner dependence | | | | | | | | | | | | | | | | | | | | | | | |
| | | 6b. Non financial analysis | | | | | | | | | | | | | | | | | | | | | | | |
| | | 6c. Key person risk | | | | | | | | | | | | | | | | | | | | | | | |
| Three - Maximise Value | 7. Exit Options | | | | | | | | | | | | | | | | | | | | | | | |
| | 8. Strategic Planning Business Model | 8a. Boutique vs Scale | | | | | | | | | | | | | | | | | | | | | | | |
| | | 8b. Efficiency or Expansion | | | | | | | | | | | | | | | | | | | | | | | |
| | | 8c. Strategic Succession Plan Document | | | | | | | | | | | | | | | | | | | | | | | |
| | 9. Strategic Financials | 9a. 5 * 5 * 5 | | | | | | | | | | | | | | | | | | | | | | | |
| | | 9b. Financial reporting package | | | | | | | | | | | | | | | | | | | | | | | |
| | 10. Systems & Procedures | 10a. HR tools & templates | | | | | | | | | | | | | | | | | | | | | | | |
| | | 10b. Systems, Policies & Procedures | | | | | | | | | | | | | | | | | | | | | | | |
| | 11. Marketing & sales | 11a. Brand Touch Points analysis | | | | | | | | | | | | | | | | | | | | | | | |
| | | 11b. Marketing plan | | | | | | | | | | | | | | | | | | | | | | | |
| | | 11c. Marketing & sales collateral | | | | | | | | | | | | | | | | | | | | | | | |
| | | 11d. CRM | | | | | | | | | | | | | | | | | | | | | | | |
| | | 11e. Sales reporting & forecasting | | | | | | | | | | | | | | | | | | | | | | | |
| | | 11f. Online strategy (including social media) | | | | | | | | | | | | | | | | | | | | | | | |
| | 12. Corporate Governance | 12a. Review business advisers (legal, accounting, insurance) | | | | | | | | | | | | | | | | | | | | | | | |
| | | 12b. Board composition & guidelines | | | | | | | | | | | | | | | | | | | | | | | |
| | | 12c. Family Council/communication | | | | | | | | | | | | | | | | | | | | | | | |
| | | 12d. Director succession | | | | | | | | | | | | | | | | | | | | | | | |
| | | 12e. Decision rights & authorities | | | | | | | | | | | | | | | | | | | | | | | |
| | 13. Ownership Mindset | | | | | | | | | | | | | | | | | | | | | | | | |
| | 14. Peak Performance Trust | | | | | | | | | | | | | | | | | | | | | | | | |
| | 15. Management Succession | 15a. Identify & recruit potential successors | | | | | | | | | | | | | | | | | | | | | | | |
| | | 15b. Management development & performance management | | | | | | | | | | | | | | | | | | | | | | | |
| Four - Extract Value | 16. Tax Planning | | | | | | | | | | | | | | | | | | | | | | | |
| | 17. Documentation | 17a. IM | | | | | | | | | | | | | | | | | | | | | | | |
| | | 17b. Due Dilligence | | | | | | | | | | | | | | | | | | | | | | | |
| | | 17c. Sale of Business | | | | | | | | | | | | | | | | | | | | | | | |
| | 18. Liquidity Event | | | | | | | | | | | | | | | | | | | | | | | | |
| Five - Manage Value | 19. Ongoing Investment Planning | | | | | | | | | | | | | | | | | | | | | | | |
| | 20. Asset Protection | | | | | | | | | | | | | | | | | | | | | | | | |
| | 21. Estate Planning | | | | | | | | | | | | | | | | | | | | | | | | |

## Letter to the Client

The next stage of the process is to send a letter to the client to outline the goals, a summary of the key results and identify the gaps that need to be addressed. There should be a meeting to discuss the recommendations and ensure the client is happy the goals set achieve the outcomes.

# • STEP 4
# FINANCIAL PLANNING

One of our favourite themes is "Begin with the end in mind." In financial planning terms, this means understanding exactly what your retirement looks like, what funding you will require to live the lifestyle you choose and who should own those assets after you sell your business, considering issues like asset protection, simplicity of operation, tax effectiveness and estate planning and other complex issues that require professional financial planning advice.

## 4.1 How much money will you need in retirement?

Many retirees greatly underestimate the amount of money they need to fund their retirement lifestyle, and there are two key statistics I regularly quote that show the importance of getting this part right.

A typical Australian male who turns age 50 is expected, on average, to live until 82, a remaining life expectancy of 32 years. This has serious implications in terms of funding retirement. It is much longer than retirees 50 years ago, who had to fund a fairly short life expectancy after work, and while medical science and technology are improving to increase our life span, our health costs increase.

Life expectancy at birth (years)

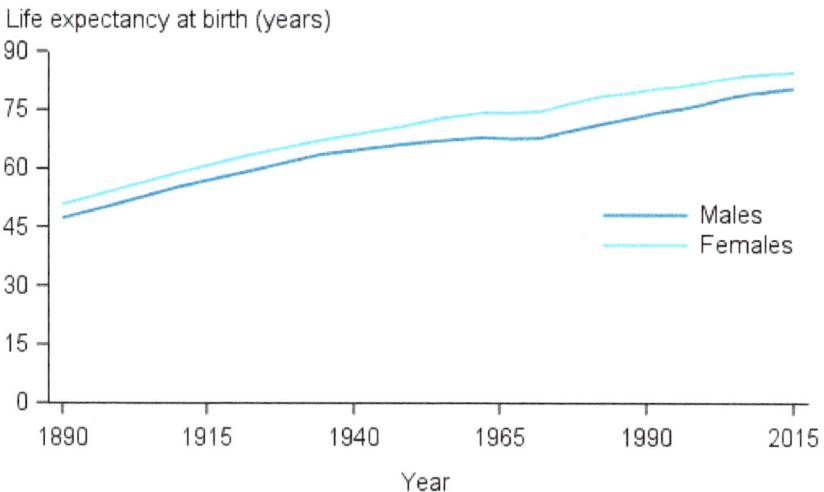

SUCCESSION

The second important thing to remember is that on average business owners spend far more money in retirement than they typically spent while running the business. Recent research studies suggest retirees spend up to 160% of preretirement spending, all due to one key factor — time. As a business owner you invariably find it difficult to take long holidays or travel overseas, but after exiting the business successfully you'll have the time to take trips and do the things that have been on your bucket list.

So we start with working out how much you need to fund your retirement, and then work backwards to see how we can get there. This will involve maximising the value of your business, looking at ways to release lump sums or ongoing income streams, and investment strategies for any other assets that you have — for example real estate, share portfolios, superannuation. So, we work with your financial planner to design an overall wealth plan. If you don't have a financial planner we can also help you find one.

Now is also a good time to get some tax advice to understand the whole picture. Ask your accountant — if you sold your business tomorrow at its current valuation, how much CGT would I have to pay? And secondly, can I improve on that? Tax advice is a crucial part of the financial planning process. Your business may be worth say $6 million, and you may have decided you need $4 million to fund your retirement. But after tax and transaction costs you may only walk away with $3 million.

There are a number of small business concessions, but you need good advice to make sure your exit is managed correctly to meet the various thresholds and conditions. We'll look at those in Step 16.

You may also think about a self-managed superannuation fund as a tax effective way to invest the proceeds from your business.

## 4.2 Protect Value

The next steps involve protecting the value that is already there through asset protection strategies, some insurances, preparing for unplanned events and de-risking the business.

## 4.3 Case Study

Personal and family information was provided as part of the initial fact find process at Step 2 and this is an important consideration for the next stage of the process.

In this stage, you will be asked specifically about your:

- objectives
- personal details
- financial dependents
- employment
- assets and liabilities
- superannuation
- insurance
- income and expenditure
- current advisers.

## Objectives

**YOUR OBJECTIVES**

Please provide as much information as you can. We will provide additional assistance in these areas during your appointment, should you need it.

*What is your main life and financial goals?*

It helps to be specific and comprehensive – you may wish to include some of the items listed in "IDEAS" below.

| IDEAS to include in your OBJECTIVES | Short Term (0-2 Years) | Priority (High, Med, Low) |
|---|---|---|
| Holidays | Work less | High |
| – Education | | |
| – Children | | |
| – Property | | |
| – Shares | | |
| – Work Arrangements | | |
| – Lumps Sums | Medium Term (3-7 Years) | |
| – Inheritance | | |
| – Self-employed | N/A | |
| – Renovations | | |
| – Retirement Recreation | | |
| – Purchases, e.g. cars, boats, jewellery | Long Term (7 Years +) Don't forget retirement income goals | |
| | Close the retirement gap. | High |
| | | |
| | | |
| | | |

*Are you on track to achieving your financial goals?*

Yes        No        Unsure_____

## Your personal details

Personal details include:

- do you smoke?
- do you have a will? If so, is it general or enduring, when was it updated, where is it located, who is the executor, have you granted anyone the power of attorney?

## Financial dependents

You need to provide details of anyone who is financially dependent on you, such as children, and include the following details:

- date of birth
- the year they are in school or university
- whether they have Austudy
- what year they are dependent on you until?

## Employment

You will need to provide information regarding your occupation and working life, such as:

- how long have you been with your current employer?
- whether you intend on changing your work status or employee in the near future?
- do you see your income earning capacity as being stable?
- do you have any other taxation structures?

## Assets and Liabilities

You need to provide an overview of what assets you own and what you currently owe, such as:

- whether you own your home
- investment properties
- motor vehicles — whether it is under a lease structure
- cash in the bank
- other investments in shares, unit trusts, cash in term deposit or any other significant assets or investments
- credit cards — include its limit, and what debt is owing on it
- personal or margin loans
- superannuation funds and plans — including any personal contributions and the current value
- trauma cover and income protection — include the annual premium, when it commenced, renewal date, the benefit value and the withdrawal value.

## Income and expenditure

An overview of the various sources of income you earn needs to be outlined. This would include:

- base salary
- commission or bonuses
- car allowance/novated lease
- social security
- rental income
- investment income.

It is important to note whether you think this income will change within the next 12 months and how much you think you can save per month without having a detrimental impact on your standard of living. Can you save any further income per month if you are motivated?

## Current advisers

The last part of your assessment is to provide details of professional advisers you use, such as:

- accountant
- solicitor
- insurance broker
- stock broker.

## • STEP 5

# UNPLANNED EVENTS

The average age of Australian business owners is 58, and sadly many business owners in their 60s can't afford to retire. Post GFC, around 50% of business owners are delaying retirement due to financial necessity. But these business owners, due to their age and potentially high stress levels, are in high risk categories for heart disease, cancers and age-related conditions.

## 5.1 What happens to your business when an unplanned event happens?

Many people avoid talking about death, wills or selling their business. And many families are left inheriting a burden. With no succession plan in place they are left with a business that can't survive without the owner. So they close the doors, or get the best price they can under the circumstances, selling off machinery or a few contracts. Some are left with an administrative nightmare because nothing is documented, compliance isn't up to date, there are debts outstanding or simply no one can log in to the business systems.

In the event of your death or serious illness, what would happen to your business? Do you have plans in place to ensure that control or ownership of the business is passed on to the successor of your choosing? And would your family be taken care of in the event of the business being sold? Is your will up to date, or would your estate be inherited by a previous spouse?

If you have worked hard to provide for your family, don't risk it by not protecting your assets. Develop a succession plan and talk to your loved ones about it so that they have somewhere to start if you are incapacitated. Think about a best case and worse case position; the best case will be a fully developed and executed succession plan that ends in a long, healthy and financially secure retirement! The worst case would be what your family would need to do in an emergency to manage or sell your business — the location of key documents, names of key people etcetera. Both will need a degree of effort on your part to get everything in order, but much less effort than it would be for a grieving family member with no previous involvement in your business.

Ideally, you will need to formulate plans to ensure that your business can survive an unplanned event such as an accident or illness. Part of this will be making sure you have a shareholders' agreement that clearly states who will manage and/or own the business in the case of your death or incapacitation.

## 5.2 Buy/Sell Agreements

If a buy/sell agreement is to be formed, then the Shareholders Agreement will usually state that both agreements must be executed at the same time.

Buy/sell agreements generally come into play in the event of an insurance 'trigger' event — that is, death, illness, accident or disablement. They allow business principals to plan for the future of the business by specifying whether the business should continue, be sold, transferred or liquidated in the event of their death or incapacitation.

The agreement may provide for the transfer of equity interests to the continuing owners by the payment of fair market value to the owner's estate (funded through life insurance) and deal with key person issues such as the elimination of debt, the extinguishment of personal guarantees and the replacement of lost revenue. A properly drafted buy/sell agreement can ensure that:

- the business value is preserved, and possibly even strengthened
- there is business stability for the continuing owners
- funds are available to allow the continuing owners to buy out the departing owner's share without putting the business in jeopardy
- funds are available for the payment of expenses such as capital gains tax (CGT) and stamp duties
- a fair price is paid to the outgoing owner or to his or her estate or financiers
- suppliers and customers are given certainty around the business's future

- the value of the business is preserved even with the departure of a principal
- business liabilities are repaid to reduce the financial burden on the business
- the risk of disputes between business owners is reduced should a trigger event ever occur.

Generally, there are two key aspects to any business succession agreement: a correct transfer arrangement and a correct funding arrangement. In any agreement it is important to establish:

- how the business will be valued, and using what methodology
- which events will trigger the agreement (these could include death, disability, resignation, bankruptcy, retirement or even criminal charges)
- what the succession obligations of the various business owners will be
- whether life insurance can and should be used to fund the payment of all or part of the purchase price.

When these considerations have been agreed, the documentation will then specify the terms and conditions of the agreement and how it is to be funded.

## 5.3 Case Study

An estate planning review forms the next part of the plan with wills, enduring powers of attorney and possible a testamentary trust being primary considerations. The Smiths also have a 32-year old daughter who does not work in the business and who has been divorced and remarried. She has children to both marriages so they are keen to look after her but at the same time protect the estate.

A review of their shareholders' agreement and buy/sell agreements was undertaken to ensure that all parties are protected in case of an unplanned event occurring (serious illness, death, incapacity). As a result, new agreements were written and insurance covers updated to reflect the increased value of the business.

An unplanned exit may occur due to:

1    Resignation
2    Divorce
3    Bankruptcy
4    Mental incapacity
5    Death
6    Total and Permanent Disability (TPD)
7    Trauma.

In the case of points 4 through to 7 funding or protection may be provisioned via the adoption of an insurance policy for principals or key persons.

The type of protection required may differ depending on the stage of the business. As a general rule, businesses will fall into one of the following categories:

- New Business — Asset Protection
  - High debt to equity
  - Owners may have;
    - Given the bank personal guarantees
    - Loaned seed capital
- Established Business — Revenue Protection
  - Established revenue patterns
  - Goodwill and turnover growing
  - Key person dependence
- Mature Business — Ownership Protection
  - Higher equity, succession issues
  - Less key person dependence
  - Shareholder/ beneficiary loan accounts.

## Consider the probability of an event triggered by Death, TPD or Trauma?

For Smith Engineering where there are three owners, there is a 72% chance that one of the owners will suffer from one of the above events. Statistically, men have a higher probably of an event occurring than women. Statistically, men have a higher probability of an event occurring than women.

## Business Owners worry about these issues:

- 47% of business owners indicated their spouse and/ or family worry more about the personal guarantee than they do
- 65% of business owners know someone who has lost personal assets as a result of a personal guarantee being called by a lender.

## Review and identify

Upon the death or permanent disability of a business principal/partner consider the following:

- Can the remaining principals service the debt?
- Will the bank continue to rely on any personal guarantee of a departing principal?
- Are personal assets at risk?
- Can the business repay the principal's loan account?
- Can the remaining partners purchase the departed partners equity in the business?
- Who will own the insurance policy?
  - The business — Consider tax consequences
  - The principals
- How are policy proceeds treated for tax purposes?
  - Death, Terminal illness — Tax Free
  - TPD, Critical Illness — Potential CGT event for business.

Using Insurance as a tool will deliver the liquidity required to allow for:

- the reduction or repayment of debt after the loss of a principal or key person which reduces interests, commitments and alleviates cash flow issues,
- repayment of principal loan accounts.

In summary, an insurance-based strategy will provide the necessary capital required to fund potential financial short comings in the event of an unplanned event. Such a strategy will protect the remaining shareholder as well as protect the departed shareholder(s) family.

## Unplanned Events Preparation Checklist

The purpose of the following questions is to assist us with ensuring all legal matters have been resolved, and identify any gaps. Consider the following:

- has the unplanned event checklist been completed?
- have lawyers been briefed?
- has a formal buy/sell agreement been finalised and signed?
- is the client aware of times when the agreement should be reviewed? This would be performed ideally annually at a strategy discussion and before a major life event
- has a suitable basis for valuing the business been reached in the documentation?
- have trigger points been determined in the documentation — such as divorce, temporary or permanent disability, resignation, retirement or criminal charges?
- have suitable funding arrangements been made that match these trigger points?
- has adequate consideration been given to taxation matters such as capital gains tax and stamp duty?
- have suitable deadlock provisions been determined in the documentation in case of shareholder dispute?
- has the documentation made suitable use of drag along/tag along provisions to protect minor and major shareholders alike in the event of major business events such as sale to an acquirer?
- have all owners been included in the process to enable consensus around the above matters?
- has the documentation been executed suitably so that it supersedes any past agreements, verbal or written?

Owners need to consider whether they are covered by life insurance and Total Permanent Disability. They also need to consider whether they have a will and powers of Attorney for all owners.

# • STEP 6
# DE-RISKING

The number one priority before selling your business is de-risking it. If you don't have time to complete a full succession strategy, focus on decreasing the risk first. The price for your business will be determined by Profit, Potential and Perceived risk, and while it's possible to improve all three, I'd argue that risk is the lever you have most control over and gives you the greatest return.

## 6.1 Risk and its effect on valuations

In valuation, there's a whole stock of methodologies and ways to value a business, but at the end of the day it comes down to two things: reward and risk. The reward is obviously the profit or the return from the business, but the risk in achieving that return is at the heart of valuations. That's true of BHP and Rio Tinto and Westpac Bank, and also the small business down the road.

Most small business owners we see don't have a handle on the risk element. They generally understand that their profit contributes to their valuation. But if we can identify all of those risks, we can show them the relationship between risk and the valuation multiple. If we can improve the risk, the valuation will increase. So that's an area we work on specifically with business owners. We also focus on WHO will buy the business to ensure the highest possible price.

## 6.2 Owner Dependence

Many small businesses are owner managed, meaning the business is completely dependent on the owner. If the owner becomes sick or takes a holiday, the business can't survive. Many business owners simply walk away because they have no one to sell the business to; they didn't have a succession plan, and therefore no succession happens.

Kell and Rigby, one of Australia's oldest building companies shut down after they failed to find a buyer. It was a family company spanning four generations over 102 years.

The construction company was a multiple winner of Master Builders Association awards and had been involved in some of the biggest projects in the state, including the War Memorial in Hyde Park and the renovation of Sydney Town Hall.

The CEO, James Kell, said the company had been negotiating a refinancing solution, but it fell through. He said the company had struggled to recover after a financial dispute over a luxury apartment complex in Rushcutters Bay in Sydney's eastern suburbs.

## 6.3 Non-financial Analysis

We looked at non-financial analysis in Step 3, where we identified and prioritised the weak points in the business. Non-financial analysis is all about finding and prioritising action on risk areas in the business. Now is the time to implement improvements in governance and compliance, strategy and planning, human resources, risk management and financial management.

For a detailed example of a client implementation plan, identifying the various work streams taken on by different experts over the succession plan timeframe, please refer to www.successionplus.com.au.

Based on our analysis of the non-financial risk items in Step 3 we now need to prioritise all those items where the business is underperforming in order to reduce risk. As the valuation is directly related to the level of risk within our business, each item identified in the scorecard needs to be prioritised according to importance and urgency. In the example earlier, I'd suggest that the absence of a shareholder's agreements/buy-sell agreement could lead to a major financial disaster if one of the shareholders becomes ill, while having an independent director on the board is less urgent or important to business survival.

The analysis highlighted that the business does not have a fixed remuneration system or employee share plan. Implementing either of these strategies involves several considerations, for example if a business does not have job descriptions and staff performance reviews in place there is little value in adding a formal remuneration review system.

Developing the succession plan often spans 18 months to two years but in managing its implementation we need to ensure that in each step of the process one of two key outcomes is achieved — either reducing risk in the business or improving performance/profitability.

## 6.4 Key Person Risk

"Steve Jobs may well be one in a billion, but he is not immortal. The company's share price has got the wobbles more than once when investors have become concerned about his health and the lack of a successor." — Emma Connors

Remember when Steve Jobs retired from Apple? Already battling cancer, Steve Jobs put in place a new management team and stood down as CEO. While the market's reaction was at first a little wobbly, Apple survived, and in fact following his subsequent death, the valuation of Apple saw unprecedented levels, becoming the most valuable company in history as at August 2012 and reaching a record US$1 trillion in August 2018.

While Apple as a business may be an unusual case, Steve Jobs' situation unfortunately is not. But he managed his succession well, developing a strong and able team around him that were able to take the reins when he no longer could. He also instilled such a strong sense of culture in the business that Apple employees were able to continue on as if he were still there, asking themselves: "What would Steve do?" Customers already loved the Apple brand and innovative product line, and would keep on buying whether Steve was there or not.

## Apple share price

In this case Steve Jobs was the CEO. In your business you may have a key person that you really can't do without — a sales manager who holds all the relationships with clients, a technical programmer or developer who manages your business systems, or a scientist who holds all of your research and development IP. Or the key person may be you.

In any size business if you have the right management team in place, loyal staff who understand your business philosophy, and ensure your customers will enjoy the same experience with or without you or your key people, you are well on the way to a successful exit. But many business owners are the key person in the business, and without them the business will fail.

If you are currently the key person in your business, how do we help you to gradually extract yourself? That will depend on the type and size of the business, but we will work with you to work out the key relationships and knowledge that you hold and develop transition steps. A key task will be to document as much as you can about your business.

McDonald's is a good example of a systemised business. What makes McDonald's so successful is that it is easily duplicated, with every McDonald's franchise running pretty much the same. The franchises run on a 'turnkey' system — the operations manuals and the procedures and systems for the running of a store are so comprehensive and logical that a new owner can literally turn the key and open the doors for trading.

Unfortunately, this is often far from the case for the typical family owned business. Much of the know-how is in the business owner's head, making it very difficult for anyone new to come in and get started. But buyers are prepared to pay more for businesses that have documented systems, policies and procedures. You might pay a multiple of one or two times for a local burger bar, but around 6 times to buy into a McDonald's franchise.

Break down the areas of the business into its key functions and areas and then keep drilling a level deeper to identify all the processes in your business. For a retail outlet or workshop, you might start with the procedures to open and close up the shop. As you write each step, keep asking yourself 'how' to make sure you are not just assuming that a staff member would know how to complete each step, for example setting the alarm system or switching on the air conditioning. Make sure you are not expecting them to get from A to C without first guiding them through step B. A good way to test this is to get someone not involved in the business to try to perform each task as they have been written (properly supervised if there is any safety risk!).

Documentation of processes requires balance between being detailed and comprehensive while not being so long that no-one will bother to read it. Number each step so that it is easy to follow and gives the reader a sense that they are progressing through the task.

Next, put the processes where everyone can access them. For larger companies this may be an intranet site, or it may just be a folder on a shared network drive. You might print them in a book on site. Whichever way you choose, make sure each process or set of instructions is easy to find — clearly titled and in a logical order. Then assign staff members to update the processes regularly, or as changes occur.

Here are some examples of documentation that you will need to create or update when implementing your succession plan:

- General instruction manuals on operating systems, opening and closing, contact details for management team, security staff
- Shareholders plan, company constitution
- Sales processes — document each step in the sales process from adding customers to your database, dealing with an order, through to invoicing, returns policy, credit policies and ongoing relationships
- Procurement — document how you go about finding suppliers, any due diligence you do on them, purchase order process, dealing with invoices
- IT systems — document which systems deal with which processes and any software licences, expiry dates etc. Now is also a good time to get someone to overhaul your systems to look for efficiencies
- Staff procedures — document processes from recruitment and induction to job descriptions, performance management processes, leave policies, workplace behaviour policies, OH&S policies and termination.

Documentation can be a laborious task, but it helps the business to run smoothly without you, allows staff to take ownership and accountability of tasks without too much one-on-one training time, and of course helps to add value to your business. You can ask each staff member to get involved in the workload by documenting the processes they are involved in, and then switching with other employees to test the procedures. Or, you can take on a contractor to take full responsibility, although note they will still need access to your team and their time.

Of course, implementing this plan early is recommended because transitioning your role to other team members takes time, but there are other important factors at play. I mentioned earlier that it is better to start the exit process when you still have a passion, drive, and energy for your business, not when you have become stale or the business is in decline. It's also important to have time to ride the waves of the capital markets — transitioning yourself out of the business as the manager means you can start to enjoy some time off before you actually sell, and means you can wait for the right buyer and the right price.

In Steps 13 and 14, we look at ways to make sure the business does not lose its key people, with various incentive plans.

## Maximise Value

The next stage is usually quite an extended one where we look at maximising the value. Your plan is in place, you have worked on de-risking your business and reducing your operational involvement, and now it's time to make the business as attractive as possible to a potential buyer.

When we first arrive at a valuation of a business very few owners say, "I'm happy with that, let's sell." They generally want and need to improve the value to fund their retirement.

The next steps show the strategies we implement to increase your valuation multiple. Note that larger businesses tend to achieve a higher multiple than small businesses, partly because the perceived risk is lower — larger businesses are expected to have a strong management team, more people to cover each other's roles, more governance, better systems and processes and less reliance on a small number of clients. Significantly growing your business may add to its ultimate value on exit. But first, we look at the different options in actually exiting your business.

## 6.5 Case Study

### Risk Assessment Presentation

Smith Engineering undertake a risk assessment. The following scales are used to determine the possibility that a given event will occur:

### Likelihood Scale

Likelihood represents the possibility that a given event will occur. It can be expressed as being almost certain to occur, likely, possibly, unlikely or rarely to occur.

It uses a rating scale from 1 to 5 showing it will almost certainly happen — or 90% or greater chance of occurring over the life of the asset or project, to a rating of 1 which is described as rare or less than 10% chance of occurring over the life of the asset or project.

### Impact Scale

Impact scale is the extent to which a risk event may affect the business.

A rating scale is also used. 5 represents an extreme impact to the business, such as:

- financial loss of $X million or more
- international long-term negative media coverage, game changing loss of market share
- significant prosecution and fines, litigation including class action, incarceration of leadership
- significant injuries or fatalities to employees or third parties such as customers or vendors.

A rating of 1 represents an incidental impact of risk to the business, such as:

- financial loss less than $100,000
- local media attention quickly remedied
- not reportable to regulator
- no injuries to employees or third parties
- isolated staff dissatisfaction.

## Vulnerability Scale

This is the susceptibility of a business to risk events, having regard to the entity's preparedness, agility and adaptability. The more vulnerable a business is to a risk, the higher the impact will be, should it occur.

The rating of 5 is for very high susceptibility down to 1 — being very low vulnerability.

Some examples of what a business can be vulnerable to when it is given a rating of 5 are:

- no scenario planning performed
- lack of enterprise level
- responses not implemented
- no contingency or crisis management in place.

Where a rating of 1 is given, the business has:

- real options deployed to maximise strategic flexibility
- high enterprise level/process level capabilities to address risks
- contingency and crisis management plans in place and rehearsed regularly.

For the Smith Engineering case study, we have only nominated a selected number of risks. Normally, we would identify 50 to 60 individual risks and hazards to create a comprehensive risk reduction program.

Smith Engineering are asked to give each of the following risks a rating in relation to the likelihood, impact and vulnerability for the possibility of these risks actually occurring:

- poor treatment of customers or workers
- lack of market integrity
- failure to advance company in an ethical manner
- lack of regular stock take of conduct risk strategies to get the best outcomes
- compromise company and customer outcomes
- not advancing ethical approach to business
- promotional and information material not accurate and understandable

- failure to change and improve information for customers
- inadequate channels to submit claims and seek redress
- based on work performance and well balanced against financial performance
- not consider customer, complexity and transparency in offerings.

We then use a "Heat Map" to illustrate the likelihood and the impact of a risk. This map highlights the speed in which the risk will actually occur.

## Business Continuity Plan (Smith Engineering)

### 1 Company Overview

In laying out the company's Business Continuity Plan (BCP), the critical business functions have been identified and prioritized. The company's BCP attempts to accurately determine the most important business functions. Business applications have been evaluated for business impact if they were delayed or failed, and an appropriate priority assigned. The aim was to effect a negative impact scenario around failure of any key business.

The functions have been evaluated for their contribution to business success in terms of:

- Brand damage
- Lost market share
- Product failure; or
- Legal/Regulatory consequences

The company has paid particular attention to the following Business Continuity areas:

1. Recovery Point Objectives (RPOs). The company's tolerance for lost data is inherent in its data risk precautions including effective file and document archive procedures to prevent losing files totally.
2. Comprehensive risk analysis has been carried out on all critical facilities.
3. The company has not overlooked the succession component of BCP planning and there is testing occurring for key role replacement. As a checkpoint in the Business Continuity Plan, the company will be selecting an alternate for each critical staff position, who will then be asked periodically to perform response and recovery functions in place of the incumbent during planned tests. This should later become a documented element in all job descriptions and performance review standards.
4. Multiple sources of critical supplies and processes are in place as a contingency.
5. Tools and training have been provided to ensure staff are well-trained and practiced and are the first line of defense in identifying situations that could become serious. Part of the plan is to teach employees to recognize the signs of an impending disruption in normal activity.

To minimise the risk to the business in the event of a disaster, the company needs to identify all asset types and resources, including:

- physical assets such as the factory and office premises, vehicle fleets, plant and equipment and IT assets, and
- non-physical assets such as personnel, company reputation and intellectual property.

The functions of the business must be able to immediately be replaced in case of a total disaster, including:

- Safety procedures
- Location of records
- Cash inflow
- Staff payment
- Alternative premises
- Maintaining contact with customers
- Obtaining plant and equipment.

The threats and risks that need to be considered, include:

1. Natural disasters — flood, cyclone, earthquake
2. Accidents — fire, severe injury to staff
3. Malicious — bomb, cyber attack
4. Market risks from suppliers, competitors and consumer trends
5. Strike action.

In the event of any of these threats occurring, the following checklists and action plans need to be implemented:

1. Plan of action for each unlikely threat or risk for the foreseeable outcomes
2. Evacuation procedures in an emergency situation to ensure all employees are safe
3. Security policy procedures to protect employees, buildings, facilities and information
4. Disaster recovery and survival checklist to assess what resources are available and what has been damaged to ensure the business survives in the short, medium and long-term outlook.

## • STEP 7
# EXIT OPTIONS

Perhaps the most important thing and probably also the most difficult thing for most small and medium business owners to get their heads around is the very important concept of beginning with the end in mind. When I ask business owners "What do you want from your business in ten years' time?" or "What is the end game for your business?" I very rarely get clear answers. Many people have never been asked to think about this important aspect.

## 7.1 Introduction

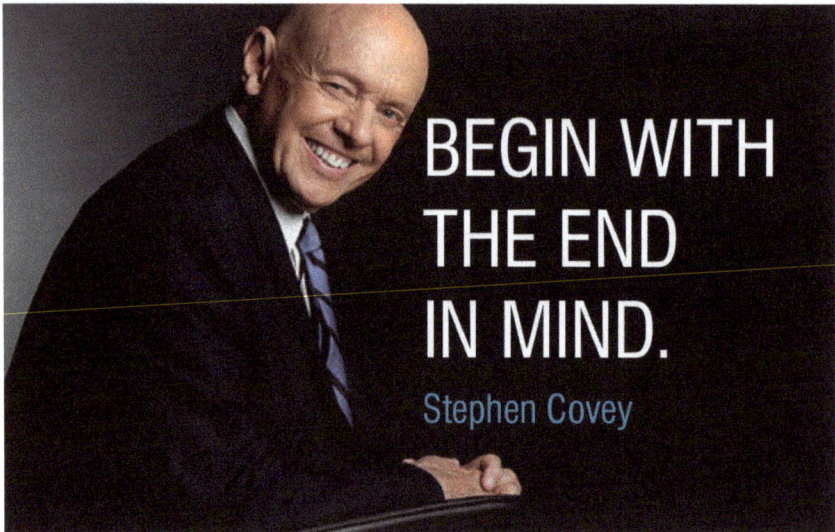

BEGIN WITH
THE END
IN MIND.
Stephen Covey

A simple analogy is I jump into a taxi outside Sydney airport. The driver asks "Where do you want me to take you, Sir?" and I reply "Not really sure, drive around for a while and we'll see what happens."

Unfortunately, many business owners operate their business using exactly this model day-to-day, driving around without really having a very clear destination in their head. Even more importantly, that destination needs to be documented and clearly communicated to key stakeholders, employees and family.

## 7.2 The 'Simple Sale'

Many business owners come to Succession Plus saying they need help through a 'simple sale' process. Unfortunately, there is no such thing as a 'simple' sale. There are sales in which the owners put in limited preparation, put an advertisement in the local paper and have a few meetings with prospective buyers ending in a contract of sale. Unfortunately, these sales often lead to big problems during the transaction or shortly after. Typically, they will be because the sale process did not allow sufficient time for the transition of the business to be managed well.

These transactions are usually based on the seller trying to achieve the maximum possible price (or in some cases of desperation, the quickest possible sale), and the buyer trying to pay the minimum possible price. The business usually transfers quickly because the previous owner wants to take their money and get out without regard for the new owner's ability to run the business profitably, effectively and efficiently.

Obviously, we don't recommend this sale process. A good succession plan is a win-win situation for the exiting and incoming shareholders. You achieve an appropriate sale value to fund your retirement, and the buyer(s) get a good stable business with future potential.

There are a number of ways to exit your business that can achieve a win-win situation. The graph below shows the options available to you and their relative time, complexity and effort to achieve. As a general rule of thumb, as the complexity and effort increases, you are rewarded with a higher price. With all options you will need to plan to achieve the best outcome, and all options will require you to get tax advice well in advance.

**Potential sale price/value**

## 7.3 Transfer of ownership between family members or friends

A business owner may transfer or sell part or all shares in the business to family members or friends. This is the least complex in terms of documentation, legal requirements and process, but certainly has its own challenges. Transferring ownership of a business from one generation to the next within a family is the ultimate management challenge, but the Australian Family and Private Business Survey 2013 (MGI Australasia), reported 48% of business owners intended to keep the business in continuous family ownership. But unfortunately, barely 26 per cent of family businesses survive into the second generation, and fewer than 14 per cent endure into the third (MGI Australasia).

Effective succession planning is especially important within family businesses since they come with additional challenges and stressors particular to the family.

When developing a succession plan within a family, we take account of factors such as:

- relationships between family members
- health of family members

- each family member's interests and skill levels
- the degree of influence family members have over each other
- competition between family members
- the degree to which various family members are involved in the business.

Succession within a family business usually involves the transfer of control and ownership — each of which should be considered separately.

Often, control succession happens by default — there will usually be one member of the next generation more active, qualified and interested in the business than his or her siblings, and usually the founder will have already spent a great deal of time grooming the likely successor over a number of years. Dividing control of the business between different successors is rarely successful, unless there are well-defined functions or business units that different family members can assume control of, or they have very defined skill sets (example finance versus marketing).

If there is competition between family members for the position, and a successor hasn't already been identified by interest, proximity or birth order, it can be useful to convene a transition team made up of senior staff (including non-family members) to choose the successor without adversely affecting the business. Giving key, non-family employees the opportunity to participate in the transition team can mean that there is increased support for the successor, which will benefit the continuity of the organisation over the long-term.

While transition of control may happen organically over time, transition of ownership requires the same careful planning and documentation as a trade sale process to minimise tax implications, and ensure that the legal reality reflects the informal intentions. A family succession plan should allow for contingency plans should a key stakeholder be incapacitated, and also be consistent with the business owner's will. In particular it should deal with future events such as divorce, partners or any step children that would not automatically inherit a share of the business, but may well be actively involved.

While this may be the least complex method in terms of documentation, make sure you get a business valuation to lock in the value of the shares at the time of transfer. This will help to minimise family dispute later, and determine the capital gains tax and stamp duty on this transfer and future capital gains tax for the new shareholders.

## 7.4 Selling the Database

If you are self-employed rather than 'running a business,' or your business has little resale value for whatever reason, you may be able to extract some value from selling your database, usually to a competitor. Some businesses have a large email database that has a high conversion rate, or are in industries that tend to have a high level of repeat business. Financial planners and mortgage brokers sell their 'book' of trail income on existing clients, whereas the trades and service industries (plumbers, electricians, hairdressers, beauticians etc) may be able to onsell their client list.

As there are no shares changing hands, the process can be much quicker and less complex than selling the whole business, but you will need advice to make sure the sale of client information is handled within legal requirements, and again to maximise the value on sale.

## 7.5 Sell to Other Shareholders

Similar to a transfer to family members, a sale to existing shareholders is less complicated than some other exit options since you already have a relationship with the buyers, and they have a good understanding of the business. Again, you will need assistance in drafting the legal documentation to make sure the sale process is smooth. You will also need a formal valuation of the business to assign a value to the shares that will also be used for capital gains tax calculations.

In this scenario your succession plan will focus on transition of control and management if the shareholders are not actively involved in the business, and as in the family transfer you will need to identify a transition team to minimise business interruption.

## 7.6 Partial Sale

A partial sale involves selling some of your shares to a third party, and is somewhere between a sale to existing shareholders/family and a trade sale, depending on the buyer. If the buyer is already involved with your business or in the same industry, the process may be similar to the family transfer.

A partial sale may be the first step to a trade sale or private equity sale. That is, the buyer makes a partial acquisition to start to build a relationship with the business, with a view to buying out the existing shares at a later date. Additional legal agreements may be required to document future milestones that will be reached, or to give the buyer the right to buy future shares using a call option. A partial sale can be a good way to free up some cash and create future options while developing the full succession and transition plan.

## 7.7 Employee Share Ownership Plan

An employee share plan allows employees to own shares in the company. This is a great way to motivate employees (since shares can be awarded in place of cash bonuses) and encourage loyalty. Once staff members are shareholders in the business it often changes their behaviour — they talk about 'we' instead of 'they' and are much more conscious of performance and decisions impacting the bottom line. Employee share plans are usually operated using a trust, which can help to fund the share purchase for employees. This is covered in more detail in Steps 13 and 14. It is also the subject of my revised book 'build it' which can be downloaded at www.successionplus.com.au.

Transferring ownership to employees is a way to manage control succession as well as ownership; the key employees needed to run the business are given incentives to stay and step up (see MBO below). Benefits such as equity participation can be powerful tools in recruitment and retention.

Again, you will need a formal valuation of the business to determine the value of shares, and legal advice in drafting an employee share plan and setting up a trust.

## 7.8 Internal Sale or Management Buyout

In my opinion, a management buyout (MBO) can be one of the most successful transactions. The current management team buys you out of your business, and continues to operate the business.

An MBO gives business owners a greater sense of certainty about the ongoing potential of their business. In most cases ownership is transferred to people that the existing owners know and have worked with. The transition can be planned over a much longer period and successors can be groomed according to the specific needs of the business and each individual's skill set.

Very few people know more about your business than those who already work in it, and will invariably have their own suggestions as to how the business can be improved. Assuming the staff are willing to participate in a management buyout, we can assume there is a reasonable match between the business, staff, values, culture and the existing owners.

Staff members who buy equity in the business and participate as an employee and a shareholder or owner are more likely to stay with the business. They are more motivated, more dedicated, loyal and focused — behaving less like employees and more like business owners. This also helps to attract other like-minded people to the business.

Management Buy-in (MBI) is becoming more popular as a Business Succession and Exit Planning tool for mid-market business owners looking to achieve a successful exit. As part of my Doctoral research (into exactly this topic), I have been looking into the various components that make for a successful implementation of a management buy-in — where key people within the business purchase equity (or a management buyout — where they purchase the entire business).

An MBI or MBO can achieve several of the key outcomes that most business owners are looking for when they prepare for an exit; which include:

- ensuring the business continues after they exit and/or retire;
- ensuring their employees (and customers/suppliers) are looked after; and
- using the sale of their asset (the business) to fund retirement.

In many ways, this is an ideal solution for mid-market businesses. Employees who are engaged and have their financial interests aligned with the owner are likely to be more productive and focused on business performance. Reducing the risk of key employees leaving also increases the value of the business (any reduction in risk leads to an increase in business value) and a predetermined sale at an agreed price with an accompanying funding model is attractive.

Over the last few months, we have developed a six-month program to implement an MBO ensuring that all of the various aspects are managed. Personal Profile Analysis (we are licensed to use this tool thru Thomas International) allows us to identify the interactions between key people, how they communicate and how they might work together (or not), and importantly, how to improve the interactions and communication. Employee Engagement includes a staff survey to determine attitudes towards the business and key issues identified by staff to improve the performance of the business. Management succession and corporate governance are also key aspects necessary to maximise the likelihood of success.

## 7.9 Trade Sale

A trade sale is the process of selling your business to another company, which may be a private company or a public listed company. You may sell to a competitor, supplier or customer that can see strategic and cost advantages in bolting the businesses together.

In many ways a trade sale can be an easier and more successful option because in most cases the people buying your business will have experience and knowledge in the industry, and have their own way of operating a business. A trade buyer is also likely to be a 'strategic buyer' which means that they may pay a higher price for the business.

## 7.10 Strategic Sale

Strategic sale refers to the price a particular buyer is willing to pay for a business above and beyond its financial value. There are many reasons that a business may hold more future value for a particular buyer. Here are some examples:

- you own a valuable piece of technology or asset
- you have penetrated a market that they want access to, or have a contract with a key client
- you have employees that they want
- they want to prevent their competitor from buying you
- having your business combined with theirs will give them the highest market share or a unique offering
- the combined businesses will bring significant economies of scale (beyond an average trade sale).

Professional buyers generally have mandates that revolve around key strategies that the company may be pursuing. Some we have seen include:

- geographic expansion
- product line addition
- vertical and horizontal integration
- economies of scale
- access to skilled employees.

These are just a few examples. Here are some facts to ponder:

1    big companies really do buy small companies
2    buyers might see different opportunities for growth than you do
3    buyers are buying your future, not your past

4    often you are too close to the daily grind to realise the significant opportunities your company can capitalise on in the hands of new ownership

5    your company probably has significant intangible assets that an experienced M&A team can leverage to attract buyers

6    you most likely have been minimising your pre-tax profits for years. Recasting allows you to present the true profitability of your organisation.

To maximise the value of a business on sale there are three things to focus on:

1    Increase profit
2    Increase the multiple (by decreasing risk and increasing potential)
3    Sell to a strategic buyer.

A good example of a strategic purchase is Instagram. Despite not making any profits and not having much future potential to make profits, Facebook bought Instagram for $1 billion, largely to knock a competitive threat out of the market. The attraction for Facebook was Instagram's momentum, fast ascension and almost cult like following with over 30 million users, which helped cement Facebook's product offering in mobile technology.

## 7.11 Sale to a listed company

The long-term price earnings average for companies listed on the ASX is 13.73. This is the valuation of the business divided by its annual earnings, which is equivalent to an earnings multiple. Obviously it varies across industries and sizes of business but let's use the average of 13.73. The long-term average for private companies is 2.5. If a private company makes $1 million dollars a year, its value, using the 2.5 average multiple, would be $2.5 million. If it was instantly listed on the ASX (which is not going to happen) we could expect a valuation of something close to $13.73 million. The gap between is called arbitrage. So we have to look into how we as small business owners can take advantage of that.

If a listed company buys a private company it benefits from that arbitrage. So it may pay say $4 million to $5 million (a multiple of four or five times) to secure the company, in the knowledge that the acquired business instantly becomes revalued at $13.73 million once added into the listed company's assets.

Selling to a listed company isn't simple — you have to position yourself for the purchase. But if you're prepared to take the time and effort to do that, the valuation difference could be significant. Our aim at Succession Plus is to attract this type of buyer.

**ASX 200 PE Ratio**

Source: Bloomberg sector PE, positive and market cap weighted

## 7.12 Merger

A merger is a joining of two entities where neither entity is deemed to control the other (conversely in a trade sale the acquiring company usually controls the new business and absorbs it into existing operations or operates it as a subsidiary). Mergers are about matching, and it is very difficult to match two businesses successfully to form a merged entity due to:

- financial disparity between the two businesses and/or their owners
- ethical and values-based clashes between the owners
- operational differences
- a poorly matched client base, for example one business might be looking for premium clients while the other is attracting low budget clients.

SUCCESSION

Typically, the synergies anticipated from merging the two businesses are not as great as originally thought. The owners can underestimate the level of involvement required in the merger or the quirks and specialities in the new business. In the meantime, they may take their focus off their existing business, with the effect of decreased profitability.

Often, the employees become confused about the business strategy, new lines of reporting and ultimately who is controlling or managing the business day-to-day. In many cases, merged businesses lose staff shortly after the merger takes place. But there are many examples of successfully merged businesses, particularly among professional practices. Mergers work best where there is a strong match between the businesses, the owners, the client bases, the systems and the internal cultures.

## 7.13 Private Equity/Venture Capital

Private Equity and Venture capital firms are institutional investors that invest in or acquire businesses with strong growth potential. Their aim is usually to grow the business and exit within three to five years, often through an IPO. If you have private equity or venture capitalists interested in your business you will need to be extremely well prepared for the negotiation and due diligence processes.

As professionals, they demand a thorough process and drive a hard bargain. Professional investors may invest into your business in the growth stage to take a minority equity stake, while giving them the option to buy out 100% at a later date. This fits in well with long-term succession planning.

## 7.14 IPO (Listing)

An initial public offering or IPO is generally a fund raising exercise rather than an exit strategy, since the business founders will usually retain some equity post listing. However it does allow you to reduce your shareholding and can be a way to achieve maximum value.

Listing on an exchange such as the ASX is an expensive, time-consuming process that rarely produces the results that business owners expect. Once listed on a publicly traded exchange the company is bound by compliance and reporting requirements to protect current and prospective shareholders, who are not involved in the day to day running of the business. Exchanges require detailed and regular reporting and disclosure, which can be costly and consume valuable resources without delivering anything of substantial value to the owners.

Listing is obviously only available to a certain size of business, and is not appropriate for all business owners.

## Exit options used by SME business owners

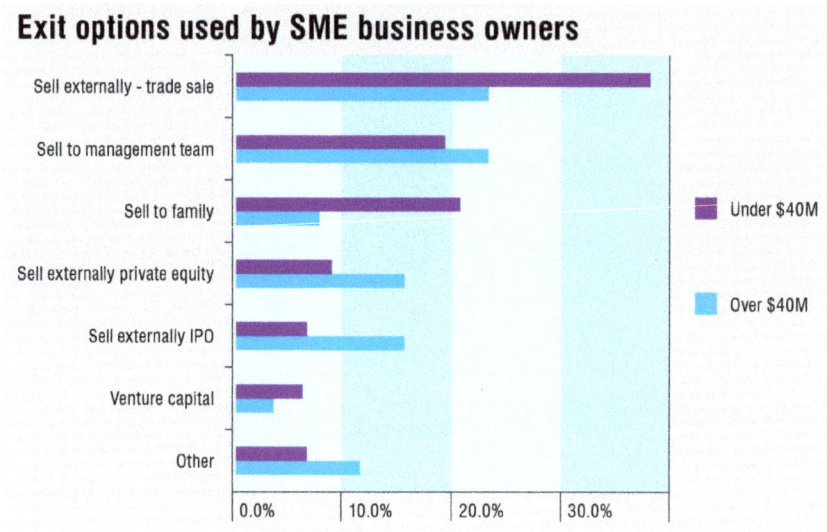

## 7.15 Funding the Transaction

When a business owner starts to sell the family business they don't often think about how the buyer will fund the business; they don't see it as their problem. And that may be true in the case of a business owner who is looking for a quick sale and who has no real interest in who buys their business, or in the new owner's ability to continue to grow the business. Business owners who want to ensure their business is transferred into the hands of the right successors may need to consider how the ideal new owners will afford to buy into the business, and this should form part of the succession planning strategy.

Understanding the various funding options will help you to understand your buyer's motivation, and therefore be more responsive in the negotiating period. Business sales, unlike houses, rarely involve simply exchanging cash for the keys on one day. Some of the more creative methods can lead to a good outcome for all parties, and most importantly facilitate the deal getting done in a tough market. Here we explore some innovative methods for funding your business sale/ acquisition, and offer some insights into the benefits of buy-in through equity participation.

In many businesses, your ideal buyer may be a young entrepreneur who is also starting a new family, buying a new house or getting married — a range of life circumstances that do not lend themselves particularly well to having surplus cash available. In some cases, it may be possible for the new owners to finance a business purchase though a home mortgage. But the downside is that if something were to happen to the value of their shares in the business their home is at risk.

Macquarie Bank, for example, offers a product called Goodwill Funding to professional practices such as legal firms and accounting practices, and businesses such as veterinary surgeries, pharmacies and real estate agencies where there is a reasonably predictable and maintainable stream of income. This funding is secured by the goodwill of the business based on its ongoing maintainable earnings and profit. It does not require property as security, but it may require directors' guarantees and security over the business assets.

Other lenders such as Investec (an investment bank) and ANZ have developed products specifically to fund management buyouts and buy-ins and internal succession. In successful businesses these products rely mainly on the business repaying the debt through its cash flow, sometimes without the need for external security. The lender will register a charge over the assets (a type of mortgage granting priority over the assets if anything goes wrong) and may even introduce some converting preference shares. These are a special type of share that basically act as a debt facility and on certain events convert to equity — so, if things are not going so well the debt converts to equity and ownership of some of the company transfers to the lender. In October 2012 Australia's Channel 9 just avoided administration by converting almost $1 billion into equity.

Another alternative is for the business itself to arrange finance for the new purchaser. This is called vendor financing, and can be arranged through business cash flow, an extension of the existing business overdraft or a new loan taken out and secured by the business for the express purpose of enabling the new purchaser to buy shares from the existing shareholders. Under this method the buyer takes ownership (or part ownership) immediately, and therefore responsibility for operating the company, but can pay for the purchase over time from the business profits. Effectively, the new owner forgoes dividends or sacrifices part of their salary until the debt is repaid.

When setting up a vendor finance agreement it is important to make sure the value of the equity and terms are matched well so that the income generated should largely fund the annual repayments.

There are some tax benefits for the purchaser when borrowing money for investment purposes, and these can make the purchase more affordable in most cases. Equally, there are some tax benefits to the vendor when cash received is staged over several years.

## 7.16 Equity Matrix

"If you think of life as like a big pie, you can try to hold the whole pie and kill yourself trying to keep it, or you can slice it up and give some to the people around you, and you still have plenty left for yourself." — Jay Leno

You don't have to sell off all of the shares in your business in one go; you can stage your exit over time. In vendor financing control and ownership changes on the transaction date, but the cash is staged over time. An alternative is to match cashflow with equity in a gradual sell down of your shares.

This works especially well with succession to family members, or to a competitor who wants you to reach a few milestones before they take on the full risk. If you do a deal with a buyer that wants a gradual acquisition, you need to get started early since this process works best over five to ten years.

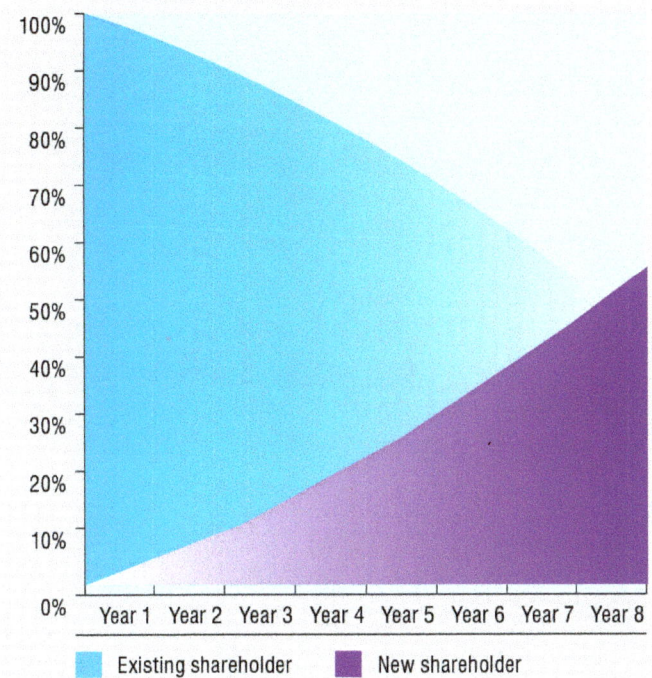

The idea is that you gradually own fewer shares in a business that is increasing in value, so the dollar value of your shareholding doesn't really fall. At the same time the buyer acquires increments of shares in a business that is increasing in value, so with each purchase they increase ownership, but pay a higher price per share.

Let's look at an example where a business owner, who owns 80% of the company, gradually sells down his equity to the 20% shareholder, his son.

129

Over the eight-year exit plan the business increases in value at 10% per year because of various value maximisation strategies.

Shareholder 1 reduces his shareholding from 80% to 20%, yet the value of that 20% is only just less than half the original value. In the meantime he has received cash payments each year at 10% of the current business value (a total of $771,000). So if he sold the additional 20% now he would have achieved $1.125m for a shareholding that was originally worth $800,000.

As the business grows in value Shareholder 2 owns 80% of a $1.8m business, but has benefited from buying those shares at a lower rate over the years. During the succession plan he has paid $771,000 for an additional 60% of the equity, now valued at $1,062,000.

As an extreme example, the early angel investors in Amazon were eventually diluted to a minuscule fraction of ownership of the company, yet they enjoyed a 4,000 times return on their invested money.

Of course this doesn't work for everyone but if you don't need a big lump sum in the next few years a gradual divestment can be a win-win situation and gives you time to reduce your involvement in the business while taking some cash out to achieve your personal financial goals — be it pay off the mortgage, help out the kids, fund medical bills or travel. Your time or effort in the business should follow a similar pattern — you train and develop shareholder two so that his knowledge gap lessens and value to the business increases over time.

| Year | Business Value | Shareholder 1 | | Shareholder 2 | | Buy/Sell Value |
|---|---|---|---|---|---|---|
| | $000 | Equity | Value | Equity | Value | $000 |
| 1 | $1,000 | 80% | $800 | 20% | $200 | $100 |
| 2 | $1,100 | 70% | $770 | 30% | $330 | $110 |
| 3 | $1,210 | 60% | $726 | 40% | $484 | $121 |
| 4 | $1,331 | 50% | $665 | 50% | $666 | $133 |
| 5 | $1,464 | 40% | $586 | 60% | $878 | $146 |
| 6 | $1,611 | 30% | $483 | 70% | $1,128 | $161 |
| 7 | $1,772 | 20% | $354 | 80% | $1,418 | |

## 7.17 Case Study

### Strategy Workbook

To build a great strategy, we need to be clear about where you want to take the business. Participating in a workshop helps us to set the direction of your business for the next 3 years.

You need to fill out a workbook to assist us in preparing for this workshop. The material in the workbook relates to getting your mind in the right space and to give us a head start so that we can make the most of the workshop.

The following questions are examples of what material is contained in the workbook:

### Year in Review

- How has your business changed in the past year? List major accomplishments of the business, as well as any challenges, relating to:
  - managing the business
  - financial consequences
  - operations of the business.

- What had you hoped to achieve but didn't?
- What do you think prevented the business from accomplishing these goals?
- What were you hoping to achieve personally?

## The Future

We ask you to provide a picture of what your business would ideally look like in three year's time and ask the following questions to help build this picture:

- What does the business do?
- Who are its main customers?
- What is your role in the business?
- Who are the new people working in the business and what do they do?
- What products or services does the business now offer?
- How much profit does it make?
- What is the atmosphere like amongst the people who work in the business?

We then ask you to imagine you have just walked through your office in three years time since your strategy session with us. You need to write down how you feel about:

- what the business has accomplished
- your role in the business
- what you are now able to do in life given the business has reached this point.

## John Smith

John provided the following information in his workbook:

### Year in Review

He was sad to lose some clients in the last couple of years. Some were asked to move on as they weren't providing any profit margin, others were no longer profitable. All staff are working a little too hard and he needs to hire more staff. Rod has improved considerably in managing and monitoring the financial performance of the business.

John had hoped to gain more business in the new design and engineering department, but hadn't due to underestimating how hard it is to roll out a new service.

Personally, John achieved a number of goals, which include:

- hiring two sales representatives
- getting Rod to build a budget for the Board's approval
- systemising the sales piece with the commencement of a live funnel that can be monitored.

In three years' time, John looked at the business and was extremely proud. He would like more leisure time and to consider the Life After Business Plan.

## Jane Smith

Jane has achieved a number of goals for the year, including:

- expanding the marketing budget
- emphasising new services to the existing clients and attracting new clients
- hired two sales representatives who now carry out these functions
- implemented new enterprise resource planning software.

Jane had hoped to replace some of the departing customers with new ones with the new service they offer, but this hasn't happened due to underestimating the amount of time it takes to successfully launch a new service.

Jane had also hoped to only work a 3-day week but that hasn't happened.

Looking at the business three years since her strategy session, Jane said the next generation of managers would have taken the business to the next level. There would be four main customers who look to Smith Engineering for a variety of services like design, engineering, consulting and support services, not just shopfitting. Jane's clients of 20 years are still around, as well as several ambitious young tradesmen. The turnover of the business is $1 million per month with a profit of $100,000 to $150,000 per month. Jane feels incredibly proud of what the business has achieved and she would have some more leisure time.

## Rod Jones

Rod has increased sales to $9 million for the year for the first time. His staff have worked well and hard throughout the year and achieving goals. He would have liked to realise a bigger dividend but needed more time. The business has hired two sales representatives to reduce the work for himself and John.

In three years' time, Rod foresees the workshop is full and the design engineering team are very busy. He is also able to step away from work for a few days at a time.

## Strategy Workshop

Having reviewed all the content of our workbooks completed by each of the shareholders, there are some obvious themes that clearly need to be incorporated into Smith Engineering's business succession and exit planning strategies. Ideally these are discussed at the workshop.

A summary of the key results, significant goals and gaps has been included below as a guide for discussion:

1   All three listed family as a key personal value.
2   The wheel of life analysis showed that all three parties have different levels of satisfaction in all areas monitored. For example, areas with the most potential for satisfaction increases for Jane were spirituality, person growth and community contribution. For John, these areas were career, spirituality and health. For Rod, these areas were leisure time and finances. These distinctions are not insurmountable, they are simply reflective of the diversity of life stage and personality among the ownership group. It is however, important to bear these distinctions in mind when approaching succession planning.

3   Financial goals varied significantly but on average, they made sense as follows:

   a   Nothing further required

   b   A little extra ($250,000) required

   c   Closure of the retirement wealth gap (target $5 million).

In terms of SMART goals (apart from the financial objectives outlined at point 3 above) — some key themes were:

- "Assistance needed from Succession Plus"
- Volunteer more and spend time with friends by reducing workweek to 3-days (1 year)
- Collect another $250,000 in dividends to enable full retirement (3 − 5 years)
- Be in a position to hand over the business in a sustainable manner (3 − 5 years)
- Transitioning to retirement (10 years)
- Closing the retirement wealth gap (10 years).

Based on this review, the discussions should centre around:

- Restructuring the current roles and responsibilities to allow John and Jane to reduce workload and enable their succession.
- Assisting John with a Life After Transition / Business Plan.
- Designing the strategic financial plan for the business to achieve personal financial goals, including Rod's retirement wealth objectives.

After a detailed review of the various exit options available, the owners agree to introduce a multi-staged approach by introducing an Employee Share Ownership Plan or ESOP (management buy-in) to attract, retain and motivate key employees and drive profit and performance, and then adopt a growth strategy (including potential expansion by acquisition) with a view to a strategic sale in 5 years.

# • STEP 8
# STRATEGIC PLANNING BUSINESS MODEL

All businesses need to have a defined business model which governs the way they operate, the pricing strategy they use and the level of service they provide to customers. The next steps are around making strategic changes to the business to achieve a higher value than most similar businesses.

## 8.1 Boutique versus Scale

A factor to consider in determining your business position and its potential value, is whether you have a scale business or a boutique business, or something in between in no man's land.

**Boutique** ⋯⫶⋯ **No Man's Land** ⋯⫶⋯ **Scale**

Boutique businesses are typically small and offer a service or product at a premium price to a relatively small client base. The value in a boutique business is typically related to its premium pricing, since if correctly managed and planned, a boutique business will be able to generate higher margins. The business can add value by developing this price advantage, becoming even more exclusive.

Here are two examples of very different boutique businesses that operate on very different models:

1    The Rockpool Bar and Grill restaurant in Sydney has a famous owner/chef, fantastic food, excellent service and a serious price list — it caters to a discerning clientele that appreciates the value of the boutique dining experience, and can afford to pay.

2    Lexus is a brand of luxury vehicles that represent prestige and wealth. Made by Toyota, they are quite distinct from the rest of the Toyota range. Lexus drivers are prepared to pay more for the Lexus experience.

Scale businesses on the other hand are larger and offer a wider range of services or products. They are often differentiated by lower prices and value for money. In a scale business volume is key to increasing value — more clients, more distribution, more products and/or more services in a business model that is cheap and easy to replicate.

Here are two examples of scale businesses using the restaurant and motor vehicle industries:

1   McDonald's is the ultimate example of a restaurant built on the scale model. Its business relies on a large number of people spending a relatively small amount of money on a standard range of products across many locations.

2   The Toyota Camry has been the best-selling mid-size car in Australia for the last 18 years. It is reliable, efficient and priced at the low end of the market, again combining high volumes with relatively low-priced vehicles.

When I first started my accounting firm, I left a large chartered firm and set up on my own. I had one large client giving me around $50,000 in fees which was really high end, international tax advice on foreign exchange trading. A very boutique, specialised, technical service. My other clients were the teacher up the road and the plumber across the road who wanted help with basic tax returns. So suddenly I was in no man's land, and it's a very difficult place to operate and a difficult offer to market. If I wanted to go and recruit a staff member, I would need someone who understands the basic PAYG rules for the school teacher, and someone who understands foreign exchange trading and capital gains tax issues.

Lots of businesses end up in no man's land so the key is to work out which end you're at and stick with it. You'll add much more value this way. Look for more clients like the ones you already have and as your service becomes clearer you will attract the right customers and staff more easily.

A potential buyer will see value in a clearly boutique or clearly scale (or scalable) business, however if your business is in no man's land it will be harder to explain how the business can differentiate itself in the market. If your business is somewhere in transition between boutique and scale, or doesn't have a strong strategy that aligns product or service with the target market, you will need to focus on this early in your succession plan.

That may mean getting some advice from a marketing expert to help you find your point of differentiation.

## 8.2 Efficiency or Expansion

If you have been happy ticking along as a small but profitable business, and are now ready to contemplate an easy life on the golf course or a cruise ship, you may not be comfortable with the idea of now pursuing significant growth. But protecting the value of your business may require you to expand or become more efficient.

**Revenue**

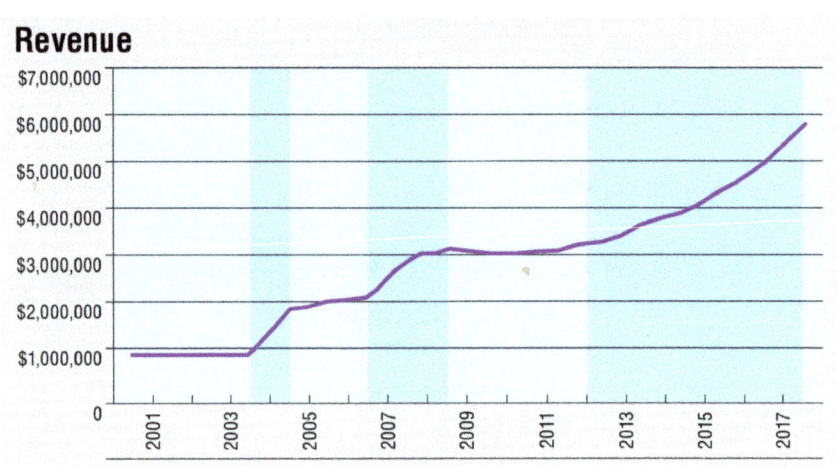

If you ask most business owners what they want to do with their business they will answer: "I want to grow it". It's an almost manic need to grow, whether or not we know why. Sometimes continual growth isn't right for the business. Often we work with clients who are unclear whether their business is in the expansion or efficiency stage. In my view, businesses simply can't do both effectively — that is you can't successfully grow and expand whilst building systemised processes and efficiencies. The two require a different mindset, different focus from team members and deliver vastly different business outcomes. A good strategic succession plan must combine and manage the timing of the stages between expansion and efficiency and ensure the business is never doing both at the same time.

In many cases, where businesses have been able to focus only on expansion they find customer complaints increase or staff turnover becomes an issue simply because they haven't built any efficiency into the system — there are no structured or documented policies and procedures. As the business grows it becomes more and more inefficient.

We had a client whose revenue reached a plateau of about $1 million for two or three years in a row. Their production capacity was about a million dollars. They were flat strapped, their warehouse was full, and their people were really busy working lots of hours. They were striving to increase revenue but were really struggling. So we explained the model of efficiency. They needed to improve their ability to perform the same $1 million more easily while, more importantly, building the capacity to increase production to $2 or $3 million.

### What do we mean by efficiency?

Train your people, take on a trainee or a new person to do the everyday tasks, upgrade your software, expand your premises if warehousing is an issue. Whilst you're doing that you're building the capacity to turn over $3 million. Then, you can go into growth stage. When you get to $3 million, we press the pause button again and we build the capacity again.

Managing our growth on that basis allows us to do two things: manage the cash flow that goes with it (because growth costs money) and allow us to maintain a level of service and product quality without compromise. If you manage your business on this basis, you can control that growth rather than letting it control you.

A Sydney client of ours was run by two brothers — one an accountant and one a sales guy. They took turns at the CEO role depending on what phase the business was in. In the efficiency phases the accountant ran the business, while in the growth phases the sales guy was in charge. This allowed them to manage the needs of the business and focus in the right place at the right time.

Another client has an entirely different management style (for example changing the agenda at monthly management meetings) depending on which phase the business is in.

The board's role is to advise the CEO and management team on which phase they should be in and how to transition between the phases over time to dramatically improve the business outcome and value. Managing this well will increase your valuation multiple.

Here are some ways to drive expansion in your business without having to reinvent the wheel.

## New market or product

Look for ways to expand what you are doing even just a little. You might add a new product or service, add a premium version of your current product or service, or find ways to reach new customers in your existing market with your existing product or service. Alternatively, you might try to enter a new but similar market. If you currently don't market your business online, now might be the time to start (although do get some advice before spending any money on this).

## Expand your database with a campaign

A low-cost way to try to increase sales is to send out a newsletter or offer to your existing database to remind your customers what you can do for them, and give them a reason to come back. You could also offer a referral reward, which will help to increase your customer numbers.

To reach a new set of target customers, try a strategic partnership with a business that has similar customers to you; for example if you have a beauty salon, you might agree with a local hairdressing salon to join forces on a special offer or mail out. A social media campaign will boost your profile, although again get advice first to ensure that your business lends itself to 'followers'.

### Make acquisitions

Acquiring another business just as you are about to exit may sound crazy or complicated, but it can instantly add scale and value. If you are able to buy a business similar to your own but in another location, you will be able to grow revenue and gross margin, potentially add some valuable skills, assets or methods, while reducing costs by taking out duplicate overheads.

Remember there will be thousands of businesses for sale over the next decade. Some business owners will be desperate to get out and will not have a succession plan in place. So there may be some solid businesses out there that you can buy at a low multiple, de-risk and improve profitability along with your own business, and then generate a higher multiple on sale.

There are several ways to fund an acquisition. Remember the seller will have the same sort of options as you do on exit, which we cover later.

## 8.3 Strategic Succession Plan

No matter how far ahead you are planning, you should have a plan that leads you from now until your successful exit. Keeping your mind on the end game will help you to stay focused. Here are some points to keep in mind when developing your plan:

- As a business owner you should always be focused on growth — even if you want to keep your business small with a limited number of customers, you need to find ways to grow profitability; adjust pricing, cut costs, add higher margin products or services. Once you make the decision to leave your business, don't take your eye off the ball. Make your business as attractive to a buyer as possible.
- The plan should let your business keep growing in whatever way is feasible, while letting you gradually withdraw. That could mean bringing in a new manager to drive growth at the same time as learning your role and gradually taking over the day to day management. If you gradually sell down shares in a growing business, your percentage of equity in the business will decrease,

but the value of those shares will increase. This is achieved by implementing an equity matrix (see previous section).

- While focusing on the big picture and your ultimate exit from the business, the plan should detail the steps along the way with clear accountability, dates and milestones. This will help you to feel a sense of achievement along the way, while ensuring that your business continues to flourish, and you are also delegating important tasks and processes.

At Succession Plus we spend a good deal of time developing your plan with you to make it work for you and your business. There is no one size fits all, with so many variables between businesses, individual needs, families, and financial goals.

Once your plan is in place we recommend that you tell your staff members what is happening. Many business owners try to hide their planned exit from their staff, but this is usually a mistake; employees can sense something is happening, start to talk amongst themselves and jump to incorrect assumptions, and get anxious that they will lose their jobs (which causes some good people to leave).

In our experience telling employees about your succession plan means they will feel their jobs are more secure, have a chance to make suggestions in the process, and get a chance to step up to more senior roles. Undoubtedly some will resist change, but the more you keep them involved generally the easier it is to avoid business disruption, and get on with achieving the tasks on your plan.

Firstly, communicate the plan in a positive and inclusive way. You may tell a select group of people first, but ideally you should get the message out to the general staff at the same time. You don't have to release full details all in one go, as you are unlikely to know yourself, but start with the overall facts, timeframe and what this means for the team and ongoing operations. For further information about this refer to our website: www.successionplus.com.au.

Let them know that you'll give them regular updates, and then deliver on this. Don't risk losing people because they perceive the organisation to be unstable, or because they feel threatened.

Make sure you have enough time to implement the plan so that staff members don't feel 'put upon' by the extra work. And encourage feedback and ideas. Depending on the size of your business you might hold some workshops to get input from various divisions of the business. If you have a small team, it is important to include everybody.

Be consistent in your message to employees, customers and the general public. You don't need a huge announcement or press release, just a brief message that says you plan to retire in the next few years and are starting a transition process to make sure the business remains a success, with the priorities being employee and customer welfare. You can then add some key dates and activities that they need to be aware of. Give them a contact to direct any questions to (you may need to appoint a specific person for this, particularly with a lot of staff), and let them know when to expect the next update.

Of course, at this point it is unlikely you will know who will buy your business, and the buyer will determine their own operational structure. The main aim at this stage is to keep the staff that you need to help you reduce your own involvement in the business in the lead up to the actual sale. The next step will be to negotiate with the buyer to take on all of the staff. This will be an easier negotiation to have if the employees are engaged and hitting business goals.

Often if managed and communicated properly employees may see increased opportunities with a larger buyer.

## 8.4 Case Study

Strategic Succession Plan

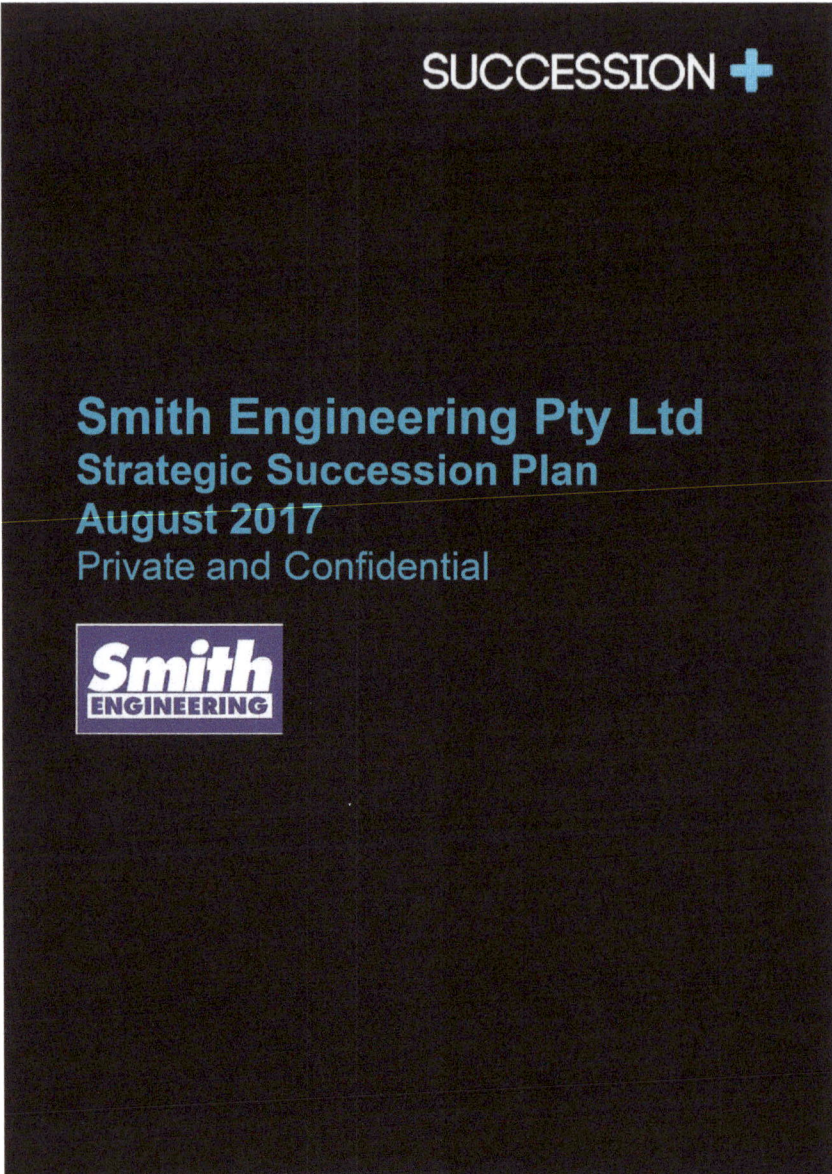

SUCCESSION ✚

# Smith Engineering Pty Ltd
## Strategic Succession Plan
## August 2017
### Private and Confidential

**Smith**
**ENGINEERING**

## 1   The Company

### 1.1   The Business

Smith Engineering constructs and installs aluminium display stands for Australian retailers.
It is based in suburban Sydney, owned by John and Jane Smith. The business was "inherited" from
Mrs Smith's father in 2000, who started the business from scratch after World War II, originally
operating from his garage.

### 1.2   Objectives

These are the major objectives planned for the next 5 years:

| | Mode | Detail |
|---|---|---|
| 2017 | Efficiency | - Implement new ERP software – MS Power BI.<br>- Implement new Marketing & Sales dashboard to enable strong growth monitoring capability. |
| 2018 | Efficiency | - Implement a formal Board structure. Particularly looking for Board members who can gain us access to desirable customers but also strong on CEO monitoring.<br>- Implement an Employee Share Ownership Plan (ESOP). Aggressive growth is forecast in the coming years. If employees are asked to be part of this, they need to educated on business principles and have access the upside in growing the business. An ESOP will also give a future buyer of John's and Jane's equity that the employees are in this for the long haul. |
| 2019 | Expansion | - Implement a multi-level marketing drive. This is tied strongly to the vision and mission statements. |
| 2020 | Efficiency | - Bed down the above. |
| 2021 | Expansion | - Acquire a competitor to accelerate growth. |

### 1.3   Staffing

Currently, the organisation has 25 full time employees, including the owners. The business has grown
from $5M in annual turnover to $8M in annual turnover over 2012 – 2016 (representing a compounded
annual growth rate of 12.47%.

### 1.4   Board of Directors

A formal Board of Directors does not yet exist, but has been identified as an important planned project
in the medium term.

## 2 Strategy Overview

### 2.1 Vision

To be the Australian retailer's first choice when fitting out their location. Our deliverables should all have subtle elements of timelessness and effortlessness.

### 2.2 Mission

- To grow to $20M in less than 10 years, by offering additional services to customers and gaining new customers.
- To use a combination of strategies, including an Employee Share Ownership Plan, to amplify the business's financial success and enable an enduring legacy for the owners John and Jane

### 2.3 Business Model

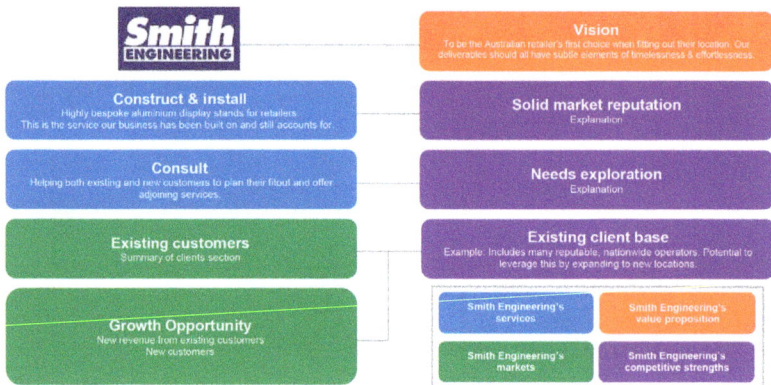

## Efficiency v Expansion

The client manages the efficiency and expansion, based on a model outline, in phases. How this management leads to a financial model and strategic budgets is highlighted in section 9.4.

## Markets

We need to identify the key markets, size and extent of the market and where the markets exist, identifying domestically and overseas.

## Price

Traditionally, we calculate our price based on cost price + 50% for our services. This is straight forward but not very creative or value added driven. Growing the consulting side of the business would be one way to add value to the business.

## Position

Our position is somewhat limiting. We are in a single location with many food chain customers. We are not in the position to meet our customer demands, who are loyal to us. We are nearing physical capacity in our Sydney location. Our staff of 25 is at the point where our information reporting and governance systems need to be updated and be more sophisticated for us to grow.

## Competitive Advantage

We group our competitors into three main groups, large, medium and small.

|  | Large | Medium | Small |
|---|---|---|---|
| Overview | Competitors of this size are frequently engaged in a variety of products and services beyond what we offer. This means they are much more likely to win high-end jobs such as airports. | Competitors of this size are similar to our size, often have similar histories, opportunities and challenges.<br><br>This space can actually fairly problematic. Small competitors have a higher degree of control over their cost structure and are not exposed to the larger competitors trying to access their market. Reputation and relationships are a key defence to these headwinds. | Competitors of this size usually struggle to offer a differentiated set of services and win projects that have a degree of sophistication that a team of 2 – 5 cannot handle.<br><br>However, if they stay small and niche, it can be a lucrative and legitimate model. |
| List of players | - Cowdroys<br>- Ingersoll Rand<br>- Harvey Norman Commercial Division | - Austaron Surfaces<br>- Nexvia<br>- Arkade Interiors<br>- Deadline ShopFitters<br>- Forward Thinking Design<br>- HJ Total Fit out | - Dynamic Door Systems<br>- Complete Shop Fitting<br>- Gibson Shop Fitters<br>- Integrated Joinery |
| Threat management | Maintaining strong relationships, strategically offering additional services to individual customers. | | |

## Marketing Plan

Our marketing plan consists of:

| | 2017 | 2018 | 2019 | 2020 | 2021 |
|---|---|---|---|---|---|
| Ideal customers | Chain retailers | Chain retailers | Chain retailers | Chain retailers | Chain retailers |
| Major Objectives | CRM for use by Sales Reps. | Marketing dashboard to monitor growth. | N/A Efficiency period. | Integrated marketing drive. | N/A Efficiency period. |
| Funnel | Maintain $90M in quotes at all times. | Maintain $90M in quotes at all times. | Maintain $110M in quotes at all times. | Maintain $110M in quotes at all times. | Maintain $140M in quotes at all times. |
| Digital | Use social media to get our brand and service set in front of as many decision makers at target companies as possible. | | | Expand marketing efforts to TV, radio, and print to galvanise social media efforts to date. | |
| Budget | $500K | $550K | $600K | $650K | $700K |
| Personnel | Jane Smith supported by John Smith and social media outsourcer. | | | Appoint a PR firm to manage entirely. | |
| Calendar | Under development – Pip Baker as project leader. | | | | |
| Collateral | | | | | |

## Operational Plan

Boutique businesses are not focused on volume, rather on premium and exclusive. They are known as having a niche market based on the highest quality. We are a boutique business.

## Risks

Risks to the business have been identified and a business continuity plan introduced.

## Succession Strategy

A recent restructure has taken place to enable better asset protection and to enhance administration. The most appropriate exit plan is one in which there would be a management buy in. Refer also to section 7.8 for Management buy-in and buy-out implementation plans.

# •STEP 9
# STRATEGIC FINANCIALS

In the early stages of your succession plan we look at the financial health of your business and other factors such as how well you manage financial information. As we maximise value we start to focus on improving financial results and reporting, which helps to improve the business valuation (i.e. increasing profit and decreasing perceived risk). In this step, we look at the recent profit and loss account for the business to establish financial stability and potential issues. Then we look for ways to quickly and easily improve profits.

## 9.1 Capacity Planning

Business capacity planning is all about proactively managing the business in terms of utilisation of resources and how efficiently they are used. Every business has a maximum capacity, in other words a maximum level of turnover that can be achieved with the employees, equipment, resources and tools available. However in the real world nothing is ever run at 100% efficiency: employees will have sick days, machines will break down or there will be delays due to inefficient operations.

Most business owners don't bother to calculate their capacity or measure the rate at which their business is performing. Let's look at an example in a professional services firm, for example an accounting practice. Let's say that with one partner, one manager, four accountants and two administration people I have the capacity to turn over $1.5 million, and at that level the business would be extremely profitable. But we will never be able to work at 100% of capacity and this accounting practice may well turn over 60 or 70% (our ideal target should be around 80% capacity).

Businesses that don't manage this capacity effectively may be pushed to the limit and turning over 90 or 95% of their capacity. But this is when other issues start — clients complain that you don't return calls, customer service levels drop, tax returns get lodged late. In a manufacturing company you might see product defaults, late deliveries or the wrong order shipped to the wrong customer. This is a symptom that the business simply doesn't have the resources to deliver its turnover.

On the other hand, if we were to run our mythical accounting practice in the running rate of 25%, quality and customer service is really good, our clients are very happy, we are probably able to over-service, however we are not making any money, invoicing only $375,000 which would not cover the costs to run the business.

There are two key things we can do to manage capacity. Firstly, in the accounting practice, to improve or grow capacity we would invest in new resources, perhaps introducing new products or employing a new staff member to concentrate on larger clients. Capacity might be able to grow from $2 million to $2.5 million.

The other variable we can adjust is the running rate — how much we actually turn over as a percentage of total capacity. To improve that we need to go into efficiency mode — systemise the business, train people, automate processes and ensure everybody is clear on the role that they play. Going back to the example of our accounting practice, we don't want fully qualified, experienced professional accountants opening the mail or sending tax assessments to clients as this is an admin task.

If we understand capacity and whether our business should be in expansion mode or efficiency mode we develop a focus for the entire business and a clear area of attention for our management team.

To help you in determining your business capacity we have created a calculation tool, which can be downloaded from our website: www.successionplus.com.au.

## 9.2 The 5x5x5 Model

This model we call 5 x 5 x 5 because it's really simple. If you went to a CEO and said "I need you to grow your profit by 25%" chances are they wouldn't be sure how to do that, or they'd already be doing it. They'll probably focus first on trying to save costs. We look at three key areas generally. Sometimes the benchmarking might identify more, but usually three is a good place to start. Three small manageable steps can deliver quite significant results, especially if you do this every year. In most businesses the following is usually achievable, and the CEO will feel comfortable aiming for small improvement targets, and can allocate responsibility for them to different parts of the business:

1    Increase revenue by 5% — whether through volume or pricing (although pricing is preferable!)

2    Increase gross margin by 5% — reducing cost to produce or serve

3    Decrease overheads by 5% — look for quick wins in underutilised space, paying out retainers unnecessarily, travel that could be replaced with conference calls, etc.

With real clients we have increased profit by 33% using this model. The key here is looking for quick wins, just sharpening what you are already doing, or adding obvious high margin services that add customer value. The well-known McDonald's' approach to increasing revenue is "Want fries with that?" At McDonald's staff members can actually be sacked for not asking that crucial question because the sale of fries is such a huge revenue and profit driver in the business.

## Here's an example:

| Profit and loss statement | 2013 $ | Current % | Improvements | Planned 2017 (3 years later) $ | Plan % |
|---|---|---|---|---|---|
| Sales | 3,000,000 | 100 | 5% Increase | 3,150,000 | 100 |
| COGS | 2,250,000 | 75 | 5% Decrease | 2,205,000 | 70 |
| Gross profit | 750,000 | 25 | | 945,000 | 30 |
| Fixed overheads | 112,500 | 15 | 5% Decrease | 94,500 | 00 |
| NET PROFIT | 637,500 | 21 | | 850,500 | 27 |
| NET PROFIT IMPROVEMENT | | | | | $213,000 |
| PERCENTAGE IMPROVEMENT | | | | | 33.41% |

No matter what stage you are at in your business or exit strategy, it is always worth a review to see where you may be able to increase profits in the business. It sounds obvious, and you may think you do this all the time, but chances are you can always find more. This is where an advisory board can be really useful; as the board members are not as close to the business they can challenge the status quo objectively.

As a result of designing our strategic financials we should be managing the business with a big picture (strategic) financial model that is focused in getting us closer to our ultimate exit strategy — this business exit target was to get the business to produce $600,000 in dividends ($300,000 per family) whilst reducing their hands-on involvement in the business.

## Revenue

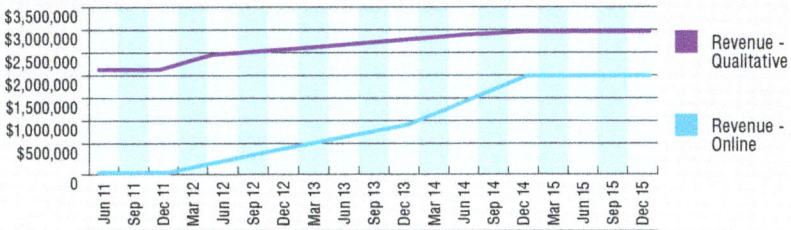

Revenue - Qualitative
Revenue - Online

## Headcount

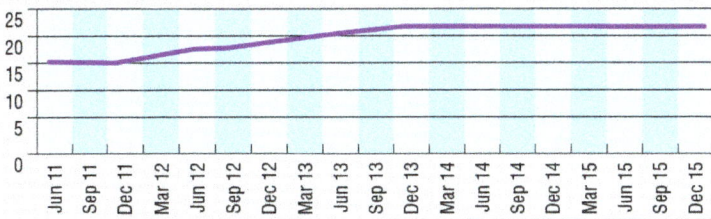

## Profit / Dividend

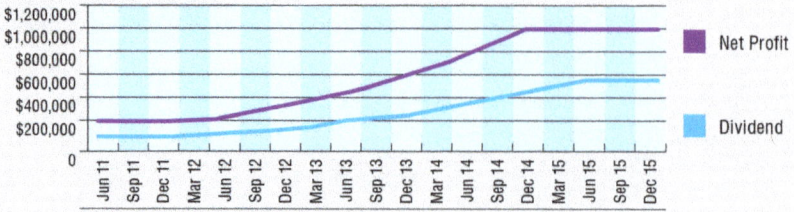

## Margin / Div ratio

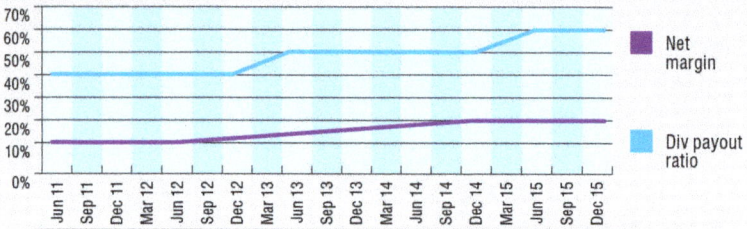

## 9.3 Financial Reporting Package

If you do not already produce or receive a monthly financial reporting pack, this is a crucial tool to implement and ensure you are on top of all the key financial and operational drivers in your business. Getting information often and promptly gives you a chance to act on any surprising results and improve profitability or efficiency. If you have started an advertising campaign over three months and can see after two weeks that it is not generating the expected outcome, you have time to change or cancel the campaign. If you only look at your financials every six to twelve months you have no way of being proactive and flexible.

A monthly reporting pack will generally include at least a profit and loss statement comparing the current month to the previous month, to budget and the same period last year to be able to easily spot trends. You may also produce a balance sheet, or a cashflow statement. You will at least need a working capital breakdown to

SUCCESSION

monitor cash, outstanding debtors, payables and inventory levels (if appropriate to your business).

Good packs start with a dashboard that highlights all of the key drivers or key performance indicators in the business in an easy to read format that is consistent each month (refer to section 9.4). This allows you to hone in on the most important figures instantly and take action, be that gross margin of a particular product or division, staff turnover, debtor days, website traffic, units sold. Even the basic off the shelf accounting packages (such as Xero) can produce most of this data at the click of a mouse. Here's an example for a manufacturing company that is focused on cashflow, sales conversion and safety (see the following Dashboard Report).

Many small businesses focus on compliance — the BAS statement, PAYG and tax returns. While these are all important they don't help you in managing the operational and financial performance of the business, and they don't help a potential buyer to understand the potential value in your business.

Your tax accountant may have been giving you some great advice over the years about reducing profits and therefore tax. When it comes to a business sale however, a business showing losses or low profits has low resale value. A quality monthly reporting pack lets you and your potential buyer see your true operating results and cashflow.

## XYZ Pty Ltd — August 2017 Dashboard Report

### Profitability

**Monthly Profit and Loss, Budget vs Actual**

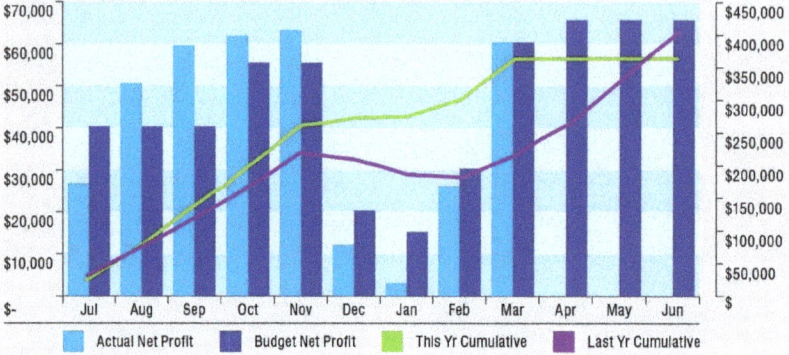

Legend: Actual Net Profit · Budget Net Profit · This Yr Cumulative · Last Yr Cumulative

### Cash Flow

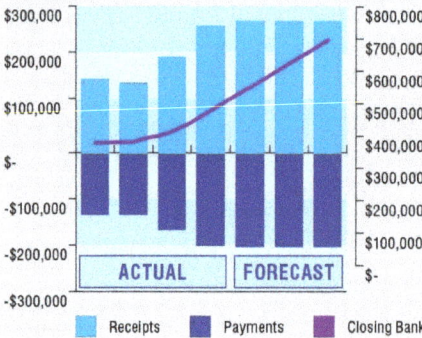

ACTUAL    FORECAST

Legend: Receipts · Payments · Closing Bank

### Operations

| | Target | Actual |
|---|---|---|
| #Enquiries | 525 | 575 |
| Conversion rate | 42% | 35% |
| #Active customers | 200 | 195 |
| Average sale value $ | $1050 | 1100 |
| Orders shipped | 245 | 220 |
| Shipping errors | 10 | 6 |

### Safety

| | Target | Actual |
|---|---|---|
| #Lost time injuries | 1 | - |
| #Hours to injuries | 10 | 5 |
| #Inspections scheduled | 3 | 4 |
| #Inspections completed | 2 | 3 |

### Working Capital

#### Aged Creditors

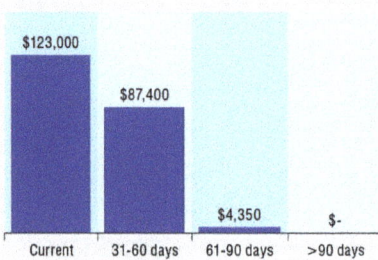

| Current | 31-60 days | 61-90 days | >90 days |
|---|---|---|---|
| $123,000 | $87,400 | $4,350 | $- |

#### Aged Debtors

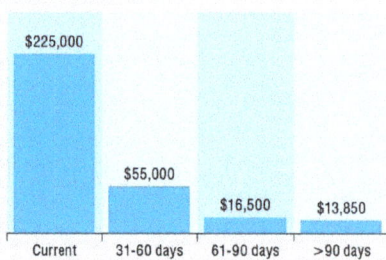

| Current | 31-60 days | 61-90 days | >90 days |
|---|---|---|---|
| $225,000 | $55,000 | $16,500 | $13,850 |

## 9.4 Case Study

### Strategic Financials

**Smith Engineering**
Strategic Financials

Current year: **2017**

| | Actual | | | | | Projected | | | | |
|---|---|---|---|---|---|---|---|---|---|---|
| | 2012 | 2013 | 2014 | 2015 | 2016 | 2017 | 2018 | 2019 | 2020 | 2021 |
| Fee Earners Headcount | 15 | 16 | 18 | 18 | 20 | 23 | 25 | 25 | 27 | 27 |
| Fee Earner Av. Salary | $75,000 | $78,000 | $81,000 | $84,000 | $87,000 | $90,000 | $93,000 | $96,000 | $99,000 | $102,000 |
| Capacity Multiplier | 3.00 | 3.00 | 3.00 | 3.20 | 3.20 | 3.20 | 3.30 | 3.40 | 3.40 | 3.70 |
| Running Rate | 65% | 74% | 73% | 84% | 71% | 71% | 78% | 84% | 72% | 70% |
| Income | $5,100,000 | $5,771,884 | $6,561,310 | $7,481,200 | $8,093,000 | $9,000,000 | $9,000,000 | $11,100,000 | $11,100,000 | $14,000,000 |
| Gross margin | 44.00% | 45.02% | 48.52% | 39.83% | 49.32% | 45.00% | 45.00% | 50.00% | 50.00% | 50.00% |
| Gross profit | $2,244,000 | $2,598,502 | $3,183,548 | $2,979,762 | $3,991,468 | $4,050,000 | $4,050,000 | $5,550,000 | $5,550,000 | $7,000,000 |
| Net Margin | 4.00% | 8.60% | 12.40% | 7.00% | 11.80% | 12.00% | 12.00% | 14.00% | 14.00% | 14.00% |
| Net Profit | $204,000 | $496,382 | $813,602 | $523,684 | $954,974 | $1,080,000 | $1,080,000 | $1,554,000 | $1,554,000 | $1,960,000 |
| Div payout ratio | 10.00% | 15.00% | 15.00% | 20.00% | 20.00% | 25.00% | 25.00% | 30.00% | 35.00% | 40.00% |
| Dividend | $20,400 | $74,457 | $122,040 | $104,737 | $190,995 | $270,000 | $270,000 | $466,200 | $543,900 | $784,000 |

**Smith Engineering**
Strategic Financials - Graphed

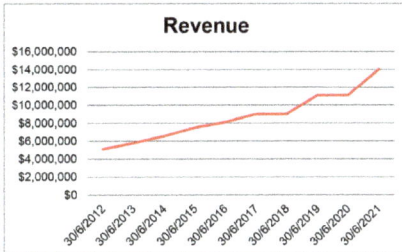

Revenue

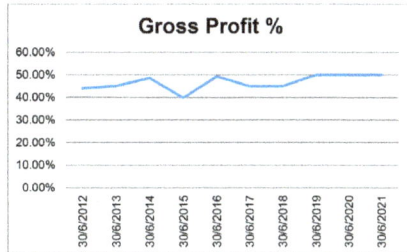

Gross Profit %

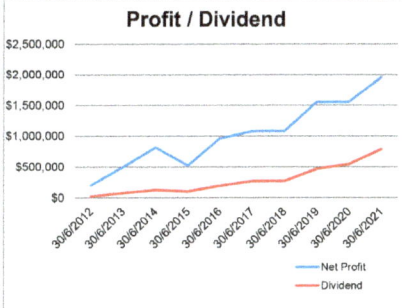

Profit / Dividend

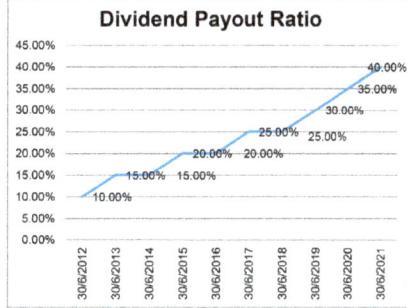

Dividend Payout Ratio

# Smith Engineering
Efficiency vs Expansion

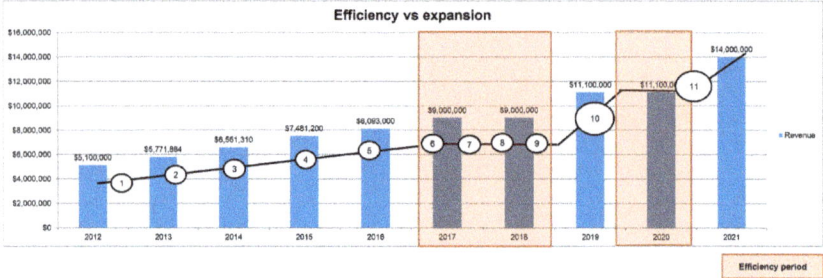

Efficiency vs expansion

Efficiency period

| Project | Name | Status | Nature | Description |
|---|---|---|---|---|
| 1 | Xero | Complete | Expansion | Moved to Xero to enable better reporting |
| 2 | Market research | Complete | Expansion | Hand consultant liaise with client base to identify new product and service opportunities |
| 3 | R&D | Complete | Expansion | Invested in R&D and then launched new products and services under "engineering & design consulting") |
| 4 | Sales reps | Complete | Expansion | Hired 2 sales reps to push new products and existing products and services |
| 5 | Marketing drive | Complete | Expansion | Expanded marketing budget to attract new customers. |
| 6 | ERP | Planned | Efficiency | New ERP software |
| 7 | Dashboard | Planned | Efficiency | Got a Sales & Marketing dashboard finalised to monitor growth. |
| 8 | Corporate gov | Planned | Efficiency | To create a proper succession plan and a business that can grow. |
| 9 | ESOP | Planned | Efficiency | To introduce staff to business ownership and attract new talent for the next round of growth. |
| 10 | Marketing drive | Planned | Expansion | For next round of growth |
| 11 | Acquisition | Planned | Expansion | For next round of growth |

# Smith Engineering
Capacity Plan

## Revenue forecast

| | Qtr 1 | Qtr 2 | Qtr 3 | Qtr 4 | Total |
|---|---|---|---|---|---|
| **Actual** | | | | | |
| 2012 | $0 | $0 | $0 | $5,100,000 | $5,100,000 |
| 2013 | $0 | $0 | $0 | $5,771,884 | $5,771,884 |
| 2014 | $0 | $0 | $0 | $6,561,310 | $6,561,310 |
| 2015 | $0 | $0 | $0 | $7,481,200 | $7,481,200 |
| 2016 | $0 | $0 | $0 | $8,093,000 | $8,093,000 |
| **Forecast** | | | | | |
| 2017 | $2,250,000 | $2,250,000 | $1,750,000 | $2,750,000 | $9,000,000 |
| 2018 | $2,250,000 | $2,250,000 | $1,750,000 | $2,750,000 | $9,000,000 |
| 2019 | $2,775,000 | $2,775,000 | $2,775,000 | $2,775,000 | $11,100,000 |
| 2020 | $2,775,000 | $2,775,000 | $2,775,000 | $2,775,000 | $11,100,000 |
| 2021 | $3,500,000 | $3,500,000 | $3,500,000 | $3,500,000 | $14,000,000 |

## Capacity

| | Qtr 1 | Qtr 2 | Qtr 3 | Qtr 4 | Total |
|---|---|---|---|---|---|
| **Actual** | | | | | |
| 2012 | $1,653,750 | $1,653,750 | $1,653,750 | $1,653,750 | $6,615,000 |
| 2013 | $1,723,345 | $1,723,345 | $1,723,345 | $1,723,345 | $6,893,381 |
| 2014 | $2,360,520 | $2,360,520 | $2,360,520 | $2,360,520 | $9,442,081 |
| 2015 | $2,412,907 | $2,412,907 | $2,412,907 | $2,412,907 | $9,651,626 |
| 2016 | $4,113,071 | $4,113,071 | $4,113,071 | $4,113,071 | $16,452,283 |
| **Forecast** | | | | | |
| 2017 | $1,791,563 | $1,791,563 | $1,791,563 | $1,791,563 | $7,166,250 |
| 2018 | $1,836,352 | $1,836,352 | $1,836,352 | $1,836,352 | $7,345,406 |
| 2019 | $2,474,739 | $2,474,739 | $2,474,739 | $2,474,739 | $9,898,956 |
| 2020 | $2,489,507 | $2,489,507 | $2,489,507 | $2,489,507 | $9,958,027 |
| 2021 | $4,177,338 | $4,177,338 | $4,177,338 | $4,177,338 | $16,709,350 |

## Multiplier

| | Qtr 1 | Qtr 2 | Qtr 3 | Qtr 4 |
|---|---|---|---|---|
| **Actual** | | | | |
| 2012 | 6 | 6 | 6 | 6 |
| 2013 | 6.1 | 6.1 | 6.1 | 6.1 |
| 2014 | 6.2 | 6.2 | 6.2 | 6.2 |
| 2015 | 6.3 | 6.3 | 6.3 | 6.3 |
| 2016 | 6.4 | 6.4 | 6.4 | 6.4 |
| **Forecast** | | | | |
| 2017 | 6.5 | 6.5 | 6.5 | 6.5 |
| 2018 | 6.5 | 6.5 | 6.5 | 6.5 |
| 2019 | 6.5 | 6.5 | 6.5 | 6.5 |
| 2020 | 6.5 | 6.5 | 6.5 | 6.5 |
| 2021 | 6.5 | 6.5 | 6.5 | 6.5 |

## Running rate

| | Qtr 1 | Qtr 2 | Qtr 3 | Qtr 4 | Full year |
|---|---|---|---|---|---|
| **Actual** | | | | | |
| 2012 | 0.00% | 0.00% | 0.00% | 308.39% | 77.10% |
| 2013 | 0.00% | 0.00% | 0.00% | 334.92% | 83.73% |
| 2014 | 0.00% | 0.00% | 0.00% | 277.96% | 69.49% |
| 2015 | 0.00% | 0.00% | 0.00% | 310.05% | 77.51% |
| 2016 | 0.00% | 0.00% | 0.00% | 196.79% | 49.19% |
| **Forecast** | | | | | |
| 2017 | 125.59% | 125.59% | 97.68% | 153.50% | 125.59% |
| 2018 | 122.53% | 122.53% | 95.30% | 149.75% | 122.53% |
| 2019 | 112.13% | 112.13% | 112.13% | 112.13% | 112.13% |
| 2020 | 111.47% | 111.47% | 111.47% | 111.47% | 111.47% |
| 2021 | 83.79% | 83.79% | 83.79% | 83.79% | 83.79% |
| **Total revenue** | $6 | $6 | $5 | $20 | |

If red, nearing overcapacity, if yellow, possibly too little revenue in either case, check the efficiency vs expansion diagram.

## Blue salaries

| | Qtr 1 | Qtr 2 | Qtr 3 | Qtr 4 | Total |
|---|---|---|---|---|---|
| **Actual** | | | | | |
| 2012 | $275,625 | $275,625 | $275,625 | $275,625 | $1,102,500 |
| 2013 | $282,516 | $282,516 | $282,516 | $282,516 | $1,130,063 |
| 2014 | $380,729 | $380,729 | $380,729 | $380,729 | $1,522,916 |
| 2015 | $383,001 | $383,001 | $383,001 | $383,001 | $1,532,004 |
| 2016 | $642,667 | $642,667 | $642,667 | $642,667 | $2,570,669 |
| **Forecast** | | | | | |
| 2017 | $275,625 | $275,625 | $275,625 | $275,625 | $1,102,500 |
| 2018 | $282,516 | $282,516 | $282,516 | $282,516 | $1,130,063 |
| 2019 | $380,729 | $380,729 | $380,729 | $380,729 | $1,522,916 |
| 2020 | $383,001 | $383,001 | $383,001 | $383,001 | $1,532,004 |
| 2021 | $642,667 | $642,667 | $642,667 | $642,667 | $2,570,669 |

SUCCESSION

# Smith Engineering
Functional Budget

| Business Management | Coordinator | Support | 2017 | 2018 | 2019 | 2020 | 2021 | Description |
|---|---|---|---|---|---|---|---|---|
| Product | Rod Jones | John Smith | $25,000 | $30,000 | $35,000 | $40,000 | $45,000 | Staff expenses plus net R&D costs |
| Positioning (incl PR) | Jane Smith | Pip Baker | $0 | $0 | $0 | $0 | $0 | Staff expense only |
| Alliances, JVs, distribution | John Smith | Rod Jones | $25,000 | $30,000 | $35,000 | $40,000 | $45,000 | Legal and consulting expenses |
| Business planning & management | Rod Jones | Steve Jobs | $0 | $0 | $0 | $0 | $0 | Staff expense only |
| Business marketing | Jane Smith | John Smith | $500,000 | $550,000 | $600,000 | $650,000 | $700,000 | Social media, TV, print etc |
| | | | **$550,000** | **$610,000** | **$670,000** | **$730,000** | **$790,000** | |

| Business Operations | Coordinator | Support | 2017 | 2018 | 2019 | 2020 | 2021 | Description |
|---|---|---|---|---|---|---|---|---|
| Staff / operations management | Rod Jones | Steve Jobs | $0 | $0 | $0 | $0 | $0 | Staff expense only |
| Training & development | Rod Jones | Steve Jobs | $50,000 | $55,000 | $60,000 | $65,000 | $70,000 | External training |
| Sales | John Smith | Sales reps | $25,000 | $30,000 | $35,000 | $40,000 | $45,000 | CRM and oncosts |
| Client services & delivery | Rod Jones | Steve Jobs | $0 | $0 | $0 | $0 | $0 | Staff expense only |
| | | | **$75,000** | **$85,000** | **$95,000** | **$105,000** | **$115,000** | |

| Business Support | Coordinator | Support | 2017 | 2018 | 2019 | 2020 | 2021 | Description |
|---|---|---|---|---|---|---|---|---|
| Information Technology | Jane Smith | Amanda Thomson | $100,000 | $105,000 | $110,000 | $115,000 | $120,000 | ERP and other software/hardware |
| Administration | Jane Smith | Amanda Thomson | $0 | $0 | $0 | $0 | $0 | Staff expense only |
| Accounting & finance | Jane Smith | Amanda Thomson | $20,000 | $22,000 | $24,000 | $26,000 | $28,000 | Accounting and consulting fees |
| Facilities management | Jane Smith | Amanda Thomson | $100,000 | $105,000 | $110,000 | $115,000 | $120,000 | Rent and cleaning etc |
| Human Resources | Rod Jones | None | $5,000 | $5,000 | $5,000 | $5,000 | $5,000 | Staff expenses mainly, minor support from HR consultant |
| Compliance & Quality | Steve Woz | Aaron Sims | $5,000 | $5,000 | $5,000 | $5,000 | $5,000 | Staff expenses mainly, maintain Quality accreditations |
| | | | **$230,000** | **$242,000** | **$254,000** | **$266,000** | **$278,000** | |

## Dashboard

Use this tool to bring all the data matrix in one place, to continuously monitor and improve your business performance.

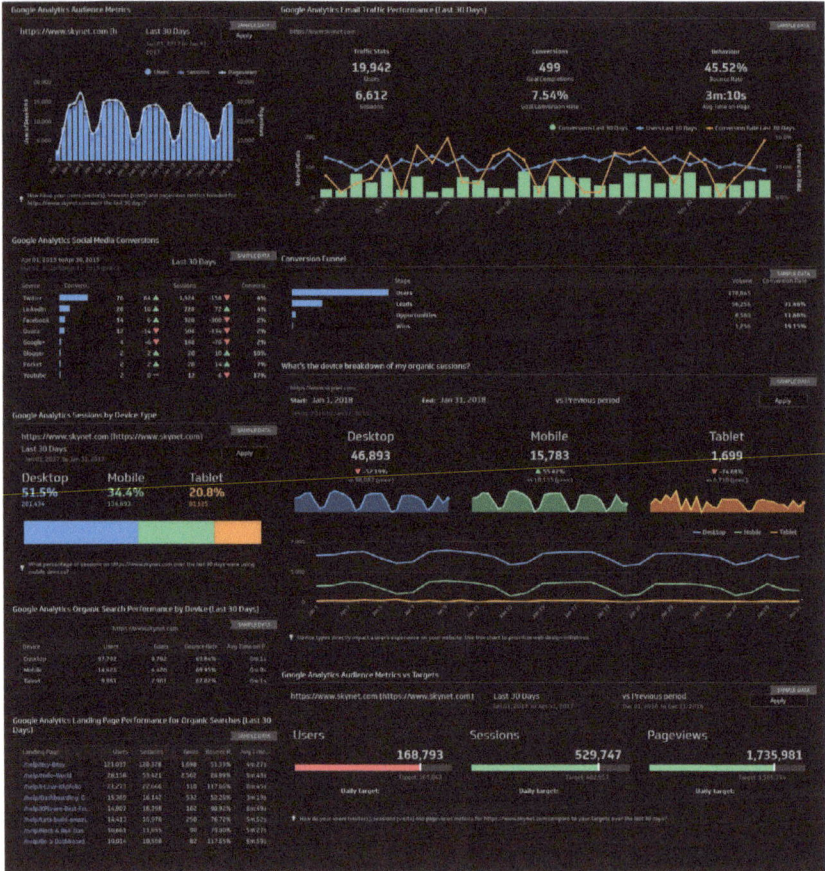

# • STEP 10
# SYSTEMS AND PROCEDURES

The benefit of systems and procedures is efficiency. Having key business tasks systemised and documented will mean the business runs smoothly no matter who is in charge. An efficient business decreases risk and therefore increases the business valuation. So first, let's look at what we would describe as an inefficient business, and then how we turn it into an efficient, lower risk business.

## 10.1 Symptoms of an inefficient business

### Key Person Reliance

The ongoing operation of the business relies heavily on an individual; even worse is the situation where key people are the business owners who are looking to exit the business.

### Management Mismatch

The skills and experience of the management team aren't suited to the business direction (for growth), and there is nothing in place to assist management succession; this is especially the case where the business owners wishing to leave the business are also the only people on the company board and in key management roles.

### Un-systemised

When business systems are not documented, are ineffective or unproven the business is usually inefficient, experiences losses and strained client relations due to poor quality work. Typically, the management team and owners of un-systemised businesses complain about having to micro-manage, and find it time consuming and expensive to train replacement staff.

### Lack of Documentation

We realise that putting a plan in place doesn't guarantee success on its own, but it does help team alignment to common goals. When external or internal changes trigger a change in business direction, the plan needs to be the blue print that is referred to and checked before deciding to switch courses. Other important documentation — for compliance and strategic reasons — includes key relationships (clients, suppliers and employees) and due-diligence documentation.

## Generating Revenue is Costly and Time Consuming

A lack of repeat or referred business is a classic indicator of the revenue generation model being ill considered or ineffective. If there is a scatter gun approach to getting sales
instead of a strategic approach, it will be costing the business dearly to get new business through the door. A heavy reliance on key customers is also a risk when it comes to reliability of future revenue.

## Lack of Reporting

If a business can't show a track record of reporting and forecasting across all areas of the business, then how can it operate autonomously? Who is making decisions and on what basis? We know that 'gut feel' is a culmination of experience, and it often does result in good decision making, but this is a very risky basis for continuing to make decisions in a business if it is to be robust against industry, market or internal 'surprises', or if it is to achieve growth or ownership succession.

## Poor Technology

Outdated or under utilised plant and equipment poses risks to business sustainability. It creates competitive vulnerability, and breeds complacency. Even if the business is doing well financially without striving for optimal efficiency and utilisation, it sure helps buffer against external changes (such as the GFC) if efficiency is a habit and valued in the business. Also relating to technology, ineffective intellectual property management presents risks and can undermine the value of a business, particularly where the intellectual property is one of the assets that give the business a competitive edge.

### Sick Finances

Personal finances mixed with business may bring short term gains in personal wealth, but these can come at a much higher long-term cost.

Remember that if you're looking to sell the business or have it valued for any reason, each dollar that's missing from the bottom line can be worth many times more dollars when it comes time to value the business. Important considerations are reliability of future revenue, basic business sustainability and capacity to finance growth. Other risks are inconsistent cash flow, poor or inconsistent profit margins, and carrying unprofitable products/services.

Each of these inefficiencies need specific action, but the two we usually recommend as priorities are HR tools and templates and documented policies and procedures. These are key to keeping staff on track and making sure you stay compliant with the various laws and regulations.

## 10.2 Human Resource Tools and Templates

Again, the most important aspect is documentation. Has everyone got employee contracts and job descriptions, for example? Do you do performance reviews? How do you work out remuneration planning and employee reward? I've got a client who mentioned to me that some of his employees have been with him 12 or 15 years and he's never updated their employment agreements from the day they started, which means the agreements are probably not legal. The number of changes to human resource (HR) and occupational health and safety (OH&S) in that period of time would be significant. So that's what we mean by looking for gaps and out of date documents. To start, get them all together in a lever arch folder. If you want to do it at an advanced level, get a secure area on a server and get all these scanned in, updated and recorded so everyone knows where they are.

SUCCESSION

## 10.3 Policies and Procedures

Ideally you have a policies and procedures manual covering each aspect of your business. They will mostly be people related but can also relate to systems and operating machinery. The standard ones are:

- Workplace behaviour
- OH&S or health and safety
- Expense claims
- Food preparation and storage
- Operating equipment and machinery
- Information technology (IT) policies — for example what employees can access in the workplace
- Security procedures and after-hours access
- Company car policy
- Staff travel
- Entertainment and after-hours events.

## 10.4 Case Study

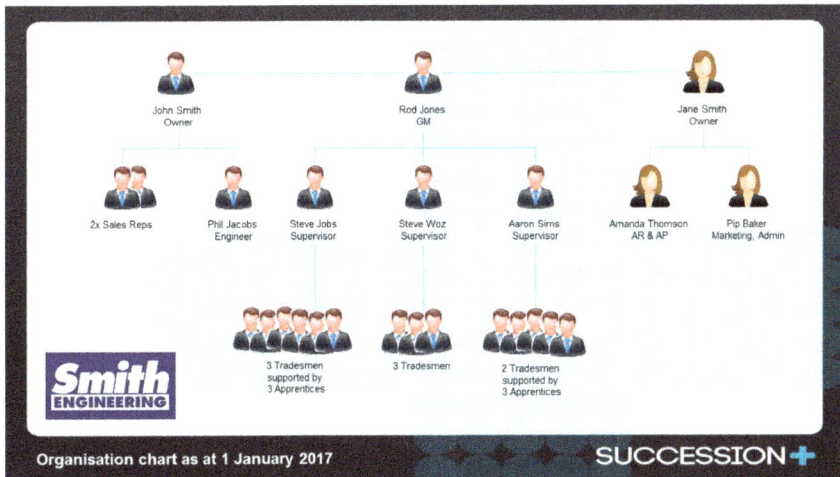

Organisation chart as at 1 January 2017

We started by building an organisational chart at Smith Engineering, which had never been done before. All owners felt it was a very useful exercise. This enabled us to introduce the concept of Functional Management.

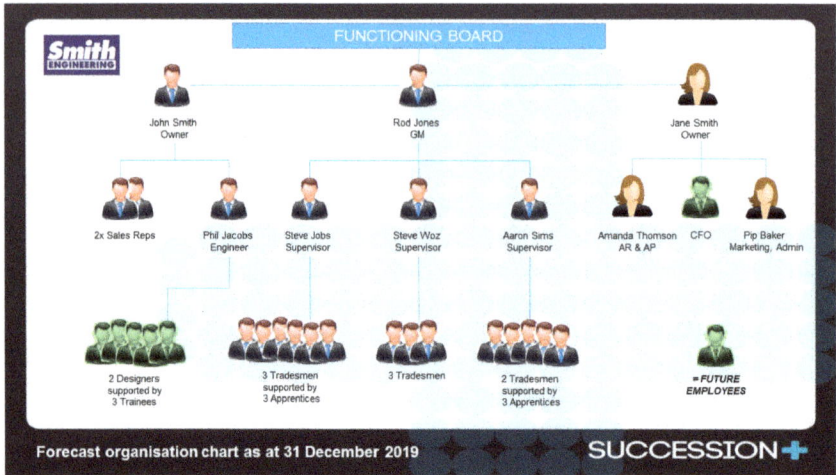

Organisational Chart in 2 years according to the Strategic Financial Planning Model

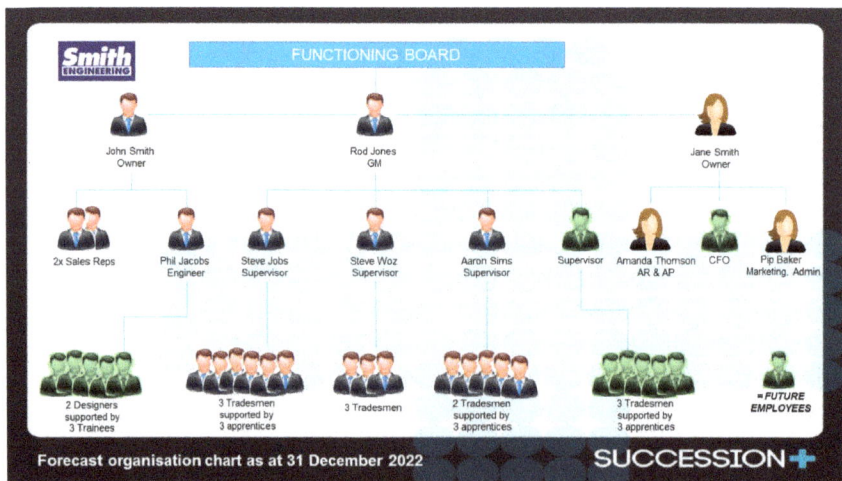

Organisational Chart in 5 years according to the Strategic Financial Planning Model

SUCCESSION

## The Functional Management Approach

Functional management complements the organisational structures. To develop it, we recommend the following steps:

- List all functions the business carries out. Organise the functions based on their relationship with revenue to the business
- Appoint a coordinator responsible for each function
- Appoint people to act as support to keep the function on track
- Identify opportunities to outsource
- Organise people's time
- Align business documents to the functional management approach.

# STEP 11

# MARKETING AND SALES

One of the key issues for any business owner is having a clear marketing and sales strategy, and unfortunately many don't. If you were very lucky at the time you purchased or started your business you may find that the demand for your product or service is adequate to keep you busy and generate enough revenue to run the business successfully. But inevitably the business grows, you employ more staff, expand to larger premises and increase your overhead costs and to compensate we need to generate additional sales.

## 11.1 How to maximise the value of your business

Most people who go into business are very good at what they do, be it as an air conditioning mechanic, process improvement specialist, or architect, but don't necessarily have marketing and sales skills.

Like so many other areas of business management, business owners often take the DIY approach and run advertisements in local papers in the hope of generating sales. But to maximise the value of the business, partly on the basis of our profitability, and partly on the basis of our professionalism, we recommend engaging some experts to design a marketing plan. This will identify accurately who the target customers are, what they like or dislike about your product, how and where they are searching for similar products or a competitor's product, and how best to communicate your message to them.

Simply getting this aspect right can dramatically change the performance of your business. A question I always ask business owners is "if I could magically generate a ridiculous amount of sales far in excess of anything you could imagine at the moment, what could you then do in your business? What potential would there be to expand, open a second location, bring in additional products or services to generate extra profits?"

Obviously, a key aspect of the marketing and sales approach would be to match every aspect of the business to the business model — a boutique accountancy practice would be expected to provide premium service, a 'luxurious' reception area, high end marketing materials as opposed to a scale-based business — which should look and feel like a highly efficient factory.

In 2012, Succession Plus undertook a client survey (thanks to our friends at Stable Research) to find out the key things our clients thought about our business, didn't know about our business or would like to see improved or added to our business. The results were largely what we expected, but we did learn that many of our clients were unaware of the breadth of our product offering, having only used Succession Plus for a specific service, for example to introduce an employee share plan.

As a result of this survey we modified our marketing materials to include different content in our monthly newsletter and added several case studies to our website to show our clients some of the other things we offer to business owners.

We typically see business owners using their own skill, talent and personality to achieve sales, and whilst this might be okay for a small business it is certainly not the way larger more professional and more valuable businesses should operate. When investors or buyers interview business owners they tend to focus on questions around how the business generates sales. The crux of these questions is to find out if there are sales systems, processes or models that generate sales, or whether sales are dependent on the owner's relationships.

A sales system/process/pipeline to generate reliable ongoing new customers is far more valuable than a talented salesperson or the owner generating all the business.

Recently, source of leads, growth hack, funnel management, click through rates etc. have all become important when we compare businesses. Buyers are very keen to understand the sources of revenue and how "automated" they are. We were recently in a due diligence process to provide five years of Google Analytics history so the buyer could have a detailed look at the web traffic and how it was generated — this is a small example but it indicates a larger issue.

Many SMEs don't have this sorted — the sales come from the owner's personal network, some marketing collateral and hopefully a good sales team — that is no longer good enough — the day the owner stops working — the leads stop!

If two similar businesses turnover $5 million but one had a fully automated marketing system with all digital assets in place, producing a constant flow of leads 24/7, and the other has to rely on a team of sale people in vehicles knocking on doors — then without doubt the first business is more valuable.

Further, this is not necessarily a massively expensive or time-consuming exercise, digital disruption provides so many tools to simplify marketing functions and it is cheap to outsource — but it should be a major part of your focus as a business owner to maximise value.

## 11.2 Top 10 Sales Tips

Sales techniques are imperative to the survival of a business. They underpin revenue growth, which is almost always the primary goal of any enterprise; not only are they fundamentally important for front line employees to harness, upper level staff often benefit from knowing these. Sales techniques are used in a vast majority of sectors, from IT to finance to marketing.

Here are the top 10 tips on sales techniques for the type of skills you need to use to gain new business and build and maintain client relationships.

### 1  Prepare

Before you make your first initial contact with the potential client, make sure you research their business thoroughly, understand their industry and take a look at what their competitors are doing. Also, do a little web research on the person you're going to be talking to.

### 2  People Skills

Some people find meeting new people easy as it comes naturally to them, but others find it difficult. Remember you're the face and personality of your company. There are many courses that can help develop your people skills and cover many aspects such as questioning and listening skills, giving and receiving criticism and praise and using assertive behaviour.

### 3   First Impressions Really Count

If you are having your first meeting, first impressions are really important. The majority of people make their first impression within 15 seconds of meeting you. To feel confident, you need to look confident. Make sure you look clean, tidy and are dressed appropriately. Do not wear jeans to your first meeting even if they are a casual company. The first meeting is always about looking and appearing smart.

### 4   Starting A Client Relationship

Once you've made the first contact, you need to build on the relationship. It is important to listen and understand their business needs. Once you've built that relationship, shown you understand, and earned their trust, you are on the right track to making them a regular customer.

### 5   Relationship Building

To build on the relationship, it is important to maintain regular contact with the client. If you don't, then they will either go to your competitor or lose trust in you. Make sure they know that they can contact you on your email, work number and mobile.

### 6   Listening to Your Client

Your client might mention a problem that they are currently experiencing at work. If you can solve this problem, don't be afraid to give them your professional advice even if they don't ask for your help. You have to be confident in finding solutions to their work issues.

### 7  Sell the Benefits

Sell the benefits of your product or service. Remember that your product or service is benefiting their business needs. You are helping them gain a flexible work schedule to make their work life a little easier on them.

### 8  Don't Rush the Sale

Never let your customer feel like they are being rushed into a sale. This is important especially if you're still building the relationship. If you can make them feel that they are in control of the relationship, you won't risk losing the client to a competitor.

### 9  Remember, A Promise is A Promise

If you promise to do something, perhaps a favour relating back to your services/product, make sure you follow through. If there is a deadline, make sure it reaches your client at least a day before. If you're forced to extend the deadline, contact the client straight away and let them know.

### 10 You're the Expert

Never forget that you're the expert in your field. Make sure the client knows that they can turn to you for advice, you understand the industry and have the knowledge to provide expert advice and share good work practices.

## 11.3 Case Study

In relation to Smith Engineering, it is important to ensure the company has a clear marketing and sales strategy. The following questions will make sure that Smith Engineering has certain systems in place to generate income.

## Marketing and Sales Questionnaire

### Branding:

1    Do you have a documented corporate identity?
2    Do you have a list of all the points at which customers are contacted by your brand?
3    Is your logo applied consistently throughout the business (size, colour, placement)?
4    Is your branding consistent with your boutique vs scale model?
5    Does this all extend to premises, staff, stationery, uniforms and of the physical manifestations elsewhere?

### Online, website, social media:

1    Do you have a consultant or employee with specialised skills in integrating your website with your social media channels?
2    Do you have an effective Search Engine Optimisation strategy?
3    Does your website carry clear calls to action that convert prospects into identifiable leads?
4    Do you actively monitor the traffic to your website?
5    Do you use an online newsletter to engage with your database?

### Public relations:

1    Do you have a consultant of employee with specialised skills in public relations?
2    Do you actively compile news-worthy matters relating to your business and relay them to the public (such as the addition of new owners or investors, hire of senior employees, acquisitions, signing of major customers suppliers, creation of strategic alliances or expansion activities)?

## Advertising:

1. Which of the following advertising channels do you use?

   Radio — Television — Infomercials — online advertising like Facebook or Google Adwords — press — fixed billboard — merchandise — in-store — celebrity branded — aerial (such as skywriting)

2. Do you actively monitor how successful each these advertising campaigns are?

3. Are they successful?

4. If they are not successful are backup strategies available?

## Marketing collateral:

1. Which of the following marketing collateral types do you have in place?

   Business cards — demonstration scripts — capability statements or product data sheets — partner or manager biographies — visual aids such as PowerPoint presentation — web content — packing slips — letterhead — brochures — books

2. Do they match your business model: boutique vs scale?

3. Are they applied consistently among your sales team?

# • STEP 12
# CORPORATE GOVERNANCE

"The best executive is the one who has sense enough to pick good men to do what he wants done, and the self-restraint to keep from meddling with them while they do it." — Theodore Roosevelt

This chapter covers the practical side of governance. Legal requirements under the Corporations Act are very specific and apply differently to public and private companies. Some items discussed below as recommended practices are in fact a requirement in public companies.

## 12.1 Review business advisers

A key to success for any small businesses is to surround yourself with the right advisers. Unfortunately, many small business owners skimp on paying for good advice in an effort to reduce costs, but it's a false economy and in the long run ends up costing you more. With bad advice you can lose money, staff, valuable resources and time. Surrounding yourself with the right advisers is vitally important in the succession planning process.

There are many different business functions involved in effective succession planning as you go through each of the five stages. All of these processes can be greatly enhanced with the involvement of a team of quality advisers that specialise in succession planning. In our role as project managers we work with business owners to coordinate the various advisers required in the development and implementation of their succession plan, bringing in the right expertise and experience at the right time. Typically, these will include:

### Tax consultant

Tax advice is crucial in succession planning. If you take action without tax advice you may end up with a higher tax bill than was necessary, and once a tax event takes place, it can't be undone. A tax adviser will help you to determine the appropriate structure for your transaction and ensure you can take advantage of all the available tax relief and concessions. Your buyer may also request certain conditions to be in place to minimise tax implications or stamp duty on their side. Be aware that once you put any arrangements in writing they can be used to determine the tax impact, even if you later change the agreement. So, again, planning upfront is key.

### Accountant

An accountant and corporate finance adviser will be involved in valuing the business, mapping the transfer of equity over time (ownership/shares), and funding the purchase.

### Lawyer

A number of agreements are required in order to correctly record everyone's understanding of how the succession plan is to work, and to ultimately sell equity. These include:

- a shareholders' agreement, which every business should have in any case
- a buy/sell agreement, or sale of business/shares agreement, which outlines the arrangements that would come into play if one shareholder is no longer able to continue in the business
- a funding agreement which would outline the funding options available to the shareholders in the event of various circumstances, for example the death of one of the parties.

### Insurance expert

It is important to have insurance not only for the business and its assets, but for key shareholders, particularly to determine what would happen in the event of trauma or death. An insurance expert will ensure the correct policies are in place, are correctly structured and regularly reviewed to ensure that the needs of the business and the individual shareholders are being met.

### Mentor

To get the best result from the business it is useful to have an objective person to help you through the process, especially if you are aiming to reach certain business goals during your succession plan. Business succession planning can be an emotional time, so a mentor can be a key player in the advisory team to keep perspective and drive accountability. One of my family-owned business clients recently found that the emotional issues were far more difficult, complicated and time-consuming than the technical aspects of the transfer from father to sons.

### Project manager

This is the role that coordinates the various technical experts. Designing the succession strategy and coordinating its implementation is vital to ensuring that the plan works effectively for everyone involved and requires a holistic perspective from someone who understands the entire process.

### Documentation experts

If you are putting your business up for sale you will need an information memorandum (IM) that outlines the business opportunity to a potential buyer. Some corporate finance advisers will offer this service, or should be able to refer you to someone who specialises in this field. Look for someone who understands the financial content of the IM as well as possessing good writing skills.

### Your network

Don't be afraid to ask for help from those around you. If you belong to any industry groups, business networking groups or have access to consultants and advisers, get the benefit of their experience.

### Advisory Board

You should have an advisory board throughout your business's life, but if you don't already have one it is a good idea to get one in place in the succession planning stage to help in the overall plan of maximising value. The advisory board will guide you and keep you accountable. It will also give a potential buyer comfort that you have governance and process in place. Advisory boards help to guide the strategic direction of the business and overall business philosophy and are involved in the bigger picture decisions. They usually don't have legal standing in decision making, but continually challenge the management team to make sure you don't make dumb or costly mistakes. They also make sure you don't become complacent, or take shortcuts, for example by not having an up to date business plan and targets.

An advisory board gives you access to serious executive input without paying for top-notch consultants. One of my clients set about recruiting an advisory board from a local network of business associates, offering selected candidates a generous amount of shares as compensation.

The selections from the talent pool were based on the fact that they identified several 'holes' to fill; financial expertise and strategy to keep them from getting bogged down in the small details of running the business. They also wanted an expert in the digital media environment, one of their target markets. The advisory board for this business concluded the business was undercharging customers, which led to improved profitability. The more you charge, the more clients value what you say and do, provided that your basic offering is of real value.

Being in business can be like riding a rollercoaster. There are some great highs, but there are also some terrible lows; these are times when advisers should act as cheerleaders. Although some advisers will only work on a fee for service, an experienced and seasoned adviser may agree to be compensated via shares and options, which may suit the business owners if cash is not readily available until after exit.

## 12.2 Board Composition and Guidelines

A typical board meeting calendar may look as follows:

| Item | Time and location | 20XX | | | | | | 20XX | | | | | |
|---|---|---|---|---|---|---|---|---|---|---|---|---|---|
| | | Jul | Aug | Sep | Oct | Nov | Dec | Jan | Feb | Mar | Apr | May | Jun |
| | 9am - 12pm boardroom, head office | 18 th | 15 th | 19 th | 17 th | 21 st | 19 th | 16 th | 20 th | 20 th | 17 th | 15 th | 19 th |
| **Strategy** | | | | | | | | | | | | | |
| Develop | 8am - 5pm seaside retreat, pretty beach | | | | | | | 17 th | | | | | |
| Adopt | | | | | | | | | | | X | | |
| Review | | | | | | | | | | | | | X |
| **Budget** | | | | | | | | | | | | | |
| Develop | | | | | | | | | | X | | | |
| Adopt | | | | | | | | | | | X | | |
| Review | 1pm - 5pm | | | | | | | | | | | | X |
| **Board performance** | | | | | | | | | | | | | |
| Evaluation | | X | | | | | | X | | | | | |
| Feedback | | | X | | | | | | X | | | | |
| Planning | | | | X | | | | | | X | | | |
| **Finance** | | | | | | | | | | | | | |
| Draft accounts | | | | X | | | | | | | | | |
| Final accounts | | | | | X | | | | | | | | |
| **Shareholders** | | | | | | | | | | | | | |
| AGM | | | | | X | | | | | | | | |
| Report | | | | | X | | | | | | | | |

*Example board calendar*

When asked about their board of directors, many owners of small and medium sized businesses frequently respond along the lines of:

"All of the owners of our business are also directors and all of us work in the business. We know the business inside-out, so we don't really need formal board meetings." Or

"As the single shareholder, director and senior executive of the business, I AM the board of directors and I know everything that matters about this business. We're really not big enough to worry

SUCCESSION

about having a formal board. I deal with the formal stuff when the accountant gives me the forms to sign each year."

In our experience, having a formal board adds value to the business throughout the business life cycle, and gives a potential buyer assurance when you are looking to exit. The purpose of the board is to drive strategy, monitor performance, provide accountability, set and monitor risk and manage the senior executive (CEO or General Manager). Boards also bring fresh ideas, insights and outlook to steer business strategy and remain objective, with the ability to step in and prevent a hindrance or complete disaster. Well chosen board members have experience from a range of industries and situations and can use that experience to maximise returns in your business.

If you are a director or are considering appointment as a director of any entity, it is well worth educating yourself on the legal duties and responsibilities. The Australian Institute of Company Directors (AICD) runs highly respected courses in this area. Below is a concise summary of the functions of the board, taken from the AICD Company Directors Course:

- Strategy formulation and approval
- CEO selection, monitoring, evaluation, remuneration and, when necessary, removal
- Ensuring that effective governance processes are in place
- Setting and monitoring corporate culture
- Control and monitoring of organisational performance
- Ensuring that appropriate risk management is in place
- Compliance with the law and the requirements of regulators
- Big picture policy formulation
- Communication with key stakeholder groups
- Crisis management.

## Characteristics of an Effective Board

An effective board will have full understanding of its roles and responsibilities, both at a board level and individual director level. The board needs to comprise a range of skills and experience, and

185

have formal processes in place to facilitate timely, efficient and relevant communication and decision making. This includes clearly documented and consistently implemented processes, policies and guidelines around board meetings, reporting, selection and removal of directors and board evaluation.

Board meetings should operate to a standard agenda, with reporting packs provided in advance of each meeting and minutes issued within 48 hours afterwards. Reporting packs include operational and financial metrics to keep the board members informed on performance, trends and any issues in advance of the meeting. At the meeting, time can be more productively focused on tackling the issues. Below is a standard board meeting agenda.

- Minutes of Previous Meeting
- Actions Arising from Previous Meeting
- Managing Director's Report
- CEO's/General Manager's Report
- CFO's/Financial Controller's Report
- Sales Pipeline Update
- Other Business
- Future Board Meeting Schedule
- Special Items (e.g. budget)
- Evaluation of Meeting.

An annual board program ensures all of the 'big items' are scheduled time in the appropriate months, for example to deal with strategy development adoption and review, budget development adoption and review, board performance review, annual account sign off, shareholder meetings and general compliance.

There is a great deal of commentary, recommendations and guidelines on what makes an effective board composition. Ultimately it comes down to what makes sense for the present and anticipated needs of the business. The number of directors on the board generally relates to the size of the company: smaller companies operate well with three to four while large public companies typically have upwards of eight. The board needs to give consideration to composition at appropriate intervals, looking at the mix of existing directors and then working out how to fill any gaps as the business develops or undergoes significant change.

As a minimum, we usually recommend our small business clients have two non-executive directors or board advisers. A non-executive director or board adviser can add significant value in terms of industry or business expertise, experience or contacts. An independent director or adviser should also be able to strengthen strategic planning, decision making and corporate governance. In larger businesses or those with complexity or particular risks the board will form committees to focus relevant board members' time on those areas. Examples are:

- Audit Committee
- Remuneration Committee
- Risk Committee
- Nomination Committee.

These committees are then governance focused and guided by their own specific Charters.

## 12.3 Family Councils/Communications

In many family owned businesses the complexities of having family members who might be shareholders, employees and managers (and obviously family members) can substantially interfere with the operations and strategic direction of the business (rarely in a good way).

I have seen many businesses where the inability to effectively manage this complex web of relationships has greatly reduced the value and performance of the business.

One of the best solutions is to introduce some sense of corporate style governance — in the case of the family business a family council can be introduced to represent the wishes, goals and strategy of the family (assumed to be major shareholders). This can avoid the issues of individuals within the family making representations to management and even directly to employees. In many cases the discipline and structure of this type of arrangement will provide a forum for open communication and a structure to allow two-way feedback, and ultimately a better result in terms of stakeholder outcomes.

## 12.4 Director Succession

In the same way that a business owner must look at ownership succession as part of an exit strategy, the board also needs to look at management succession of its directors as a key part of the puzzle.

There are several recent and well publicised cases of public company succession issues involving directors — some quite good examples where the plan has been outlined and communicated for some time and the successor well prepared. Others not so good where succession was not managed and an unplanned event forced a rapid change on the business, which it was ill equipped and badly prepared to handle.

In smaller businesses owners need to carefully separate ownership succession and management succession and ensure they have the most suitable successors for both, as they are often not the same person despite the founder traditionally fulfilling both roles.

### Richard Pratt — Visy Packaging Succession Plan

Richard Pratt died in 2009 after a long battle with prostate cancer. Pratt spent five years carefully planning his succession to ease himself out of the day-to-day running of Visy and leave his family well looked after.

Pratt's son Anthony assumed the role of leader of the Visy empire, and inherited Pratt Inudstries USA. The family investment vehicle, Thorney Holdings, went to daughter, Heloise and her husband, Alex Waislitz, while Visy Industrial Packaging was left to daughter, Fiona and her husband, Raphael Geminder. Each business had been manage by the successors for the past few years. Visy's $3 billion Australian manufacturing group, was split equally between the three oldest children, while Pratt's youngest daughter, Paula had a Sydney mansion and cash held in trust until she turns 18.

Pratt and his family also brought in a team of non-family board members, led by former Foster's boss, John Murphy as chief executive and another Foster's boss, Ted Kunkel as chairman.

## 12.5 Decision Rights and Authorities

Between the directors, owners, management team and shareholders it is important to know who makes what decisions, and what happens when a shareholding changes or there is a dispute between shareholders.

### Shareholders' Agreements

The Shareholders Agreement is really like a corporate rulebook that sets out issues such as:

- how the company will run
- how the profits of the company will be divided
- how decisions will be made
- what happens in a deadlock if the directors or shareholders can't agree.

When playing a game, you may not need to refer to the rulebook from play to play, but when you don't agree with a call, the rulebook has the final word — and it is the same with a Shareholders' Agreement. You and your fellow shareholders/ directors make the day-to-day decisions about the company and its business, but if at some point you don't agree with each other, then you can refer to the agreement for a ruling.

The Shareholders' Agreement should cover the most important aspects of running a company, including:

### Directors

How many directors should there be? Who may be a director? How are they nominated, appointed or removed? What quorum of directors is needed to make a decision? Does the chairperson have a casting vote? How is a managing director appointed?

### Who makes the decisions?

Should it be the directors, who are appointed by the shareholders? Should it be the shareholders themselves? If so, will they have different classes of shares that entitle them to different voting rights? Or will it be a combination of both depending on the particular decisions that need to be made? When the shareholders are also the directors it is practical for the directors to make the decisions on a day-to-day basis. A directors' meeting can be called quickly and most questions (or motions as they are properly called) can be passed by simple majority vote. The types of decisions that could be made based on a majority vote include:

- removing a director or appointing a new director. Depending on the circumstances, this can be a substantial decision if the director is an executive director and shareholder
- appointing a manager to the business
- buying low-value equipment, for example, equipment under $10,000.

When the decisions are more important, particularly when they involve a major or ongoing financial commitment, or a change in the direction of the business, it may be wise to require an absolute consensus in order to make the decision.

**Examples of decisions that might require a consensus include:**

- decisions to expand the business by buying another business
- decisions to expand the business by taking on additional funding.

These voting rules can apply to directors, shareholders or partly to shareholders and partly to directors, depending on the decisions under consideration.

## How do you break a deadlock?

When the relationship between shareholders breaks down to the extent that the company cannot be run effectively, you have a deadlock. This is when the Shareholders' Agreement is invaluable.

In a deadlock situation, the Shareholders' Agreement will set out the rules under which a shareholder can request the other shareholders buy his or her shares to allow him or her to leave the company. This may be a mandatory provision so that the other shareholders must buy him out. If none of the shareholders wants to remain involved in the company, and they want to get out of the relationship altogether, they can apply to the court for a winding up order and the company will be wound up and deregistered. A liquidator is usually appointed to make sure all the debts are paid and then any surplus is distributed to the shareholders in accordance with the Shareholders' Agreement.

## How Do You Break Up?

A Shareholders' Agreement should always set out the rules for what happens when a shareholder wants to sell their shares, whether or not there is a deadlock. Usually the Shareholders Agreement contains pre-emptive rights, which means the exiting shareholder must first offer his/her shares to the other shareholders. If the remaining shareholders don't want to buy the shares, the outgoing shareholder can sell them to a third party.

Remember the shareholders of a company are the owners. They can make decisions every day without ever having to look to the Shareholders' Agreement. And, if they all agree, they can even make decisions that contradict the Shareholders' Agreement. It is only when there is a disagreement that you need to refer back to the rulebook — and if things have reached that point, you had better be sure that the rules work.

## Dividend Policy

Including the basis for dividend distribution and how it is calculated.

## Matters Requiring Unanimous Approval, Special Resolution or Ordinary Resolution

Decisions made have varying degrees of importance in terms of how the outcomes of those decisions may impact the shareholders and/ or the wellbeing of the business. Some decisions can only be made at a meeting of shareholders, while others are delegated to the Board of Directors. Usually reflecting the degree of importance, the Shareholders Agreement will set out how these decisions are made, under the following headings and may be as follows:

- Unanimous means everyone must agree

- A Special Resolution is defined in the agreement, typically falls in the range of 60 — 75% e.g. a resolution passed by more than 74% of directors/shareholders
- An Ordinary Resolution is also defined in the agreement, typically this is a resolution passed by more than 50% of directors/shareholders. Examples of decisions that may require unanimous approval of shareholders:
  - Amending the company constitution
  - Entering into a scheme of arrangement with creditors
  - Giving a guarantee or other form of security by the company. Decisions that would usually require either Special or Ordinary resolution of shareholders:
  - Change in issued share capital
  - Securing debt finance above a set threshold
  - Amending the dividend policy
  - Acquisition of other businesses.

## The Business
- Purpose of the business (usually to make profit)
- Usually includes special terms given that shareholders are also often key people in the business e.g may include a requirement to contribute skills to the benefit and advantage of the business, and non-compete clause
- Right to examine financial accounts
- Nominated Accountant
- Nominated Banker
- Registered Office
- Frequency and Notice Period of Board Meetings
- Requirement and Frequency of updated Business Plan and Budget.

## Transfer of Shares and Pre-Emption
How shares may be transferred under a range of different circumstances:
- Planned exits
- Unplanned exits

- Who shares can be transferred to
- Whether shares are to first be offered to remaining shareholders
- Basis of valuation of shares
- What happens concurrent with the transfer of shares e.g. resignation as director, returning company records
- Repayments and guarantees
- What happens with any amount owed by the Company to the Shareholder
- What happens with personal guarantees given by the Shareholder.

## Breach Exit

Sets out the circumstances that warrant expulsion of a shareholder. Typically:

- Breach of the Shareholder Agreement
- Criminal conviction involving fraud, dishonesty or serious harm to another person
- Bankruptcy
- Action or negligence resulting in harm to the business
- How the expulsion takes effect
- Basis of valuation of shares in the event of breach exit.

## Drag Along

This clause mainly prevents minority shareholders from blocking the sale of the business. This clause basically gives the majority shareholder the right to force other shareholders to sell to a buyer. Of course, the basis for valuing shares must also be set and agreed here, and the buyer must pay no less than that price.

## Tag Along

This clause protects shareholders in two ways:

- From all of a sudden finding themselves in business with someone they don't want to be in business with!
- If a partial sale, giving all shareholders the opportunity to sell some of their shares.

If a shareholder finds a buyer, then under this clause, the other shareholders have the right to 'tag along' i.e to force the buyer to buy their shares as well, in full or in part, as the case may be. The shares must be purchased on the same terms as agreed with the original selling shareholder.

## Other 'standard' clauses

- Confidentiality
- Governing law and jurisdiction
- Variations to the Deed of Agreement
- Successors
- Termination
- Duration
- Notices
- Stamp Duty and Costs
- Inconsistency
- Waiver
- Cumulative Rights
- Execution by Counterparts
- Non-Solicitation
- Not Induce Breach
- Entering into Competition
- Dispute Resolution
- Entire Understanding.

## Shares in the Company

Entitlement of Shareholders to the capital of the company, and their voting 'voice', usually proportionate to the number of shares held, the issue of new shares, quorum of shareholders and basis for changes to Company Constitution, which must usually be unanimous.

## Types of Buy/Sell Agreement Structures

### Heads of Agreement

This is an agreement rather than a legal contract and the legal enforceability of these types of agreements is doubtful. However it does show a level of intent.

### Mutual Wills

Mutual wills are between two parties (usually spouses) who bequeath their business assets to the surviving party in the event of either of their deaths.

### Conditional Contracts

This is a contract conditional on a particular trigger event. Caution should be taken with these types of agreements; if poorly drafted there can be stamp duty payable on the full value of the business depending on the state jurisdiction. In addition, the signing of a conditional contract may in itself trigger a capital gains tax (CGT) event, or establish the timing for the occurrence of a CGT event.

### Share Buy-backs and Redemption Agreements

Under this type of arrangement, the company redeems the shares held by the shareholder when a trigger event occurs. The source of funds under this arrangement is the company. The share buy-back arrangement must cater specifically for Corporations Act requirements and tax implications, which includes the proceeds being treated as an unfranked dividend and the CGT cost base being affected.

### Put and Call Options

'Put' and 'call' options are widely recognised as the most efficient way of structuring a buy/sell agreement. A put option allows the executor of the estate to 'put' the business interest to the surviving party (or a nominated party to the agreement) and legally binds that person to buy. A call option allows the surviving party to 'call' upon the ceasing owner (or the executor of his/her estate) to transfer the business interest and legally binds them to sell. The transfer is always carried out at a price predetermined under the agreement.

The use of put and call options ensures the CGT liability in respect of the transfer is triggered on the actual transfer, not when the agreement is entered into. It overcomes a CGT issue that can arise with conditional contracts. The use of put and call options provides increased flexibility and tax effectiveness of the arrangement for the business partners and beneficiaries.

## Funding Arrangements

There are a number of ways to provide funding for a buy/sell agreement, including the use of a Peak Performance Trust. Generally, life insurance can provide all or at least part of the funds required to allow business owners to satisfy their obligations under a buy/ sell agreement should an insurance related trigger event occur, and this should prevent the continuing owners from having to borrow money, liquidate assets or deplete the reserves of the business or their personal wealth. Once the type of life insurance policy required has been determined, the requirements of the buy/sell agreement establish how the policy **should be held. The methods of ownership typically include:**

## Cross ownership

Under a cross-ownership agreement, each of the business owners holds a policy on the life of each of the other business owners, with the proceeds being payable to the continuing owners. The proceeds are used to purchase the departing owner's interest in the business from his or her estate. With cross-ownership it is important to recognise that without a legal agreement in place the surviving owners cannot force the estate to sell their share of the business in most cases.

### Company ownership

This can only occur within a company entity and should be considered as a funding arrangement where the legal agreement is the share buy-back or corporate entity redemption agreement. There are several adverse tax consequences with this approach, and as a result it is not used very often.

### Insurance trust

In this scenario the trustee owns the policies on behalf of the business owners. This may be a suitable option in circumstances where the owners enter and leave the business regularly. However, there are also several adverse tax consequences with this approach.

### Self-ownership

Self-ownership is generally considered to be the most practical funding method due to its portability, tax effectiveness, ease of administration and simplicity in engaging new business partners in the agreement. Each of the business principals owns a policy on his or her own life with the proceeds payable to the estate of the deceased principal. The agreement entails the insurance proceeds funding the purchase price, so as to give the continuing owners a market value cost and the deceased owner's estate market value proceeds from the sale. This option is only available where a buy/sell agreement is used as a legal arrangement.

## 12.6 Case Study

A new board was introduced with Mr. Smith (Snr) as the Chairman, Rod Jones, representative of employees and the company's accountant as an independent, Non-Executive Director.

An agenda is set and given to the board members before the meeting takes place, along with any material that needs to be reviewed by the attendees prior to the meeting. The meeting would normally include the following topics:

- Minutes of the previous meeting
- Agenda for this meeting
- Actions from the previous meeting
- Financial controller's/finance manager's report
- General Manager's report
- Strategy review and update
- Corporate projects — progress to date.

Special items would also be raised at the meeting as well as setting a date for the next meeting.

Minutes are to be taken of the meeting to document the topics discussed as well as any actions arising from the meeting.

## Position Responsibilities

Usually, the main responsibilities are:

- Strategy formulation and approval.
- CEO selection, monitoring, evaluation, remuneration and when necessary, removal.
- Ensuring effective governance processes are in place and followed.
- Setting and monitoring corporate culture (top down).
- Control and monitoring of organisational performance.
- Ensuring that appropriate risk management is in place.
- Compliance with the law and the requirements of regulators.
- Ensuring adequate resources are made available to enable the management team to meet the strategy (financial, staffing, equipment, etc.)
- Big picture policy formulation
- Provide accountability and timely information to shareholders.
- Communication with key stakeholder groups.
- Crisis management.

Here are some additional guiding notes on the key functions.

| Functional Area | Director's Role |
|---|---|
| Strategic Direction | Participate with management in setting:<br>• policies<br>• goals<br>• strategies<br>• performance targets<br>Design these to meet commercial and community expectations.<br>It is the director's role to understand, test and endorse the company's strategy |
| Resources | Ensure sufficient resources are made available to management to achieve the strategic plan:<br>• money<br>• management<br>• manpower<br>• materials<br>• suitable CEO<br>Ensure the application of shareholder assets for the right purpose and in the right way. |
| Performance | Monitor the organisation's performance against its strategies and targets.<br>(This is the area where most effort is typically focussed).<br>(It is important to also monitor the effectiveness of the strategy, and if it becomes apparent that the strategy is not working, review it!) |
| Compliance | Ensure there are adequate processes in place to comply with legal and accounting requirements.<br>(It is first necessary to diligently go about identifying the relevant legal and accounting requirements, and then tasking suitably qualified managers to attain compliance with those requirements).<br>Ensure a compliance culture from top down. |
| Risk | Agree and establish and appropriate risk appetite for the company.<br>Clearly identify the risks, and ensure appropriate processes are in place to manage the risks.<br>It is not adequate to just have a risk management system in place. It is essential to ensure that it is adequately covering all areas, and that it is being put into practice. It is the responsibility of management to actually implement the framework. |
| Accountability to Shareholders | Report progress to the shareholders: the right scope and amount of information, and the frequency and channel of reporting.<br>The board is responsible for aligning the interests shareholders, board, management and employees. |

Directors differ from management:

- Directors act only as a group.
- Directors (generally speaking) operate on a longer-term time frame and at a more strategic level than managers.
- Directors are responsible for ensuring everything is done.
- Directors are accountable for culture.

| | Directors | Management |
|---|---|---|
| Risk | Set risk appetite | Ensure risks are managed |
| Strategy | Set strategic direction and vision | Devise strategic plan and implement it |
| Culture | Set the 'tone' and require management to demonstrate appropriate values | Develops and adheres to codes of conduct/codes of values |

## Board Skills Self-Assessment Matrix

At Succession Plus, we use a matrix tool to analyse the relevant skills/experience and qualifications of the board and potential board members. This is important in identifying gaps and shortfalls.

Some of the skills, experience and qualifications we look for include:

- Industry knowledge and experience including:
  - company's key markets
  - experience with consulting services and products
  - knowledge of company's services and professional services background
- Technical skills and expertise, such as:
  - Accounting and financial literacy
  - Marketing and business development
  - Sector exposure
  - Intellectual property
  - Integrated business systems
- Governance competencies, for example:
  - Private company and professional services board experience
  - Strong leadership/board chair experience
  - Executive performance management

- Behavioural competencies, such as:
    - Integrity and high ethical standards
    - Team player/collaborative
    - Cultural fit/ability to work with directors
    - Effective communication skills
    - Innovative thinking.

Once the selection criteria is determined for recruiting a Non-Executive Board member for Smith Engineering, it is presented at the next board meeting for endorsement and then a plan for the recruitment process is confirmed.

The skills matrix template evaluates the individual skills of each director as well as for the whole board. This is an important consideration in that the selection and recruitment of a Non-Executive Director/Chairperson needs to bring skills and expertise to build on the current strengths and address any assessed gaps in skill of the whole board.

## • STEP 13

# OWNERSHIP MINDSET

One of the biggest issues for most business owners is people — and whilst we have all heard the quotes about our people being our biggest asset, I often speak to business owners who consider their people to be their biggest issue or liability.

## 13.1 Think and act like business owners

In December 2011, I listened to Brad Hams of Ownership Thinking speak at the Exit Planning Institute conference in Florida. His presentation was about getting your people to 'think and act like business owners' by finding better ways to attract, retain and motivate your key people — the by-line of my book on employee share plans. To download a free eBook, refer to
https://services.successionplus.com.au/ebook/build-craig-west/.
You can also register to watch a free webinar on Employee Share Ownership Plans.

Ownership Mindset is a business model which provides design, advice and consulting to businesses who wish to engage employees and create a 'culture of accountability and purpose'. The goal of Ownership Mindset (OM) is to create an organisation of employees who think and act like owners. It's not only about making money, however. OM is also an excellent cultural model and retention strategy. Companies practicing OM retain employees at a 200% better rate than companies that don't.

There are four components of Ownership Mindset. We have customised the principles of ownership thinking and added several new tools to create an ownership mindset program. This is shown in the diagram below:

## Personnel
### PPA, Team Audit & Staff Survey

Ownership Mindset creates an environment that promotes learning and development, while increasing visibility and accountability. Your best people will excel, and your poorest performers are generally self-selected out by their peers.

## Knowledge
### Financial & Business Training

Employees are taught the fundamentals of business and finance, so that they are better equipped to make decisions that are financially sound.

### Systems
### Forecasting with KPIs

Rather than focusing only on lagging financial measures, an emphasis is placed on identifying the most critical leading, activity-based measures (Key Performance Indicator, or KPIs), and utilising those KPIs to forecast results on a regular, formal basis.

### The Right Incentives
### Plans tied to business performance/Employee Share Plans

The process of employee education and focusing on the right measures in an environment of high visibility and accountability will increase your organisation's profitability, guaranteed. We can now design and implement a broad-based incentive plan, because it is self-funding.

In the succession and exit planning process, better engaging your team to drive performance within the business will always add value. Most buyers are far more attracted to businesses that are run by motivated and incentivised employees than those that need to be run by owners.

## 13.2 Case study — NPG

The best way to demonstrate how Ownership Mindset works is to follow an example of a company that has successfully implemented the strategy.

In August 2011, our long-term client, NPG was facing a few major issues. It was heavily reliant on the three owners, the staff were disengaged, which frustrated the owners, and nobody was clear about the vision and future of the business. The owners had some clear personal goals. They wanted to continue receiving solid income from the business without having to be there every day. They wanted to be able to semi retire and take a few months off or work part time, while continuing to build value in the business. And finally they wanted to reduce their personal risk and liability.

The owners recognised that they had some business challenges that would make it difficult to achieve their personal goals. Firstly, they were having difficulty attracting and retaining staff with the right skills and right attitude/cultural fit, and could not get staff to think about the company's wellbeing as well as their own. They found it tough to find the right remuneration and incentives strategy for their disengaged, blue collar work environment. This was exacerbated by disharmony between two departments of the business and cashflow restraints.

The owners needed to take significant action, and with the help of Ownership Mindset they began with four major steps.

1   Defined the overall strategy and vision
2   Improved people management and communication
3   Implemented ownership mindset to move the company towards a business of 'business people'
4   Appointed an independent General Manager to reduce the reliance on owners and move the company forwards.

With these four actions, the business became cohesive and productive. Staff members understood the vision and strategy of the business and the owners, and gained a clearer understanding of what was expected of them. They felt more included and informed through monthly company-wide information sessions. All employees were educated in business ownership and began receiving information about the performance of the business. A self-funded incentive plan will replace their Christmas bonus.

There is more 'we' than 'me' thinking in the culture, and a greater sense of purpose, visibility and accountability. The two owners closest to retirement appointed and began grooming their successors.

In 2012, we reviewed progress with Bob, one of the owners. He highlighted the following list of achievements:

•   Insurance coverage improvements underway
•   Resourcing gaps filled
•   Accountant appointed
•   Sales and resourcing 3 year forecast prepared

- Shareholders arrangements worked through
- Goals clarified
- Monthly staff meetings in place
- Monthly management meetings in place.

*Just three months on from implementing Ownership Mindset in our business, we are thrilled to see that our employees are shifting from indifference and a sense of entitlement, to a team who are really engaged and proactive. Before Ownership Mindset, absenteeism was a massive problem for us. Not only were staff using up all of their sick leave, but often they just wouldn't show up, leaving us understaffed and unable to meet our customers' deadlines. If they didn't need the cash, they would just take leave without pay. We were losing a lot of money because of it!*

*Since kicking off our Ownership Mindset program, absenteeism has already dropped by at least one third! Overall, productivity is higher and our employees are taking more interest in the financial well-being of the business. Instead of all the responsibility falling to the owners, our leadership team are really on top of what's going on in their areas of the business: they understand their numbers and are sharing the issues and challenges we face in running the business. Overall, it's a great sense of relief for us as owners. We really feel like we're 'sharing the insomnia' that comes with running the business. We're positive that, by doing business the Ownership Mindset way, our profit is going to soar and we'll all be having more fun working together as a result!*

The benefits of Ownership Mindset can be seen almost immediately, and the best part is that they last. And it's not just about money. The culture of accountability, winning and team alignment drives staff to achieve long-term goals. Once they are engaged and understand how they can affect the performance of the business, they are motivated to keep on making improvements. There are many other success stories. One US IT consulting and management services business doubled its 2011 profit in 2012, just 1.5 years after implementing Ownership Mindset.

A cabinetry business recovered $21,000 in its first 3 months after implementing a Rapid Improvement Plan.

Many owners that have implemented an Ownership Mindset strategy have reported a 'natural shedding of dead wood', typically employees who weren't willing to be held accountable. Their departure was normally to the great relief of their hard-working, culturally-aligned co-workers.

## 13.3 Case Study — Garrett Sullivan, Kaikor Construction Associates, Inc.

In 1985, Garrett Sullivan and his business partner started a construction company, Kaikor Construction Associates, Inc. Seven years later, his business partner retired. Garrett built the business to annual revenue of $20-25 million per year, predominantly working on government contracts such as bridges, concrete buildings, parking structures and parking lots. He found success when he benchmarked the business against heavy highway contractors in the less than $50 million category and worked hard to get results in the top 25% (a Best in Class ranking in the construction industry).

In 2009, Garrett went to the Annual Ownership Thinking conference. Although he had already been sharing some financial information with his staff, had a bonus plan in place, regularly looked at Key Performance Indicators (KPIs) and was consistently benchmarking, he found that the Ownership Mindset Management System put structure and organisation around those activities. He believed Ownership Mindset promoted a deeper understanding of the financial information being shared with the employees and helped his team understand how they could impact the bottom line.

Garrett set a stretch profit target of 35% in January and began implementing an Ownership Mindset Plan, with staff receiving training and full financial information. By May, the financial results indicated that they were on track and remained strong as the year progressed. By November, the Senior Management Team decided to award a 50% 'deposit' on the incentive payout the week before Christmas, emphasising that the payment was the result of the employees' continuous efforts, and not a Christmas bonus. The company closed out the year achieving their stretch profit target.

As the Ownership Mindset culture continued to grow, Garrett held a quarterly meeting with all employees to review the financials. He also introduced activities such as a financial planner to talk about personal wealth management and financial boot camp for the non-financially literate employee. Ownership Mindset topics were also encouraged in business communication, for example the weekly foreman's meeting and the company's bi-monthly newsletter. In the second year, the company doubled its profit and continued to do well for the next three years. Around this time, Garrett found that he had fulfilled all of his goals for the business. He had built the company to a standalone business no longer dependent on him, and he had invested in his employees' development to help them realise personal and professional dreams. It was time to move on and allow other team members the opportunity to step up in the business by taking real equity ownership. The senior managers were very clear: they wanted to buy it. However, they didn't have the cash to buy the business outright.

### 'New Company/Old Company Buyout'

A concept called 'New Company/Old Company Buyout' was structured, which enabled the business to be sold gradually, over an agreed five-year period.

First, a new company was formed with the senior managers having a minority stake and Garrett having a controlling interest. New and existing contracts were assigned to the new company, while the new company paid the 'old' company for use of all business assets and premises. After the third year, the new company had enough retained earnings and cash to buy all of the equipment. And when one of the new employee-owners needed to cash out for personal reasons, the other senior manager bought his interest.

The buyout plan worked extremely well and was accelerated in the fourth year. Only one issue remains to be solved; the unearned profit on the outstanding $34 million of uncompleted contracts. It was agreed that one-third of this profit would be paid to Garrett in quarterly payments if he continued to work as an employee for a year (at his current rate of pay with all benefits).

Once Garrett's employment ended he maintained ownership of the building and parking lot and rented it to the business. The structure enabled him to 'cut ties' without any future liabilities beyond his direct control.

The combined payments included three years of office and equipment rental charges, building and parking lot rental fees (still ongoing), and the final equity payout. Garrett estimates this was equivalent to achieving at least 3-4 times earnings value, typical of the construction industry. However, he is quick to point out that earnings were higher than previously due to the success of the Ownership Mindset Management System program.

Garrett still sits on the board and consults with the business, while the old company holds his real estate investments. He has one reflection on what he could have done differently:

"I wish I had acted sooner on implementing Ownership Mindset, as even though we were in the top 25% in our industry class in net income and return on equity, I think we could have been much higher."

## 13.4 Case Study — Ownership Mindset

### Ownership Mindset Survey

To refine implementation of Ownership Mindset in each company, an initial survey is conducted to get a base line of information. Below are some examples of questions asked, rating each question, from strongly agree to strongly disagree:

- I believe that the leadership team at our company is performing well
- I understand the difference between profit and cash and could explain how the company could be profitable yet have a negative cash flow

- When our company's financial results improve, employees' compensation improves
- I know if we are meeting the expectations of our owners
- I know what the most important measures are that our company should focus on to be successful
- We should increase the financial information we provide to our employees
- I generally know what the potential payouts of my incentive plan is and the goals that must be met for those payouts.

The next part of the survey is to provide suggestions for issues currently facing your company, in particular for:

- operational issues
- financial issues
- people issues
- opportunities to make significant improvements
- incentive plans.

## Personal Profile Analysis

The purpose of Personal Profile Analysis (PPA), a form of psychometric testing, is to increase people's awareness of themselves and others around the organisation, so they can more effectively cooperative in the work environment.

William Moulton Marston was the father of the DISC theory but also known as early developer of the polygraph lie detector test. Marston also invented the Wonder Woman character, being an advocate for women's rights.

He incorporated four personality types into his model: Dominance, Influence, Steadiness and Compliance (or sometimes referred to as conscientiousness). All people are a blend of these four personality types, and typically show traits from one or two in particular.

Our process calls for:

1 Individual PPA Assessments
2 A Team Audit.

DISC profiles help you and your team:

1   Increase your self-knowledge: how you respond to conflict, what motivates you, what causes you stress and how you solve problems
2   Improve working relationships by recognising the communication needs of team members
3   Facilitate better teamwork and minimise team conflict
4   Develop stronger sales skills by identifying and responding to customer styles
5   Manage more effectively by understanding the dispositions and priorities of employees and team members
6   Become more self-knowledgeable, well-rounded and effective leaders.

| Dominance | Person places emphasis on accomplishing results, the bottom line, confidence | • Sees the big picture<br>• Can be blunt<br>• Accepts challenges<br>• Gets straight to the point |
|---|---|---|
| Influence | Person places emphasis on influencing or persuading others, openness, relationships | • Shows enthusiasm<br>• Is optimistic<br>• Likes to collaborate<br>• Dislikes being ignored |
| Steadiness | Person places emphasis on cooperation, sincerity, dependability | • Doesn't like to be rushed<br>• Calm manner<br>• Calm approach<br>• Supportive actions |
| Compliance | Person places emphasis on quality and accuracy, expertise, competency | • Enjoys independence<br>• Objective reasoning<br>• Wants the details<br>• Fears being wrong |

## Terminology related to PPA

They use the analogy of a tree, below the line factors serve as support factors that make up a person's primary attributes. Highs are above the line which are determined by working strengths, fears, motivators and value of the organisation.

## PPA Assessment

When individuals are examined under the Thomas tools, we are looking to see if there are substantial discrepancies between the work mask (how we operate in the work environment) and behaviour under pressure (a more natural representation of the person's character). If there is a major discrepancy, unsustainable methods of coping may be enabling this. So we look at:

- Dominance
- Influence
- Steadiness
- Compliance.

## Putting it all together

PPAs altogether is called a PPA profile. A team profile is an energetic group of people who are committed to achieving common objectives who work well together and enjoy doing so and who produce high quality results.

## Groups vs Teams

In a business setting, teams are more desirable than groups, we want to strive to be a team. The process helps us to discover which one we are more like.

With a group you have:

- One individual in charge
- Individual accountability
- Separation of thinkers and workers
- Managerial control
- Excellence through division of work — each person focuses on a narrow set of tasks
- Measurement of individual performance.

In teams you have:

- Shared leadership
- Joint accountability, mutual support and trust
- Team members who think and work together

- Purpose and modus operandi decided upon and fine tuned by the team
- Some tasks done interchangeably by team members who teach one another skills
- Tough goals that make the team battle together with collective excitement about achieving the goals.

## Team Culture

How do we work together?

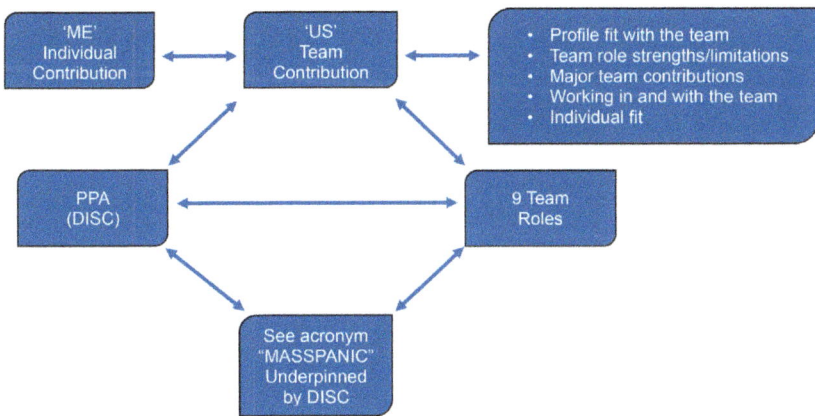

All good teams have each one of the following acronym to avoid MASS PANIC:

- Motivator
- Analyser
- Supporter
- Specialiser
- Pioneer
- Anchor
- Networker
- Innovator
- Concluder.

The process helps us answer these questions:

1. Whether we have all of these attributes on our team
2. Whether any are missing
3. Whether have concentrations of attributes and therefore conflicts.

Team Audit (online tool via Thomas International)

Smith Engineering Case — Actual Team Culture

Team Strengths

This team readily communicates facts and information both verbally and in writing. It will promote itself well, can influence and persuade others and creates favourable impressions. This group places great importance on accuracy and precision and continually works towards maintaining a high level of quality and standards.

Being non-aggressive, the group creates a non-confrontational environment. It uses knowledge and expertise to convince others to its point of view and encourages people to work to given standards and organisational policies.

This friendly team endeavours to involve people in order to create a culture of quality and precision.

Team Reaction to Change

The team is likely to view change cautiously. However, since it continually seeks to improve standards, it will accept change once the benefits to the organisation are assured. However, once agreed, the action process must be communicated well and the timescales set should be realistic and achievable. The team is unlikely to take risks, but once it is confident and the details and procedures are in place, it will go forward with enthusiasm.

Preferred Team Leader

The ideal person to lead this team will be people oriented and have the ability to encourage and motivate through personal knowledge and expertise. Such a person should exercise some caution when making decisions and not be tempted to take short cut methods. A friendly working environment should be provided, which is preferably free from confrontational issues.

## Team Value

The environment in which a team works, the level at which it operates and the value it brings to the organisation are vital factors in its success or failure.

The value this team brings to the organisation is as follows:

- Involving people and applying logic in order to achieve results
- Ability to communicate both internally and externally
- Creating an environment which develops and follows systems
- Working with and through people in administrative or specialist areas
- Providing technical and specialist support
- Making favourable impressions and encouraging involvement.

## Team Limitations

All teams have strengths which bring value to the organisation, but equally they also have limitations. This team's limitations are that they may:

- Talk about what needs to be done
- Feel rejected and lose confidence when their decisions, feelings and ideas are not considered
- Be too optimistic in setting and quantifying goals.

## Employee Agreement to Incentive Plan

## Purpose of the Incentive Plan

The purpose of the incentive plan (Plan) is to provide an incentive that encourages alignment of the team with the goals of the business, rewards team performance and increases the retention of team players.

## Plan Design & Definition of Terms

The Plan is designed to provide rewards that are self-funded and unlimited: it is anticipated that all employees will strive to increase the profitability of the business in the knowledge that they will share in the additional profit.

Through the Plan, the owners will share the profits of the business that are in excess of what the business needs to pay taxes, retire debt, reinvest in the business and provide owners with a reasonable return on investment. We define this minimum point as the Profit Threshold.

When the Profit Threshold is exceeded, we will then share part of the extra profit (i.e. part of the amount of profit above the Profit Threshold) Share of Extra Profit. The resulting $ amount of profit available to share with employees is the Incentive Pool.

Each year, the Profit Threshold will be reviewed as well as the % Share of Extra Profit to reflect the goals of the business, industry trends and market conditions.

## How the Plan Works

For the first year of the incentive, the company will agree to:

- Profit Threshold of <Insert Percentage>
- Share <Insert Percentage> of Extra Profit.

Since business profit fluctuates substantially from month-to-month, quarter-to-quarter and even between half year periods, it is important to manage how incentives are paid out so that the company doesn't end up overpaying and/or falling short of cash. Incentives will be paid out on the following basis:

- Reward Interval: <Interval>
- <Period/interval> there is a Mid Term Payout Cap of <Percentage> This means the company pays out part of the Incentive Pool up to this profit point and bank (i.e. hold in reserve) any amount above the Mid Term Payout Cap until we have the full year result.
- < Period/ interval> there is no Payout Cap. The full year payout is based on the full year figures.

While Extra Profit of <Insert Percentage> will be retained in the first payout period, there is no maximum to how much can be shared at the full year result.

## Eligibility for the Plan

Employees who are Eligible to be in the plan ("Eligible Employee") are those who:

- Have provided continuous service as a permanent employee of the company or at least 90 days.
- Have accepted and signed the terms of the agreement.
- Are not employed on a casual, contract or labour hire arrangement with the company.

## Calculation of Payment

Calculation of payment is as follows:

- Payout for the first period is based on the 6 months commencing <Start Date> and ending < End Date>.
- Payout for the second period is based on the full year figures to <Date>.
- Each eligible employee will receive the same reward payment if Profit Threshold is exceeded.
- New employees who meet the 90-day service minimum, but who were not employed for the full Reward Interval, will receive a pro-rated payment based on their commencement date.
- Incentive Pool will be distributed among all permanent employees based on full or prorated part-time status.
- Incentives are taxable wages.
- There is currently no cap on the plan.
- Net Profit (EBIT) amounts are determined using the accrual accounting method.
- There is a cap on the first period's reward payment ("Mid Term Payout Cap"). No more than 2% of sales in that period may be made as a reward payment to employees as a whole. This measure is in place to ensure that the incentive plan does not cause cash flow problems for the business.
- Employee may elect to contribute bonus amounts to their superannuation fund, if eligible.

Payment will be made as follows:

- Must be an Eligible Employee of the company on the date that the Incentive Payout(s) is actually paid.

Future Years

It is anticipated that the plan will continue in future years with the likely modifications being adjustment to:

- Profit Threshold
- Mid Term Payout Cap
- Reward Intervals.

## Changes to the company incentive plan

In the event of a significant change in the business climate or product lines, or for revenue recognition and/or account management purposes, or because of other unforeseen circumstances, the company reserves the right to make any changes to this company incentive compensation plan deemed necessary at the sole discretion of company management. Such changes will be provided in writing, before or after the fact, as appropriate, to ensure its consistency with overall corporate objectives, requirements, and business conditions.

# • STEP 14

# PEAK PERFORMANCE TRUST

The Peak Performance Trust (PPT) is an Employee Share Ownership Plan (ESOP) developed specifically to meet the needs of small to medium-sized businesses. If there's any business sector that truly benefits from having employees who are motivated to think and act more like business owners, it is the SMEs. But traditional employee incentive vehicles were designed for large corporates and are complicated, expensive, difficult to establish and administer, and largely inappropriate for smaller privately-owned companies.

## 14.1 Introduction

The Peak Performance Trust (PPT) was developed to offer smaller companies a tool that delivers all the benefits of a sophisticated employee incentive scheme, but without the expense or complexity. The PPT is simple, effective and good value.

Employee Share Ownership Plans, or ESOPs, are a mechanism used to allow employees to own equity in the company they work for, with the express intention that they will think and act like business owners.

The primary objective is to create a structure with which employees' lifestyle and financial goals are aligned with business objectives. The result? A cohesive and committed team that is single-minded about working toward and sharing the benefits of a successful and profitable business.

ESOP companies have improved performance, higher profits and better staff retention than other businesses. The ability to attract, retain and motivate people to peak performance means being able to attract and retain business — and it is a major source of competitive advantage. In fact, it can mean the difference between success and failure.

Described by CPA Australia's In the Black magazine as an 'ingenious funding mechanism' for exit strategies, the PPT links increased profits to performance payments made into a trust on behalf of employees, building an employee's stake in the business.

Imagine if your employees were as focused, driven, and as motivated about your business as you are — imagine if they came up with new ideas and cost savings regularly and imagine if they were as interested in profit as you. Sounds like Utopia but it is possible and in fact it is happening with businesses that effectively use Employee Share Ownership Plans. The research tells us that businesses that combine employee ownership with a participative management style grow 8-11% faster (National Centre for Employee Ownership) than they otherwise would have. ESOPs are a great way to:

- Attract, retain and motivate key employees
- Improve business performance — profitability, staff retention, productivity
- Build an internal succession plan for staff and business owners.

"Employee ownership is a different way of thinking about business. It targets long-term sustainability by recognising that employee/ owners are more committed to developing innovative products and processes. The result is competitive advantage and lasting success, in good times and bad." — Sir Stuart Hampson, former Chair of the John Lewis Partnership (the largest ESOP in the world with over 80,000 employees in the plan)

## 14.2 Why do workers get into an ESOP?

In a recent Melbourne University study, a group of employees were asked certain questions and below are what they ranked as the most important elements of an ESOP:

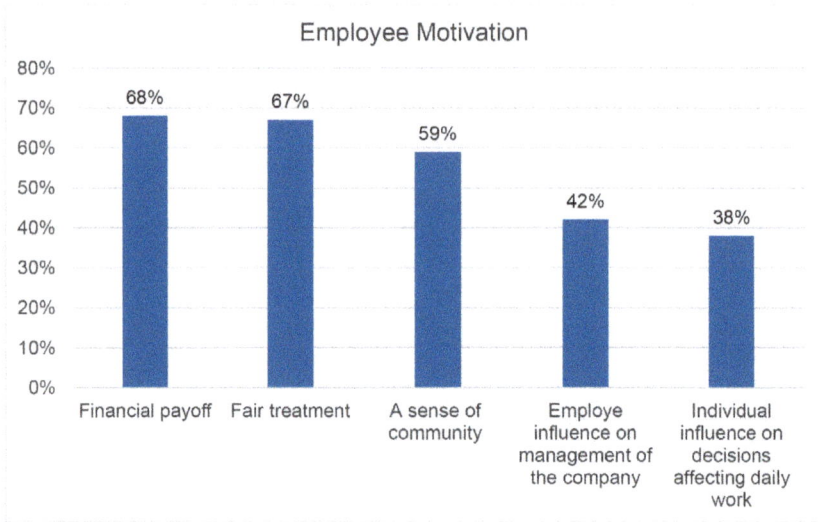

Source: Michelle Brown, Rowan Minson, Ann O'Connell and Ian Ramsay

Why Do Employees Participate in Employee Share Ownership Plans?

Employee Share Ownership Project, Melbourne Law School, The University of Melbourne, 2011

ESOPS are used for several reasons:

1   Savings Vehicle — most ESOP plans have a long-term focus (3–7 years), allowing employees to accumulate savings through acquiring and holding shares

2   Participation — ESOP participants tend to experience a greater sense of community and involvement with the decision-making process, leading to increases in employee engagement levels.

3   Succession Planning — an ESOP can be an effective employee buy-out instrument when the owner(s) want to retire (or change their business direction) and need to sell.

4   Funding Retirement — ESOPs can give founders the ability to extract cash prior to retirement.

Academic Research on the Impact of ESOPs:

• ESOPs appear to increase sales, employment and sales per employee
(Drs. Joseph R. Blasi and Doulas L. Kruse
School of Management and Labor Relations Rutgers University).

- ESOP companies that combine employee ownership with a participative management style grow 8-11% per year faster than they otherwise would have been expected to grow based on pre-ESOP performance
  (National Center for Employee Ownership, Harvard Business Review September/October 1987).
- Compared to 500 private non-ESOP companies, ESOP companies paid better benefits, had twice the retirement income for employees, and paid higher wages than their non-ESOP counterparts.
  (Wealth and Income Consequences of Employee Ownership: A Comparative Study from Washington State, Kardas, Peter A., Scharft, Adria L., Keogh, Jim, November 1998).
- Studies between ESOPs and productivity growth have found greater productivity and profitability in the first few years after a company adopts an ESOP
  (Dr. Doulas L. Kruse, School of Management and Labor Relations, Rutgers University, 1995).
- The number of ESOPs in the UK increased by 10% during 2012
- (National Centre for Employee Ownership, February 2013).

## Ladder to Equity

Whilst the research undoubtedly shows an increase in employees looking for equity in the business they work for — Australia lags behind on the world stage in providing a mechanism to achieve this. According to recent research in both the United States and Europe, a little over 30% of employees have some kind of equity interest in the business they work for, whilst in Australia that number is around 8%.

A simple mechanism to manage the transition through various stages is the issue. It is not simple, nor smart, to simply take an employee and provide them with equity — and thus the ladder becomes important.

As Warren Buffet says — "Employees are keen to climb the ladder to equity — but someone needs to provide the ladder."

## Progressive Staged Approach

Employee Earnings → Income Model → Profit Share → Equity → Control

- Employee Earnings — Earning (salary/wage/hourly rates etc.) — this is where most employees start (and stay).
- Income Model — The first step on the ladder then is to boost that income and this is quite common. We often see companies paying bonuses, commissions on sales, incentives etc. to increase an employee's income. This is a great step to link performance with reward.
- Profit Share — Most equity plans begin with this simple step and in fact many end at this step. Simply providing a share of profits to employees is a great additional incentive as they are directly rewarded as a result of the financial performance of the company in the same way that a business owner typically would be. This step changes the focus from personal to team performance.
- Equity — Whilst there are many equity plans available, our models provide a formal structured mechanism to incorporate profit share, equity and control into any business succession plan. This allows employees to transition into an equity ownership position within the business they work for and encourages long-term strategic thinking.
- Control — Often this step is never utilised though on occasion has substantial benefits in terms of succession, not only in terms of ownership but also of business management. Ultimately, control means that employees can be transitioned through the earlier four stages and end up in a position of control. This may mean that they take over general management or become CEO of the company. It may also be that they end up with a seat on the board at some future date however, this step is not to be rushed.

If managed correctly, the ladder is a great methodology to identify opportunities to progressively transition employees to think and act like business owners and motivate key employees in the long term.

Note however that the transition should be managed carefully with KPIs and performance criteria to proceed up the ladder. Such plans can fall over without logical steps listed out for employees or where businesses miss steps trying to fast track progression.

## 14.3 Background to Employee Share Ownership Plans — International

Employee Share Ownership Plans (ESOPs) are very popular in the United States, the United Kingdom and Europe but have not yet gained momentum in Australia despite legislative changes and evolution since the 1970s. ESOPs benefit private businesses by:

* Funding an exit
* Delivering improvements in performance
* Achieving business continuity after the owners exit
* Allowing a tax effective transfer of ownership.

In the United States nearly half of all ESOPs are used by private firms to buy out an owner. It also positions the business as a more competitive employer and therefore attracts and retains key staff. Half of business owners surveyed said securing the right talent/finding competent staff was the number one issue while retaining them was ranked at 16%.

The following diagram shows statistics on ESOPs in the USA and the growth in number of ESOPS since they were introduced around the 1980s.

### What do ESOPs look like?

Currently, there are about 8,000 ESOPs with 11 million employees and approximately $1.3 trillion in employee Owned equity. ESOP companies are incredibly diverse: there are ESOPs in almost every industry, ranging from just a few employees to over 150,000, spread throughout the nation. This diagram provides a brief summary of what the ESOP community looks like.

## What do ESOPs look like?

Currently, there are about 10,900 ESOPs and equivalent plans employing more than 11 million U.S. employees. ESOP companies are incredibly diverse: there are ESOPs in almost every industry, ranging from just a few employees to over 150,000, spread throughout the nation. This infographic provides a brief summary of what the ESOP community looks like.

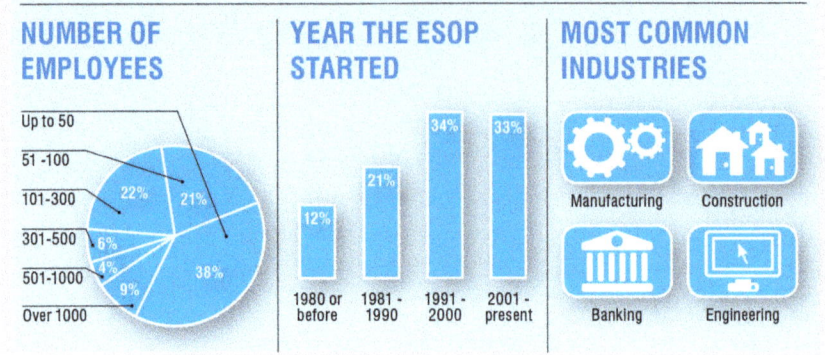

### NUMBER OF EMPLOYEES

Up to 50
51 -100
101-300 — 22% 21%
301-500 — 6%
501-1000 — 4%
9% 38%
Over 1000

### YEAR THE ESOP STARTED

34% 33%
21%
12%
1980 or before | 1981 - 1990 | 1991 - 2000 | 2001 - present

### MOST COMMON INDUSTRIES

Manufacturing     Construction

Banking          Engineering

ESOPs are particularly suited to a business exit because they allow more flexibility in the exit timeline, offer a structured and smooth transition and are an attractive alternative to selling on the open market.

## 14.4 Employee Share Ownership Plans in Australia

Employee share plans have been operating in Australia since the mid-1960s with both IBM and Ajax Fasteners operating schemes with varying success. The plans were first embodied in legislation in 1974 and have led to evolving significance and increasing support amongst business, and the gradual evolution of the legislation.

Support for employee share plans continued when in 1996 The Hon John Howard MP delivered a policy statement, Employee Share Ownership Plans Initiatives. The subsequent Howard government increased tax concessions for employees in ESOPs and also relaxed the conditions to allow more companies to launch an employee share plan.

Implementing an employee share plan to facilitate an exit strategy is gaining popularity in Australia and especially amongst small to medium enterprises. There are potentially great benefits to the business owner, the employees and the business due to improved retention, motivation, performance, productivity and profitability.

In a sale situation the PPT is also a clear demonstrator of the company's performance and the health of its financial assets since it shows the company's ability to pay funds over a period of time based on performance targets being achieved.

There is no single model or hard and fast rules, but ESOPs generally fall into two broad categories — giving benefits to executives or benefits to general employees. To facilitate a business exit, we will look in more detail at transferring ownership to employees through a Peak Performance Trust.

## 14.5 A strategic approach to remuneration

Transforming employees into committed shareholders of your business involves developing a remuneration system that reflects your organisation's philosophy, objectives and values. The way that you reward your staff members influences their thinking, behaviour and performance.

For example, a company that pays bonuses or commissions to individuals for monthly or quarterly results encourages employees to focus on short term individual results, and not on the longer-term business strategy. If the reward is capped, staff may hold and roll over sales from one period to the next rather than doing more than is necessary to achieve each bonus.

Employee remuneration is about more than just money — it is about motivation and reward, which contribute to increased levels of productivity and morale. A strategically planned remuneration system helps to align your employees' personal and financial goals with your business goals and encourages an ownership mindset.

A good plan will combine a competitive base salary package with a short-term bonus based on individual performance, and a component that relies on long-term performance and team work.

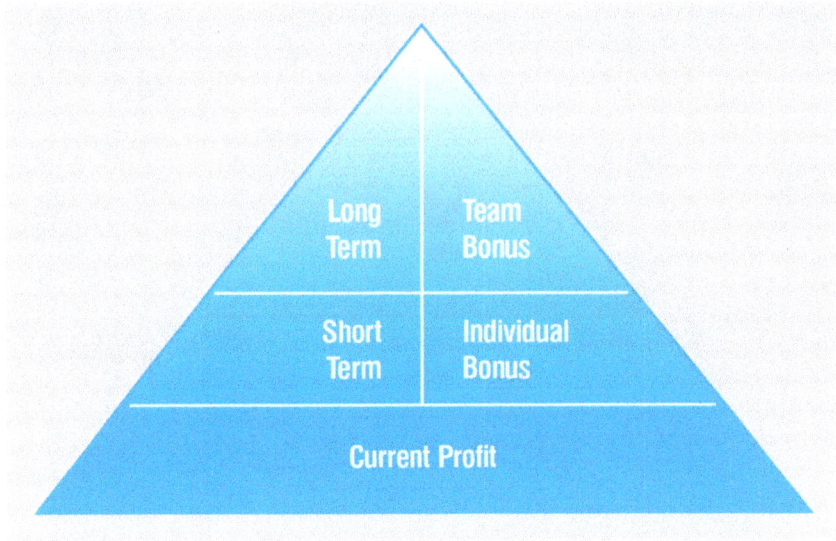

## 14.6 Peak Performance Trust

**What would it mean to your business if your employees were as committed to achieving success as you are?**

One of the most innovative vehicles through which to provide employee share ownership is a customised Peak Performance Trust (PPT) — a new type of ESOP that has been developed by, and is only available through Succession Plus.

With a PPT, the employer creates an investment trust into which it makes contributions on behalf of, and for the benefit of its employees. It makes a commitment to investing a predetermined amount of money into the trust on a regular basis, contingent upon participating employees achieving determined performance outcomes. As the profits increase, so too does the percentage share that employees can benefit from. If profits are not increased, then no further allocation of funds is made to the PPT.

Here's how the PPT works:

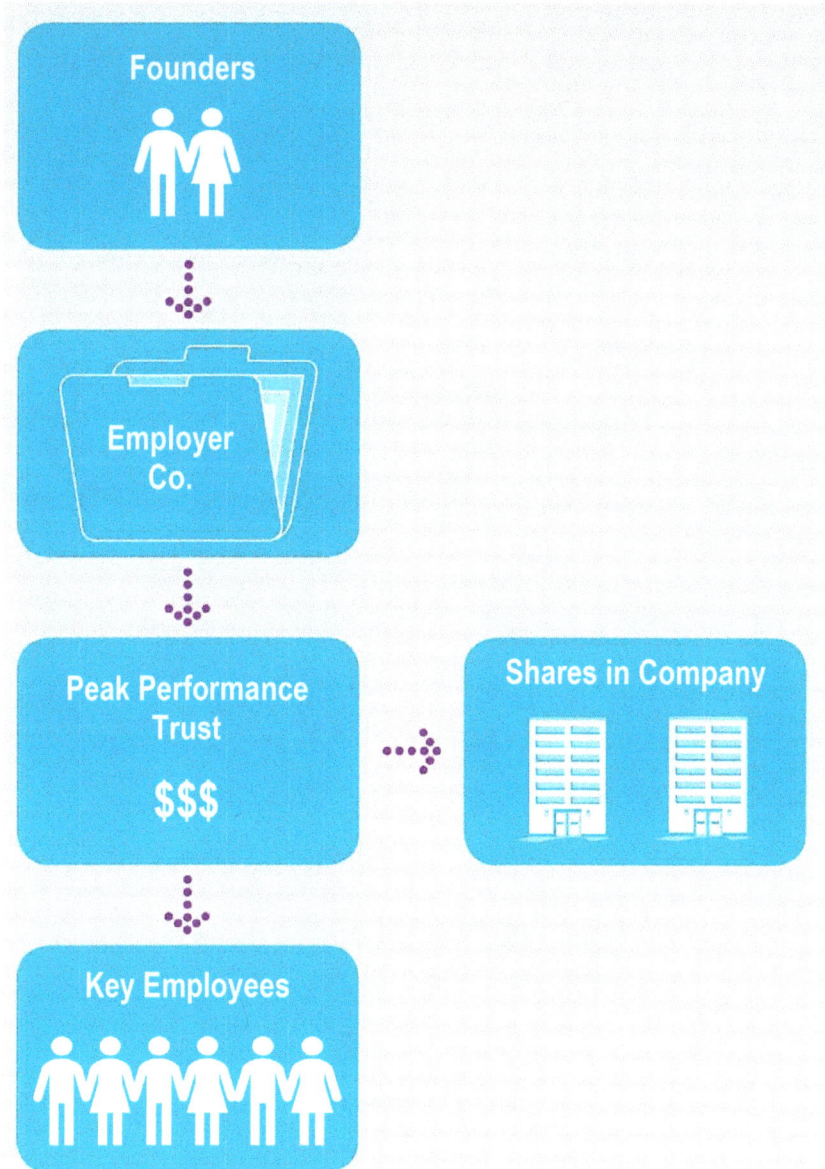

1    The Employer will invite key employees to participate in the PPT. Qualification is usually at least partly related to years of employment.

2    A net profit benchmark and a percentage of profits above this benchmark to be contributed to the PPT is calculated. For

example, the Employer could pay 25% of the net profits generated by the Employer over $500,000. If the Employer's net profits for the year are $600,000, then 25% of $100,000 (i.e. $25,000) will be contributed to the PPT.

3    The Trustee will use this contribution to allow employees to invest in shares in the Employer.

4    Because the PPT has a share in the Employer, and Employees have a unit in the PPT, increased profits will result in an increased value of each employee's indirect share in the Employer. Furthermore, because this is the only type of investment allowed under the deed, the equity value of the trust will always match the equity value of the Employer.

5    Dividends will also be paid annually to employees in proportion to the units held.

6    The only members allowed under the plan rules are employees — so if someone leaves they are automatically excluded and their units redeemed or sold.

7    Qualifying periods are normally set up to govern the "disqualifying discount" — the amount that an employee is "penalised" if they "leave early."

## 14.7 Using a PPT in your remuneration strategy

As an employer you make contributions on behalf of, and for the benefit of, your employees into your PPT. Your business makes a commitment to investing a predetermined amount of money into the trust on a regular basis, contingent upon participating employees achieving predetermined performance targets. As the profits increase, so too does the percentage share that employees can benefit from, and vice versa.

The benefits of a PPT are considerable for employees and employers, ensuring complete alignment between financial and lifestyle goals. The PPT is the ultimate 'golden handcuff' for staff as it links financial reward to achieving long-term results.

The following simple rules will help you to make the most of your PPT and motivate your staff:

- Simple — well thought out and easy for all staff to understand
- Applicable — applies to all staff consistently (although you can choose to offer greater reward to particular levels or for particular relevant outcomes for which employees have control)
- Reliable — once communicated does not change often
- Transparent — communicated clearly and without ambiguity. All performance indicators must be able to be measured objectively and progress communicated regularly
- Supported — the system must be supported by all company owners, board and management.

## 14.8 Using a PPT for your succession plan

A PPT can provide a facility to fund an ongoing succession planning arrangement where money set aside in the trust is used to fund the purchase of a proportion of the business. In this way, the purchase is directly linked to the performance of the business and becomes largely self-funding.

There are two options when using a PPT in a succession plan. The first allows indirect ownership in the company. Qualifying company profits are transferred to the PPT, which then buys shares in the company. The employees own units in the PPT, making them indirect equity holders in the company.

This option has the benefit of involving all staff in ownership of the trust and can greatly simplify the business ownership structure. The trust becomes the majority shareholder without complicated ownership structures or the compliance burden of dealing with many minority shareholders.

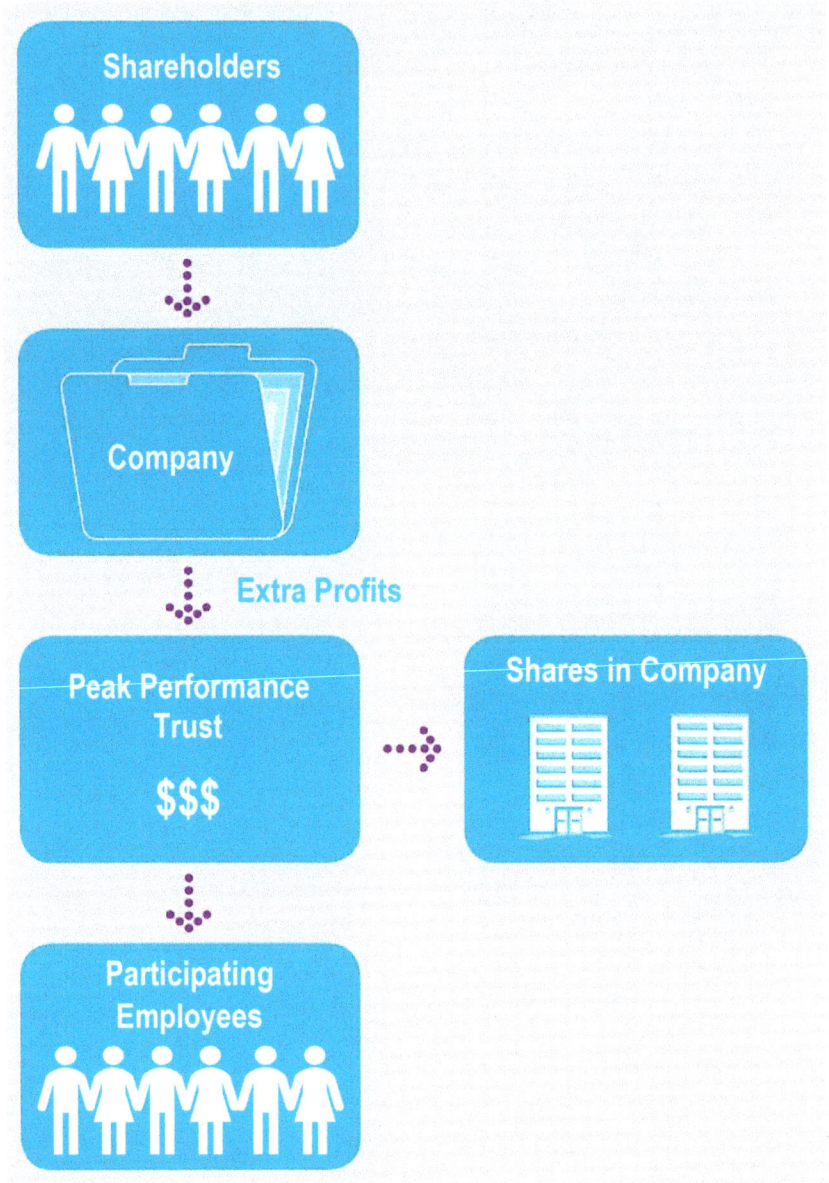

The second option allows individuals to become direct shareholders in the company. The profits directed into the PPT are used to make loans to employees so that they can buy shares.

## 14.9 The inner workings of a PPT

The principle of the PPT is to reward profit-increasing performance, meaning bonus payments are only made into the trust where performance criteria has been met. The most common use of a PPT is a bonus reward scheme in which a minimum net profit target is determined, based on financial projections for your business. Once the minimum target is achieved, the company contributes a predetermined amount of additional profits to the bonus pool.

The PPT is managed by a corporate trustee with specific investment powers and is restricted to only investing in shares in the employer company. We recommend that the directors of the corporate trustee include:

- two employee representatives (employees that are participating in the plan)
- one employer representative (a director or owner of the company) and an independent adviser (accountant, lawyer or representative of Succession Plus).

### Eligibility

It is preferable to include as many people in the organisation as possible, within predetermined criteria. This should specify a minimum period of employment, vesting arrangements (i.e how long shares are held before the benefits can be realised) and what happens if an employee leaves the company. One of the benefits of the PPT is that eligibility and vesting periods are completely up to you, however you must ensure these are decided upfront, documented clearly and communicated clearly to all employees.

Being a flexible structure the PPT can be customised to measure and reward different performance criteria in different businesses, so it is important to determine which aspects of individual and overall performance you want to reward.

Income in a PPT is distributed to participating employees annually, based on the number of units held at the beginning of each financial year, and on how much those contributions have earned during the year. It is usual for employees to have served a minimum period of employment before being invited to participate in a PPT, and to remain with the company for a specified period of time before they are able to extract the maximum benefit.

Generally, the minimum period of service before being invited to participate will be twelve months, but at times you may want to waive this condition for certain individuals, for example an employee to extend an under-performing employee's probationary period or to attract or retain a particularly high-performing member of staff.

## Disqualifying discount

We recommend implementing a minimum period, based on a sliding scale, to be served before employees are entitled to draw benefit from the PPT, for example:

- End of Years 1 to 3 — no benefit
- End of Year 4 — access to Year 1 benefit
- End of Year 5 — access to Years 2 and 3 benefit

Under this scenario, an employee who leaves will miss out on the balance of the last two years' contributions, but the penalty might be reduced after five years and eliminated altogether after ten years of service.

There is virtually no limit to the way these conditions can be managed within a PPT, so it is possible to create some very innovative scenarios. One of our clients decided to offer 20% of the employee's account within the first five years, and 100% from year six.

## Establishing targets

In order to transfer funds into the PPT you will need to set targets for your employees to meet. This involves having a good understanding of the potential future performance of your business, and the areas that employees can influence to drive performance.

We start by looking at current profit drivers, and where the business should focus to motivate improvement. If you don't identify the key profit drivers and include them in the PPT, you may incentivise staff to focus on the wrong outcomes. For example, many businesses nominate sales volume as a KPI, but this can motivate staff to lower unit price, which ultimately decreases margin and affects bottom line profit.

## Unit allocation

Participating employees are allocated units in the PPT based on the contributions directly made by, or apportioned to, each person. The proportion of bonus allocated to individuals is determined using a points system, which can be calculated in a number of ways. Most commonly points are allocated based on the employee's total remuneration for the year (including short-term incentive payments), and their length of service.

> **Example**
>
> An employee has been with the company for five years and is on a current salary of $60,000
>
> 1 point of every $1,000 = 60 points
>
> 1 point of each year of service = 5 points
>
> Total points = 65.

For example, an employee might be allocated one point for every $1,000 in earnings (including incentives) and one additional point for each year of service. This method of points' allocation takes into consideration seniority (based on salary) and loyalty to the company (based on length of service). But there are many other ways that points can be calculated, depending on the needs of the organisation.

For some clients we have created allocation methodologies based solely on salary. For others we have created allocations based on multiple considerations, and one client uses three measures: overall business profitability, team sales and individual sales. This rewards individual, intra-team and inter-team performance and sends a very clear signal to employees about the types of behaviours and results expected and valued by the organisation, driving a culture where everyone works together for mutual benefit. In other cases, clients have elected to allocate units equally amongst all employees.

## Information and systems

It is essential to launch the PPT with clear communication and then have the appropriate systems to manage, monitor and communicate results. Staff seminars are ideal to introduce the PPT, along with a handbook and legal documentation. If employees don't understand the plan or what they can do to influence its outcome, they will be discouraged and demotivated.

Once launched, information about the performance of the organisation and the PPT should be communicated to employee shareholders regularly, along with communication from management explaining where improvements can be made. Employees should receive quarterly statements outlining the fund's performance, contributions they have received and the investments the fund has made on their behalf.

A common misconception among business owners is that they need to provide extensive information. It is actually far more effective for staff to understand and focus on improving the business's key financial drivers. One of my clients, a sales-based business, simply reports on sales versus targets, which is enough to lead staff to achieve the targets.

We often discover that companies do not have the necessary systems in place to manage a PPT. Managing your business and the PPTs performance reporting may need some investment in infrastructure to allow thorough budgeting, costing, financial modelling and identifying KPIs. A simple accounting system can be all that is needed to ensure the PPT is integrated with the business, and allows easy tracking and reporting of the trust's performance.

## Additional investments

Employees can make contributions to the PPT over and above the employee contributions. Because the PPT is designed to earn income on its assets, investments into the trust are considered to be capital, and are therefore not taxable in the hands of the trustee. Examples are salary sacrifice and savings.

## 14.10 Benefits of a PPT in succession planning

According to a recent report in the San Francisco Chronicle, "Employee Share Ownership Plans may help businesses stay open as boomers retire." The article discusses the fact that baby boomers own half of the privately held businesses that have employees. In every year, nearly 4,000,000 across the United States retire.

Selling isn't always an option. According to the report, only 20% of small businesses that list themselves for sale actually find a buyer. More than 85% of business owners do not have a succession plan which outlines who will take over the business when they no longer want to (or are no longer able to) run the company, according to a report released by Project Equity last week. Passing the small business onto other family members (family/generational succession) may be possible (about 15% of the owners actually do this) but it's not always viable. In many cases, the companies simply close.

Employee ownership often works "it's not as big a shift as people sometimes assume" due to the fact that it's a shared form of entrepreneurship and differing skills amongst employees actually helps. The structure is designed to protect the employees (from each other and external issues) and provide certainty about how the plan works and what rules the owners operate under.

The benefits of a PPT in succession planning include:
- Affordable for the business
- Encourages ongoing profit improvement through rewards linked to performance
- Tax effective for both the business and participating employees
- Supports employee development
- Rewards employees who make a substantial contribution to the business
- Easily understood, controlled and managed
- Appropriate for both the long and short term

- Complies with all current and likely Australian taxation and legal requirements
- Gives the company a competitive advantage in recruiting, motivating and retaining high performance staff
- Assists employees to achieve their financial and lifestyle goals
- Improves the attractiveness and value of the business to prospective new third-party owners by demonstrating that key employees are likely to remain with the company and are committed to achieving results
- A useful and accurate measure of a company's financial performance.

## 14.11 ESOPs and Gen Y

A workshop on generation Y in the workplace raised an interesting statistic; 72% of the Generation Y population want to own their own business. Back in my dad's generation less than 12% of school leavers wanted to run their own business — most people wanted to go and work for a big bank or a corporate and stay there till they were 65 then retire on a good retirement plan.

If you have Generation Y employees this is an important thing to know, as they may leave to pursue their goals if equity ownership is not an option. However, another interesting statistic was that over 90% of those wanting to own a business said they didn't want to own it on their own. Generation Y workers look for freedom and flexibility and the opportunity to have three months off to travel to Europe.

Most baby boomers look at that and think it's all too hard, they get it too easy or they are too much risk. But the fact is this is the way our workforce is heading, and rather than fight it we need to look for ways to accommodate it so that we can retain good people.

Most 30 year olds can't afford to start their own business or buy one. So, an employee share plan gives younger employees the opportunity to part own a business while enjoying the security and lifestyle that comes with being an employee. And over the next five to ten years, that employee has an opportunity to build equity and gradually take over ownership of the business, if they want it. In 2011 one of our clients, an LJ Hooker real estate office (referred to earlier), won the Employee Share Plan of the Year award for two reasons. Firstly, their sick days went down by 84%. Secondly not one person had left the business in the five years. For real estate agents that's ridiculous, it just doesn't happen. But this was all down to the ESOP. Everyone on the team was in it for the long haul. It will most likely take around 14 years for the eight team members to completely own the business. But no one is in a hurry; they are mostly in their 40s and are comfortable with a slow, long-term plan that will deliver value because everyone is set on the same performance goals.

C-Mac GM Steve Grylak was presented with the national award for best SME Employee Share Plan in 2012. The C-Mac engineering plant in Girraween, Western Sydney offered an employee owned share plan (ESOP) to all employees. As a result, the business has seen an increase in employee engagement and an 18% hike in productivity at the plant. And longer term the risk of losing skilled employees will significantly decrease.

"Being a board member has definitely given me a much different perspective on the way the business runs. I now have a lot more respect for the decision makers and have found that a lot of the day to day issues aren't as clear cut as they seem." an employee remarked.

"Being on the board has also given me some new-found confidence in the business. Now I see all the measures and processes that are set up to make sure the business doesn't fail. I've found it quite interesting so far and can only imagine it will get more exciting."

"It has definitely made people think about their futures with the company and not just the next week or day. Most people understand it is a long-term process and aren't expecting to 'get rich quick' or anything like that ... I will be constantly on the lookout to improve the business. I will also carry a sense of pride when representing the company during or even after work hours."

To learn more about how an ESOP could be part of an exit or succession strategy, refer to our website at www.successionplus.com. au.

## 14.12 Technical Guide to The Peak Performance Trust

This section outlines the technical, legal and taxation aspects of the Peak Performance Trust (PPT) and is based on Private Binding Rulings issued by the Australian Taxation Office in December 2017 and January 2018.

### What is the Peak Performance Trust?

The PPT is an Employee Share Scheme as defined by Section 83A and sub-section 995-1(1) of the Income Tax Assessment Act 1997 (ITAA), which has been designed by Succession Plus for its clients, who are predominantly mid-market professional services businesses, to attract, retain and motivate key employees.

The PPT has the following features:

- An employer or employee makes a request to set up a Peak Performance Trust (PPT)
- The PPT will have a corporate trustee which will manage the affairs of the PPT
- Both the employer and one or more employees will be able to make contributions to the PPT
- Each employee will be invited to join the trust based on predetermined selection criteria and will be allocated units in the trust
- Typically, the employer will agree to make a contribution to the trust annually based on a profit share formula
- The trustee (based on the rules outlined in the trust deed) will have strictly limited investment powers which will restrict the PPT to only investing in shares in the employer entity (or holding company)
- The PPT units will convey the same rights as owning direct shares to the unit holders

- Under the terms of the trust deed all employee units which are the result of an employer contribution are subject to the disqualifying events and disqualifying discounts
- Income (i.e. dividends paid by the employer company to the PPT) of the PPT, must be distributed to unit holders on an annual basis, though this may happen more frequently, based on the number of units held by the employee.

## What are the tax implications of the Peak Performance Trust?

### Taxation treatment for Employers
### (ATO ruling reference — 1051314640866)

- The employer contributions to the PPT will be deductible in accordance with section 8-1 of the ITAA 1997
- The contributions will be deductible in the income year in which the shares acquired using the contribution are allocated to a participant
- No fringe benefits tax will apply as the trust is a qualifying employee share trust and paragraph (ha) in subsection 136 (1) of the FBTAA provides a specific exclusion
- No SGC, workers compensation or payroll tax will apply to the contributions
- The ATO has agreed that the general anti-avoidance provisions under part IVA of the ITAA will not apply

### Taxation treatment for Employees
### (ATO ruling reference — 1051323914120)

Units acquired via employer contributions

- Where the employee receives units in the PPT as an incentive by the employer and has not paid a consideration for the units then division 83A will apply to the acquisition. This provision allows the ESS tax rules to apply (not normal income tax rules)
- Under these rules, the employees qualify to defer income taxation on the acquisition of units. This is because the disqualifying events

and disqualifying discount mean there is a real risk of forfeiture for the purposes of subsection 83A — 105(3)

- Taxation can be deferred until the earliest of the following (deferred taxing point):
    - the time when there is no real risk of forfeiture.
    - The time when the employment ceases.
    - The end of the 15-year period starting when the employee acquired the interest
- This also allows the employee to ignore capital gains tax on any capital gain (or loss) on redemption of units, up until the deferred taxing point
- Once a deferred taxing point arises, the cost base is reset at that time to the current market value
- Section 83A — 125 operates to reset the cost base of the unit at its current market value unless the deferred taxing point occurs at the time the unit is disposed of.

Tax example for a typical employee:

- For example, John receives units worth $5,000 on 1/3/18, on 1/3/28 the disqualifying discount (which operates over 10 years) no longer applies to those units and so this date becomes the deferred taxing point In March 2028 the units are now worth $7,500. John retires in 2038 and sells his units for $10,000
- John needs to include income of $7,500 in his 2028 income tax return (this amount will be provided in an ESS statement issued by the Peak Performance Trust) and this amount will be taxed at his marginal tax rate
- John can ignore the $2,500 capital gain for taxation purposes and the cost base of the units now becomes $7,500
- When John retires and sells the units he will pay Capital Gains tax on the gain — $10,000–$7,500 — this will be included in his 2038 income tax return and taxed at his marginal rates less any applicable CGT discounts etc.

Units acquired at market value by the employee:

- Where the employee acquires additional units in the trust and pays market value consideration for the units Division 83A will not apply.
- There is no income taxation affect when an employee acquires additional units at market value.
- Where the employee has paid market value for the acquisition of additional units a capital gains tax liability will arise upon the sale of those units.

Tax example for an employee — Income on units:

- During 2019 FY, whilst John has held the units in the PPT, the employer has declared a dividend payable to the PPT of $6,000, the proportion of dividend payable on John's units is $300. This dividend is fully franked (though this may not always be the case) and the trustee of the PPT must pay this out to unitholders.
- John must include income of $300 in his 2019 income tax return, he will also declare a franking credit of $100 and will be taxed on the $400 income at his marginal rate (less any franking credit).

### Taxation treatment for the PPT
### (ATO ruling reference — 1051338012860)

- Contributions to the PPT are not taxable income of the PPT.
- Income received by the PPT (dividends from the employer entity) are income and must be distributed to unitholders.
- Expenses incurred in managing the PPT (for example, Bank fees) are deductible to the PPT.

## 14.13 Case Study

Smith Engineering is an Australian based company group which currently has over 100 employees nationally.

The Employer has decided to introduce the Employee Share Plan (the Plan) as a mechanism for rewarding, retaining and motivating its employees.

The Employer has the following reasons for introducing the Plan:

- Provide a mechanism for rewarding staff for their loyalty and effort in a structured, equitable and transparent manner
- Assist to engender responsibility for the performance of our business throughout our employees and provide a mechanism that rewards staff for our collective and individual contributions.

The Employer will operate the Plan through a trust (the Trust). The Trustee Company is owned by two of the current owners and directors of the Smith Engineering Company. They also act as directors of the Trustee Company.

It is intended that the Trust will be used to acquire fully paid ordinary shares in the capital of the Employer (Shares) for employees pursuant to the Plan. The Trust provides an arm's-length vehicle through which Shares can be acquired and held on behalf of employees, providing the liquidity of employee held shares in a simple flexible manner. In effect, this aspect allows the Employer to satisfy corporate law requirements relating to companies dealing in their own shares. The Trust provides the following benefits to the Employer:

1   Allows key shareholders to keep control over company ownership
2   Registration of shares in the Trustee's name provides control over identity of shareholders, preventing a sale to unrelated persons
3   If the Employer is sold, it is easier to "mop-up" employee shareholders
4   Enables the disqualification event and disqualification discount provisions to be enforced in a simple manner through the Trust.

# MANAGEMENT SUCCESSION

When you are ready to sell your business, a buyer is not likely to appear in a puff of smoke. You will need to do some groundwork well in advance to identify potential interested parties.

## 15.1 Introduction

While for many family businesses succession to family members is an obvious choice, the 44% of surveyed respondents in a recent Family Business Australia survey who expected to sell their business now or later, gave the following reasons:

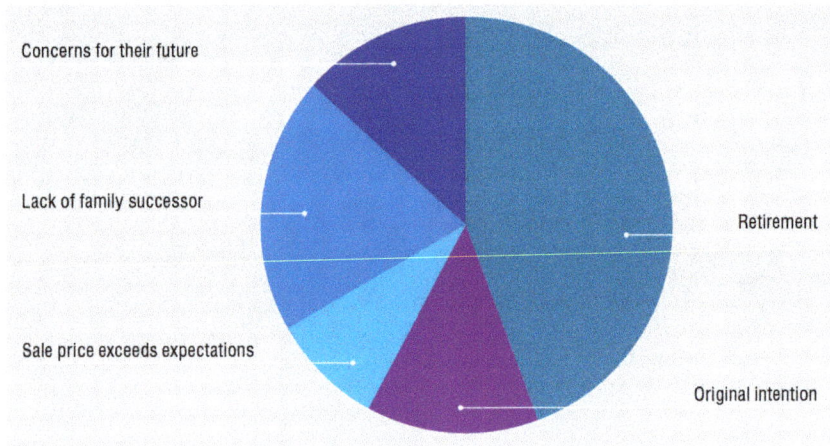

## 15.2 Identify/recruit potential successors

The survey also showed that many business owners worry more about who will run the business, rather than who will buy it.

Many business owners who planned to pass the business down to their children find that their children are not interested in the business, have followed alternative career paths, or choose to live inter-state or overseas. So, the business owner has to look at existing staff members or external recruitment for a future CEO. However, many of the exit options in Step 7 allow transfer of control as well as management, which may influence how you identify potential buyers.

An important concept to understand about succession planning is that it is not just an exit strategy — for the person assuming responsibility or buying into the business it is an entry. Therefore, the transition will need to be handled carefully to ensure that not only do you get a smooth exit, but the business continues to operate well for the new owner, whether it is run via your existing management team or someone else.

The most suitable buyer for your business is not simply the person prepared to pay the most money, or with the financial capacity at the time you want to sell. It should also be the person that presents the best long-term potential for maximising the value of the business and ensuring a win/win transaction.

Make a list of your key successor attributes to clarify what you are looking for before you approach anyone.

## Successor Checklist

I advise clients to prepare a checklist of all the important qualities that the future owners of their business must have, and to rank prospective successors against these criteria. The checklist should include specific skills and areas of expertise as well as values, financial capacity and other measures that are important in achieving a successful match between the prospective buyer, the current owners and the business. This process helps to deliver an unbiased view of each potential successor and the likelihood of them being successful in the role of new business owner. It also highlights those areas where the existing business owners should be focusing their attention in training potential successors.

To prepare an effective successor checklist, list the required attributes of potential new owners. At a summary level your checklist may look like this, although you would actually assess each assessor on many detailed areas:

| | Candidate 1 | Candidate 2 | Candidate 3 |
|---|:---:|:---:|:---:|
| Sales skills and experience | ✔ | ✔ | ✔ |
| Technical knowledge | ✔ | ✔ | ✘ |
| Financial management knowledge | ✔ | ✔ | ✔ |
| Service history (length of employment) | ✘ | ✔ | ✔ |
| Qualifications and experience | ✔ | ✘ | ✔ |
| Other skills / experience / characteristics | ✔ | ✔ | ✘ |

## 15.3 Management development and performance

Clearly a key factor of transitioning yourself out of the business relies on having strong team members to take over. This may mean bringing on additional staff, but a good succession plan will seek to promote from within where possible, rewarding loyalty and making the most of people who already know your business well.

As part of your succession plan you may need a Human Resources adviser to help you plan the ideal organisation chart for the future, the key roles you need to fill, and then assess your current talent pool. Again, it is important not to alienate or worry staff during this process, but instead give staff a chance to be rewarded, and potentially uncover skills or ambition that you didn't know about. Even employees you thought were unhappy or underperforming may suddenly show an interest in being trained and groomed for a new role, particularly in conjunction with a share or reward scheme.

The staff members that you identify as important to your current team do not have to tick all the boxes right now, but they should show some or all of the following characteristics, depending on their proposed role:

- Willingness and ability to learn
- Aligned to business culture and values
- Good customer service ethic
- Open to new ideas, and able to contribute ideas
- Able to manage staff well (if applicable)
- Reliable in terms of attendance and productivity
- Team player.

It is also useful to have a good mix of skills in the team, for example at least one person who is good at administration, process and compliance, and another who takes a creative approach to problem solving to generate more income for the business.

Once you have identified your key team members you will need to give them some incentive to stay throughout the transition period. The incentive you offer will depend on factors such as how far ahead your exit is planned, the nature of the business and industry norms, the availability of other job offers for your key people and the range of people you want to keep in terms of seniority, skills and pay levels. Some of your staff may be close to retirement themselves but will be willing to work for a few extra years if they have job security and the prospect of earning additional reward.

Don't be afraid to ask your staff what would motivate them. That doesn't mean you have to give them everything they ask for, but at least you can design a package that is attractive to them. Most employees will ask for something relatively simple — usually worth the cost when comparing that with the knowledge lost if that person leaves, and the time and cost to recruit and train a replacement.

Common incentive plans that we have seen are:

- Bonus payments awarded at key milestones in the transition period
- Bonus payments for achieving target results along the transition plan (this could be for example in achieving increased revenue, or for each task completed on the non-financial improvement list, such as getting the legal documents up to date or writing key process documents)

- Employee share plan awarding company shares instead of cash bonuses
- Non-financial rewards for achievements such as time off or gifts (for example each month of the succession plan the person contributing most to the combined effort receives a dinner voucher or a weekend away)
- Training programs to help staff get to the next level, or to develop an area of interest, for example online marketing, advanced IT skills, sales training, or networking events to learn and share ideas
- Flexible working hours — employees with families in particular may be willing to commit to several years with the business if you are able to accommodate their personal commitments.

For bonus and share schemes and the more formal rewards listed above, you may need new or amended employee contracts, with the help of an employment lawyer. Again, you can't make any promises to staff beyond the date that you lose control of the business, but you can make a contractual agreement regarding their terms of employment up to that date.

The more of a team effort you make your succession plan, the more the team will get on board and make it happen. A happy and engaged team will only add value to your business.

## Extract Value

The fourth stage is the actual transaction, or the liquidity event. We've built up value and maximised it, and now we actually get it out. That is what will fund retirement. So we look at the options to exit and how we actually execute them. We start to set the wheels in motion for the change in control and/or ownership. This may happen anything from a few months after preparing your succession plan to several years later, with the business looking very different.

Throughout your succession plan you will have been on the look-out for potential buyers and potentially engaging them along the way to get a feel for their propensity to buy. They may even have given you some tips on what they would look for in a business investment. You may not have one specific buyer in mind, but plan to approach a few companies in your industry. The further removed the potential buyer is from your current business, the more thorough and impressive your marketing needs to be. A potential buyer will expect to see detailed information that articulates the value of the investment opportunity, and stands up to scrutiny. Likewise, in most cases, the higher your target sales price, the more information you are expected to provide.

Finding buyers may be a targeted face to face approach, you might use a business broker or corporate finance adviser, or you might advertise your business for sale on line.

## 15.4 Case Study

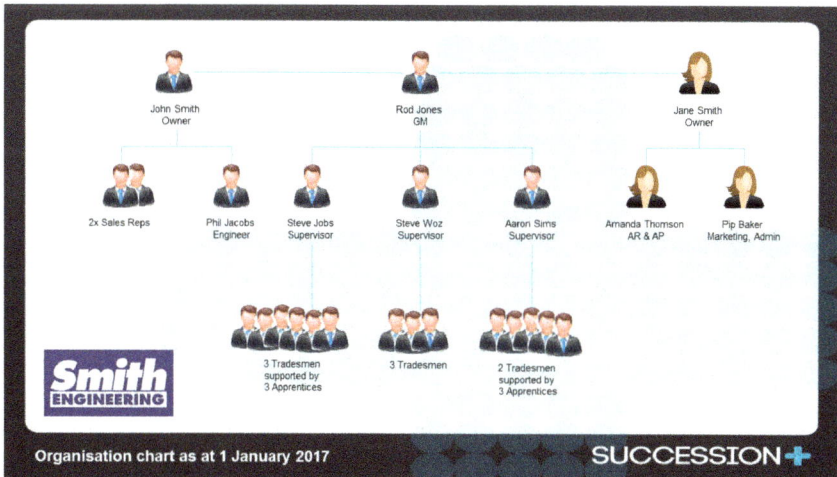

Organisation chart as at 1 January 2017

We started by building an organisational chart at Smith Engineering — which had never been done before, all owners felt it was a very useful exercise.

This enabled us to introduce the concept of Functional Management.

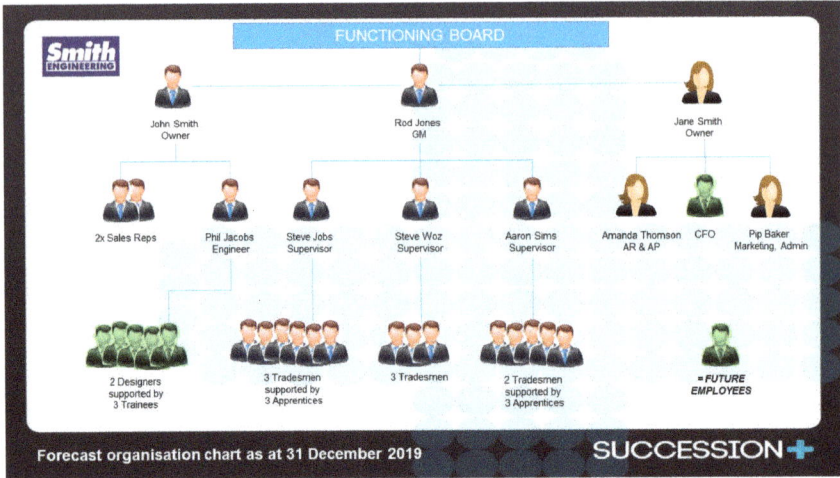

Organisational Chart in 2 years — according to Strategic Financial
Planning Model

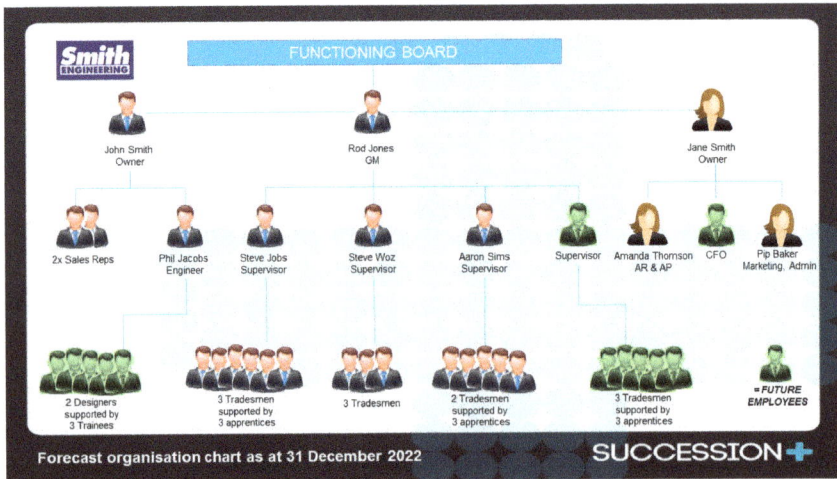

Organisational Chart in 5 years — according to Strategic Financial
Planning Model

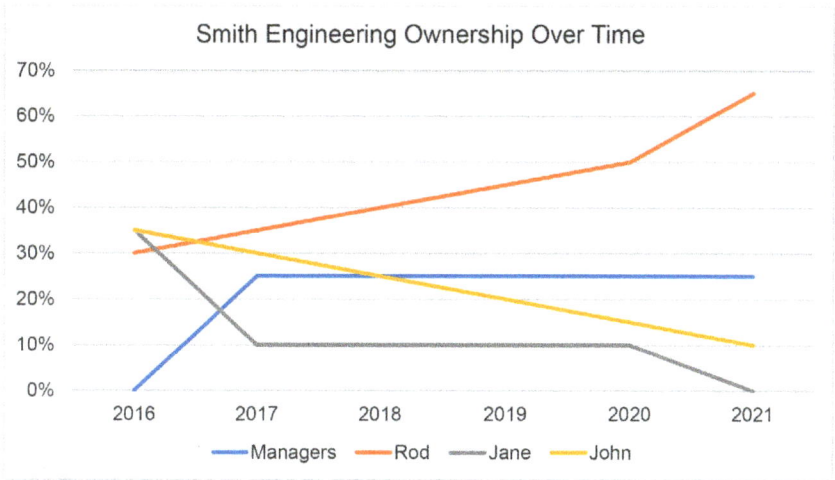

Smith Engineering Ownership Over Time

|  | 2016 | 2017 | 2018 | 2019 | 2020 | 2021 |
|---|---|---|---|---|---|---|
| Managers | 0% | 25% | 25% | 25% | 25% | 25% |
| Rod | 30% | 35% | 40% | 45% | 50% | 65% |
| Jane | 35% | 10% | 10% | 10% | 10% | 0% |
| John | 35% | 30% | 25% | 20% | 15% | 10% |

# • STEP 16
# TAX PLANNING

"The hardest thing in the world to understand is income tax." — Albert Einstein

The tax event comes fairly late in the process, when the transaction actually happens, but do get tax advice before you start on your succession plan. Seek out good tax advice when you have a preliminary business valuation, and you still have time to make the necessary changes to ensure you qualify for concessions and get the best tax outcome.

## 16.1 Introduction

The most important taxation issue in succession planning is capital gains tax (CGT). Tax has been payable on most capital gains since 1985 in Australia, and the sale of equity in a business falls into this category (in most cases). If the shares or business were first owned prior to 1985, then they may be CGT exempt. CGT is probably the most complicated area of taxation law in Australia and the issues are many and varied. Unfortunately this means that CGT advice is generally based on 'if, then' scenarios — so until you get into the specifics of your individual situation, there's little generic advice that will apply.

Tax rules also change often. The good news is that there are some reliefs and exemptions available when selling your business.

## 16.2 50 percent CGT discount for individuals

When calculating the taxable gain on the sale of shares in a business, individuals can choose between two methods:

1   the indexation method (indexed to September 1999)
2   50 per cent discount on the nominal capital gain on assets that have been held for at least twelve months.

The CGT exemption is only available to individuals, so where a person operates a business through a company and that company sells the business assets, the 50 per cent CGT discount is not available. Where the shares are owned by a trust, special rules apply.

Certain events do not qualify for the CGT discount, including:

- granting rights or options
- creating contractual rights
- creation of trusts
- granting or changing leases.

Where the discount does apply, it can work in conjunction with other exemptions.

## 16.3 Small business tax concessions

Small business tax concessions are available if the following conditions are met:

1   The net value of the assets of the business and its connected entities must not exceed $6 million
2   The asset must be an 'active' asset
3   If the asset is a share in a company or an interest in a trust, there are two further basic conditions that must be satisfied:
    - there must be a controlling individual shareholder; and
    - the individual disposing of the share, or the interest in the trust, must also satisfy the CGT concession stakeholder test.

A capital gain is reduced by 50 per cent if these basic conditions are satisfied. If the capital gain has already been reduced by the 50 per cent discount that applies to individuals, the small business concession reduction applies to that reduced gain — only 25 per cent of the original nominal gain is taxed. The capital gain can be further reduced by the small business retirement exemption, a small business rollover, or both. The 15-year exemption has priority over this concession.

## 16.4 15-year exemption

A small business entity can disregard a capital gain arising from a CGT asset that it has owned for at least 15 years if certain conditions are met, including:

### Small business retirement exemption

A taxpayer can choose to disregard a capital gain from a CGT asset of a small business if the capital proceeds from its disposal are used in connection with retirement. Again, there are a series of conditions and requirements to be met and they also relate to some of the other concessions.

### Small business rollover

A small business rollover allows taxpayers to defer a capital gain from active small business assets if a replacement asset is acquired within a period starting one-year before and ending two years after the disposal of a rollover asset in an income year, and if several other conditions are also met.

### Using the CGT concessions

In practice, a combination of these CGT concessions could be used to enhance a business succession outcome, although the outcomes will vary according to individual circumstances. No wonder even Einstein was confused. The benefits of seeking good tax advice early on in the process cannot be over stated.

## 16.5 GST and business succession

The disposal of business assets may attract goods and services tax (GST). The GST Act requires that for the supply to be GST free it must qualify as a going concern, and comprise all of the things necessary for the continued operation of the enterprise, which may be arguable if, for example, certain assets used in the enterprise are retained by the existing entity. Other requirements for agreements and registrations should also be noted.

## 16.6 Stamp duty

Stamp duty issues tend to go hand-in-glove with succession planning. Some of the basic stamp duty issues arise where:

- there is a transfer of assets between one entity/person and another entity/person
- there is a declaration of trust or transfer of property to a trust
- resettlement occurs, that is, where the assets held in one trust are transferred into a newly created trust
- there is a transfer of assets on the death of a person
- buy/sell agreements are entered into.

Stamp duty is a state-based tax and so treatment can vary depending upon your location.

## 16.7 Tax for the acquirer

The purchaser will also have to deal with tax implications when acquiring the business. These include:

### Dividend franking

The Australian system allows some relief from double taxation on dividends; that is if a company has paid tax on its profits and it distributes those profits to shareholders as dividends, Australian shareholders will only pay the difference (if any) between the company tax rate and their marginal tax rate.

### Deductible interest

The interest incurred on loans used to fund business investments is a deductible income tax expense and can be offset against salary/wages or dividends (other income).

### Capital gains

The purchase price of the shares on acquisition (and each parcel of equity in a staged acquisition) will be used to determine the cost base for a future capital gains tax event on a future sale or transfer.

## 16.8 Superannuation

There is much debate about the benefit of superannuation for business owners, but it is well worth considering using superannuation as a way to protect your assets and minimise tax.

Many business owners back themselves to the hilt in building their business, believing that the value of the business will mean superannuation contributions pale into insignificance. Of course, research also tells us that less than half of business owners extract enough value from their business to fund retirement. Many business owners are scared of the legal and compliance complexities of owning and running a self-managed superannuation fund, but with the right advice this is a manageable investment vehicle and the benefits far outweigh the increased effort, time and cost.

Contribution caps have made it difficult to get large sums into superannuation to generate a tax-effective income stream in retirement. With many family businesses owned and run jointly by husband and wife, the CGT cap contribution is a welcome opportunity available to both parties. When combined with the general contribution caps, a CGT cap contribution may allow a retiring couple to sell the family business, make contributions to superannuation in excess of $3.3 million and start a tax-free income stream.

## 16.9 Case Study

When it comes to tax planning, there are four main considerations:
1  Who will participate in the sale
2  When the sale is to take place
3  Whether or not you choose to sell shares in a company, or individual assets to your buyer
4  Whether or not you can use CGT and other tax concessions.

In 2018, we sat down with John and Jane who were contemplating a sale. Rod Jones was doing a great job as CEO, the company was growing and hitting profitability targets, morale was high because

Ownership Mindset (refer tosection 13.1) and the Peak Performance Trust (see section 14.7) had really taken root in the culture of the business.

We had mentioned to them both in the past that it is unwise to wait for the bad times to try to sell a business, as many owners do.

Jane was the one who talked about it with John first. She knew they had each achieved all they needed to on the personal front financially. They jointly decided that they would like to exit by way of sale in the next 18 months.

They decided to exit together. They also had a tag-along clause in their Shareholder Agreement, which meant the other owners (Rod and the managers through the Peak Performance Trust), would also be eligible to participate. Moreover, they also had a right of first refusal.

|  | John | Jane | Rod | Managers |
|---|---|---|---|---|
| Ownership in 2018 (today) | 25% | 10% | 40% | 25% |
| Ownership in 2020 (intended sale date) | 15% | 10% | 50% | 25% |

Jane and John called a special meeting together where it was decided mutually that:

1   John and Jane would work with Succession Plus to find a buyer for their shares
2   Rod considered participating in the sale partially, around half his shareholding, in order to take some cash off the table. But in the end decided against it, being young enough and inclined to continue accumulating ownership
3   The managers would not participate. Their own entries and exits are conducted within the Peak Performance Trust Structure and it is in the company's (and buyer's) best interests to keep ownership around the 25% level for the foreseeable future.

We therefore assumed that the sale would take place 1 July 2020 with Jane and John selling a combined 25%. The tax plan became as follows:

| Option 1 — Sale of Shares | |
|---|---|
| Share sale proceeds — 25% of the shares | $1,500,000 |
| Less cost base of shares | ($250) |
| Capital gain | $1,499,750 |
| Less 50% CGT discount | ($749,875) |
| Less Retirement Exemption ($500,000 each) | ($1,000,000) |
| Capital Gains Tax | Effectively nil |

| Option 2 — Sale of Assets |
|---|
| Not applicable in the circumstances. It would be impossible to sell a quarter of the assets without fundamentally disrupting the business. |

# DOCUMENTATION

Documentation is one of the key aspects of any transaction — many deals fall over at this point if the documentation is not accurate, up to date and efficiently organised.

## 17.1 Introduction

Once you have a buyer interested in your business, they will undertake due diligence to make sure everything that you have represented so far is true, and that there are no hidden liabilities or problems in the business. Although it may sound scary due diligence is good — the prospective buyer would not go to the effort and expense of going through this process unless they were committed to making the purchase. Either way, the best way to prepare for due diligence is to do reverse or vendor due diligence on yourself (or engage a Due Diligence expert to help you).

This is an important step because many deals fall over in the due diligence phase if the buyer uncovers something in the business that detracts from the value. In the formal due diligence process, anything the buyer finds that you haven't disclosed or doesn't stack up against what you've said so far gives them grounds to re-negotiate the price.

## 17.2 Due Diligence

Reverse Due Diligence (DD) gives you a chance to make sure everything is in order and consistent and tidy up any loose ends in time, such as expired licences, out of date software, leases on premises. The more prepared you are, the less painful the process will be.

We use an online due diligence package called Ansarada which allows us to upload a carefully organised package of documents, indexed and cross referenced, holding all of the vital information about the business.

## 17.3 Information Memorandum

When you first approach a potential buyer, you are likely to use a one-page document to summarise your business and present it as an attractive investment opportunity. Interested parties are likely to ask for your financial information, and some other critical operational details. The standard documentation is an 'Information Memorandum' (IM).

An IM is similar to a business plan but is written to the potential buyer. It is more about the benefits of the business as an investment opportunity than a path to achieving business goals. While you may be able to write the IM yourself using a standard template, it is well worth the investment getting this done professionally to make your business as attractive as possible. A poor IM will end up in the rubbish bin, and that potential buyer will be lost. Look for experts in transactions, finance and writing (as with any type of adviser we've mentioned, we are happy to recommend people). The cost of this expertise will be more than recovered in your sale price.

The IM is largely a sale brochure outlining the business, its advantage in the market place, strategic position and why a buyer would want to buy this business. In most cases this is the main criteria for decision making by the buyer — at least in the initial filtering stage of selecting companies worthy of further investigation/work.

Typically, the IM will contain an overview of your business, the market you operate in, the market you currently reach and your business model. It will also contain summaries of your team, your product or services and the advantages you offer to your customers compared with the competition. It will show your historical financial results, typically for three years, and may also include projected results for the next one to two years to give the buyer a sense of the potential in the business. The IM then gives instructions for any interested parties to take action, which we'll look at in the next section.

## 17.4 Legal Documentation

As with all commercial or business contracts there are obviously lots of key areas that need to be addressed, and much of this is an aspect of agreement between a vendor and a buyer. In most cases there are two stages of documentation: pre-sale or exit and transactional.

Prior to sale we work closely with clients to prepare an IM (as above), which is the starting point in attracting potential buyers to the business. Once discussions start, all parties to a potential sale sign a non-disclosure agreement (NDA) which prevents them from disclosing confidential information or, for example, approaching the business's customers, suppliers or employees.

Next, we will generally enter into a non-binding indicative offer (NBIO), basically an exchange of letters which confirms the proposed terms of the transaction. This is also often referred to as a 'term sheet'. At this stage it is important to note that the agreements are conditional and therefore fairly easy to walk away from.

Due diligence is typically a condition — i.e an agreement is made subject to the buyer undertaking a far more detailed review of the business. The agreement may specify the items the buyer wishes to review, for example contracts, historical financials, agreements with suppliers, licences and leases.

## 17.5 Case Study

We were able to take a lot of the material we helped Smith Engineering prepare to date and upcycle it into an "Information Memorandum". This is a glossy document designed to inform and encourage potential buyers to make a Non-Binding Indicative Offer. A few samples from the Smith Engineering IM are as follows:

## Index

In addition, we compiled an overview document to highlight the key aspects and "attract" the right buyer. See below for the Smith Engineering overview.

# INVESTMENT OVERVIEW

## COMPANY

**BUSINESS STAGE**

Mature

**SECTOR**

Light manufacture

**LOCATION**

Sydney

**YEAR FOUNDED**

1950

**TURNOVER**

2016: AUS$8.09M
2017: AUS$8.87M
2018: AUS$9.12M
2019: AUS$11.43M
2020: AUS$11.00M (estimated)
2021: AUS$11.10M (forecast)
2022: AUS$14.00M (forecast)

**EBIT**

2016: AUS$954K
2017: AUS$997K
2018: AUS$804K
2019: AUS$1.54M
2020: AUS$1.55M (estimated)
2021: AUS$1.96M (forecast)
2022: AUS$1.960M (forecast)

## CONTACT

Craig West
CEO & Founder
cwest@successionplus.com.au
Phone: +61 412 196 787

## EXECUTIVE SUMMARY

The business is an Australian owned and operated display stand designer and installer. Customers are primarily large retail chains who have a high volume of routine fit-outs and refurbishments.

## COMPETITIVE ADVANTAGES

- Strong relationships with major incumbent customers and suppliers
- Decades of combined experience in in-house designs and install services
- Approximately 8% market share
- An Enterprise Bargaining Agreement to continue the stable relationship with the employee group as a whole.

## KEY INVESTMENT HIGHLIGHTS

- A strong GM is in place, with a near majority ownership interest.
- An Employee Share Ownership Plan is in place, accounting for 25% of ownership ensuring key staff will remain.
- Well positioned for growth through new services invested in recent years.

## CORPORATE STRUCTURE

The specific owners are selling because they are approaching retirement. The business is well-positioned for growth and a larger player, with resources, is ideally placed to capitalise on it.

We also put together a dataroom for when buyers proved themselves serious enough to document a Non-Binding Indicative Offer, to give them an enhanced degree of comfort.

In all, we included around 180 documents organised into the 14 folders shown below, into an online portal that we confidentially restricted access to just these buyers. Importantly this system also manages an audit trail of questions and answers to reduce future disputes.

The process was quite smooth and aided the process getting the buyers to final Terms Sheets and ultimately an offer accepted by John and Jane.

| 01 | Corporate Governance | > |
|----|----------------------|---|
| 02 | Strategy and Planning | > |
| 03 | Financial Information | > |
| 04 | Clients | > |
| 05 | Strategic Partnerships | > |
| 06 | Personnel | > |
| 07 | Suppliers | > |
| 08 | Plant and Equipment | > |
| 09 | Premises | > |
| 10 | Policies and Procedures | > |
| 11 | Management | > |
| 12 | IT Systems | > |
| 13 | Marketing Collateral | > |
| 14 | Intellectual Property | > |

# • STEP 18
# LIQUIDITY EVENT

Once you have marketed your opportunity and used your Information Memorandum to get interest in your business, the aim is to form an agreement with your preferred buyer, or potentially several buyers. For the next step of the process, you will need a lawyer to help you with various agreements.

## 18.1 Finding a buyer

Your potential buyer will likely be in your current network. We've already covered the possibility of a management buy-out or employee share scheme to transfer ownership to people who already know your business well, care about the business and probably have ideas to improve it. This is an option well worth considering as it allows you to gradually work your way out of the business, dealing only with people you already know and trust.

If that isn't an option, the next most likely group of buyers are your competitors, who will be able to combine your business with theirs to achieve a bigger overall business, grow market share and decrease costs, removing duplicated staff or systems. Your suppliers are also potential buyers, particularly if you are a key customer they don't want to lose. By buying your business they instead get access to your customers, cut out the middle man and increase profits.

Similarly, your customer may buy your business because your product or service is crucial to their business and they can't risk losing supply, for example you manufacture patented packaging materials that they use for a high-profile product. Trade buyers may be bigger businesses than yours, but likely to be in the same or related industry. It is worth doing some research to find out which companies in your business are 'acquisitive' — a Google search should be enough to get you started. Most companies issue a press release after an acquisition, which will usually tell you what they paid for it. Find out what sort of multiples the company is prepared to pay, and how your business compares to any recent acquisitions. Most importantly, think strategic — who is your business most useful or valuable to?

Refer to the case study at 18.5 below to see an example of how to find a buyer.

## 18.2 Approaching a buyer

One of the key differences with the Succession Plus approach, compared to a 'typical business broker', is that we never advertise our businesses for sale. Our key benefit is being able to attract the 'right' buyer for a business by buyer research and building relationships with businesses in acquisition mode, ideally a listed company or a strategic buyer (see Step 7) to attract a higher price. We may approach a private equity firm we have previously worked with or an international investor.

This buyer approach is significant and a substantial differentiator in our business so we need to get it right. Firstly, this is about research and understanding very carefully what the buyer is looking for — in some of our most successful cases we have been able to 'build' the business to match almost exactly what the buyer is looking for!

In today's market, buyers are plentiful, but they are fussy — they are all looking for growth. One valid option is an acquisition, but unlike in 2006 buyers are more discerning and far more focused on the exact match they require to grow their business.

Refer to the case study below at 18.5 to see how to approach a buyer.

## 18.3 Legal agreements

Once you have marketed your opportunity and used your information memorandum to get interest in your business, the aim is to form an agreement with your preferred buyer, or potentially several buyers. You will also probably enter into a confidentiality or non-disclosure agreement (since you are potentially giving competitors insights into your business), and/or an exclusivity agreement.

You or your advisers will then usually meet with the buyer or their representatives to talk further about the opportunity and negotiate a price. This is your chance to shine and give the buyer comfort that yours is a low risk opportunity, pushing up the valuation multiple. You might sign a Heads of Agreement at this stage, in which the buyer states an intention to purchase shares in the business at an agreed price, subject to the findings of the due diligence.

You'll then have to make information available to the buyer and their advisers. This can be quite a formal process, depending on your business and the sort of buyer you are dealing with. You might just prepare some files for the buyer to access, or you may set up a data room with strict access levels. More commonly, you will have all the documents online in a virtual data room, using software such as Ansarada, an excellent custom-designed solution to manage the sale process.

Once you reach an agreement on price and terms you will need to effect the sale in a buy/sell agreement, detailing how and when the shares will change ownership, the sale price, how and when the funds will change hands, and any conditions upon which the agreement is made. You will need this agreement for all types of sale including for MBOs, employee share schemes and sales to existing shareholders and family members. It may seem like a very formal way to pass your business on to your children, particularly if they already work in the business, but ultimately you are selling shares in the business, and this does need to be recorded correctly to ensure future proof of ownership, and for tax purposes. The agreement may be requested for stamp duty purposes, so do make sure you get advice well in advance.

## 18.4 Project timeline

The sale process will typically take around six months to complete, with the first two months spent in preparation.

### Sale of business project timeline

| Step | Project | Duration | W1 | W2 | W3 | W4 | W5 | W6 | W7 | W8 | W9 | W10 | W11 | W12 | W13 | W14 | W15 | W16 | W17 | W18 | W19 | W20 | W21 | W22 | W23 | W24 | W25 | W26 |
|---|---|---|---|---|---|---|---|---|---|---|---|---|---|---|---|---|---|---|---|---|---|---|---|---|---|---|---|---|
| | | | | | | | | | | QUARTER 1 | | | | | | | | QUARTER 2 | | | | | | | | | | |
| 1 Exit options | 1a Buyer profile | 1w | ■ | | | | | | | | | | | | | | | | | | | | | | | | | |
| 2 Tax planning | 2a Tax analysis | 1w | | ■ | | | | | | | | | | | | | | | | | | | | | | | | |
| | 2b Tax advice | 1w | | | ■ | | | | | | | | | | | | | | | | | | | | | | | |
| | 2c Restructuring (if appropriate) | 1w | | | | ■ | | | | | | | | | | | | | | | | | | | | | | |
| 3 Due diligence | 3a Request & compile information | 2w | ■ | ■ | | | | | | | | | | | | | | | | | | | | | | | | |
| | 3b Reverse due diligence | 2w | | | ■ | ■ | | | | | | | | | | | | | | | | | | | | | | |
| | 3c Issues & gap resolution | 2w | | | | | ■ | ■ | | | | | | | | | | | | | | | | | | | | |
| | 3d Finalise compilation | 2w | | | | | | | ■ | ■ | | | | | | | | | | | | | | | | | | |
| | 3e Set up online due diligence room | 1w | | | | | | | | | ■ | | | | | | | | | | | | | | | | | |
| | 3f Upload documents | 1w | | | | | | | | | | ■ | | | | | | | | | | | | | | | | |
| | 3g Set up access permissions | 1w | | | | | | | | | | | ■ | | | | | | | | | | | | | | | |
| 4 Liquidity memorandum event | 4a Prepare information memorandum | 6w | | | | | | | | | | | ■ | ■ | ■ | ■ | ■ | ■ | | | | | | | | | | |
| | 4b Identify strategic buyer | 3w | | | | | | | | | | | | ■ | ■ | ■ | | | | | | | | | | | | |
| | 4c Approach buyer/s | 2w | | | | | | | | | | | | | | | ■ | ■ | | | | | | | | | | |
| | 4d Sign NDA | 1w | | | | | | | | | | | | | | | | | ■ | | | | | | | | | |
| | 4e Negotiate & sign term sheet | 1w | | | | | | | | | | | | | | | | | | ■ | | | | | | | | |
| | 4f Buyer due diligence | 2w | | | | | | | | | | | | | | | | | | ■ | ■ | | | | | | | |
| | 4g Draft & finalise sales contracts | 2w | | | | | | | | | | | | | | | | | | | | ■ | ■ | | | | | |
| 5 Pre-settlement | 5a Stock take | 2w | | | | | | | | | | | | | | | | | | | | | ■ | ■ | | | | |
| | 5b Employment contracts | 1w | | | | | | | | | | | | | | | | | | | | | | | ■ | | | |
| | 5c Leave liabilities | 1w | | | | | | | | | | | | | | | | | | | | | | | | ■ | | |
| | 5d Other settlement items | 2w | | | | | | | | | | | | | | | | | | | | | | | | ■ | ■ | |
| 6 Settlement | | 1d | | | | | | | | | | | | | | | | | | | | | | | | | | ■ |

## 18.5 Case Study

Smith Engineering Buyer Register

Date: 1 April 2020

| Target name | Contact | NDA signed | IM sent | Correspondence |
|---|---|---|---|---|
| Shearwater Private Equity (Sydney) | Toby Ronson (CEO) | 15/3 | 15/3 | 14/3: sent an email to Tony summarising opportunity. 15/3: received signed NDA, sent Toby IM. 16/3: Toby called and asked some questions. Asked Tony to complete a non-binding Indicative Offer to gain access to the dataroom. 25/3: Tony forwarded us a Non-Binding Indicative Offer. Opened access to dataroom to Toby and his team. They are currently compiling a series of questions for us to respond to. |
| Thompson Engineering (Vic) | Faith Thompson (co-owner) | N/A | N/A | 18/3: sent an email to Faith summarising opportunity. Thompson Engineering is a similar sized business in the same space as Smith Engineering but headquartered in Melbourne. John and Jane approved contacting Thompson, believing there may be scope for an eventual merger. 19/3: Faith declined the opportunity owing to disinclination toward interstate expansion. |

| Target name | Contact | NDA signed | IM sent | Correspondence |
|---|---|---|---|---|
| Johnson Engineering (NZ) | Ron Swanson (MD) | 18/3 | 21/3 | 18/3: sent an email to Ron summarising opportunity. 21/3: Ron asked for, accepted and signed an NDA. Sent the IM the very same day. 22/3: Ron called to ask some questions and suggested they have been considering an acquisition in Australia to gain a toe-hold in the larger market but also expressed a desire for outright rather than partial acquisition. Nonetheless, he agreed to make a Non-Binding Indicative Offer on a partial purchase basis to gain access to the dataroom. This is currently with Ron and his team under development. |
| Peabody Engineering (WA) | Dave Schultz (CEO) | N/A | N/A | 18/3: sent an email to Dave summarising opportunity. Similar rationale to Thompson Engineering for the approach. 23/3: Peabody declined the opportunity owing to having recently been purchased by a conglomerate itself. |

| Target name | Contact | NDA signed | IM sent | Correspondence |
|---|---|---|---|---|
| Philips Engineering (ACT) | Steve Philips (founder) | N/A | N/A | 18/3: sent an email to Steve summarising opportunity. Similar rationale to Thompson Engineering and Peabody Engineering for the approach. 27/3: Steve declined the opportunity owing to having recently made an acquisition and currently no bandwidth to look at another. |

The above is a sample of the buyer register we put together for Smith Engineering. As you can see, we kept detailed notes on progress and correspondence. This allowed us to keep John, Jane and Rod abreast of all developments routinely, but also keep each of the participants moving at a similar clip to one another.

This latter point is important because we always like to have multiple parties bidding for the same business, it creates some competitive tension. Here, Shearwater Private Equity and Johnson Engineering of New Zealand both showed substantiated interest.

Offers compared:

| Shearwater Private Equity | Johnson Engineering |
|---|---|
| • Purchase of the full 25% between John and Jane<br>• $1.8M in total<br>• 75% up-front<br>• Another 10% in 12 months if the business achieves $1.5M EBITDA in 2020 financial year<br>• Another 15% in 24 months if the business achieves $1.5M EBITDA in 2021 financial year | • Purchase of the full 25% between John and Jane<br>• $2M in total<br>• 50% up-front<br>• Another 50% in 12 months if the business achieves $1.5M EBITDA in 2020 financial year |

The above shows a common issue in business sales — price paid is only good if it is accompanied by acceptable terms.

Ultimately, Jane and opted to sell down to Shearwater on the basis of:

- They have a strong and proven team of consultants who can slot right in assisting with the Business Plan
- They have a reputation for being patient capital — they seek "boring" investments without the need to exit at a huge multiple (which is not achievable with Smith Engineering because of its ownership structure)
- They are located nearby — headquarters in Sydney.

The lower total amount offered was not considered to be a major issue.

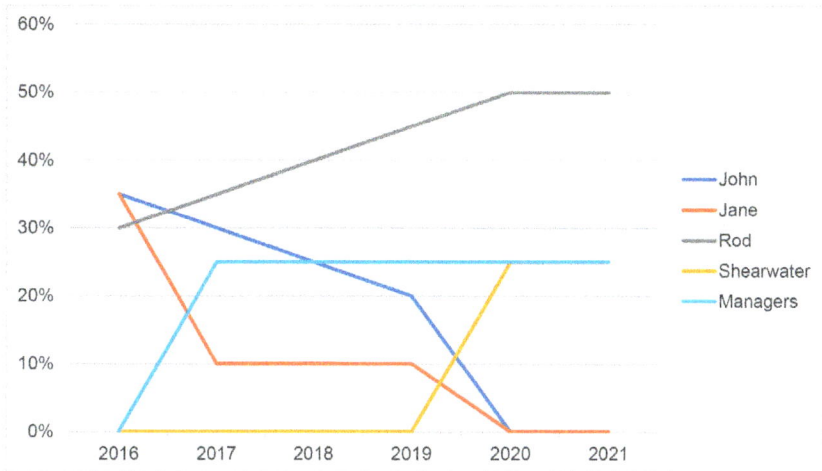

After the transaction, ownership of Smith Engineering was as follows:

- 50% Rod
- 25% Management
- 25% Shearwater Private Equity.

A business owner's finances change significantly after a successful exit (hopefully with a substantial sum of money in the bank). It is important to reorganise your financial affairs to maximise your future income.

## 19.1 Life after an exit

The last stage after your business sale is to take a brief look at how you manage the cash that you have extracted. You are now an investor rather than a business owner, with potentially a significant sum to invest and provide for a long retirement.

So, we look at asset protection, estate planning and investment strategies to ensure you have the ongoing income stream that you need.

The average 50-year-old male in 2018 can expect to live until 82 so if you retire at the typical age of 65 you can expect to live another 17 years and need substantial capital to fund your retirement, particularly in an environment of low interest rate returns and fluctuating markets.

The reality is most business owners have been used to using their business cashflow to prop up personal income as and when required, and in many cases vice versa. This is no longer possible as we no longer own the business. So, we need to think about engaging the help of an expert in the area of financial planning to ensure our assets are owned in the right entity (see Step 20 on asset protection), and that the assets are reasonably capital secured.

For example, we don't want our entire investment portfolio in high-risk growth stocks such as gold exploration stocks (which may well quadruple in value if gold is found but may also achieve zero value) but stocks that are able to supply a reliable income to fund your retirement going forward for the next 10 or 20 years.

In many cases using a self-managed super fund (not just at retirement but throughout business ownership and leading up to retirement) can produce significant advantages in terms of asset protection and taxation.

## 19.2 Case Study

Because we were anticipating a major change to the composition of assets in John and Jane's wealth structure, we reviewed their position with the help of John and Jane's financial planner, Wes Anderson.

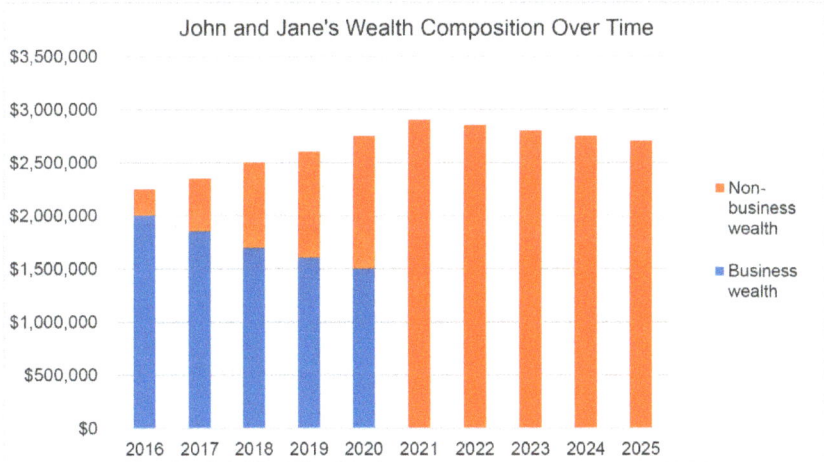

John and Jane's Wealth Composition Over Time

We mapped this out ahead of the deal with Shearwater to ensure John and Jane's retirement plans would not be jeopardised by accepting their offer.

They were able to gain comfort that their retirement lifestyle and wellbeing needs would be suitably funded by accepting the offer from Shearwater.

# • STEP 20
# ASSET PROTECTION

Asset protection is a means of using business practices and structures to create barriers between your assets and the risks faced by your business or yourself. It's part of an insurance strategy to make sure that everything you build is protected.

## 20.1 Time to review your assets

While you may have set up an effective structure for your business, your divestment or retirement is the time to review your assets to see whether your structure is still appropriate. Your assets may be in jeopardy in retirement because of the way they are invested or owned. The decisions we make in estate planning will also affect the ownership of assets and therefore our ability to protect them, and will also affect your retirement income in terms of investment planning. Because these are all interrelated it is important to get good advice to balance the needs of tax planning, investment planning and asset protection.

When you are in business your asset protection strategy aims to protect your assets from risk and, most importantly from being sued. One way to protect yourself is to take out insurance policies. A key component of the legal aspects of selling a business is to minimise the potential future threat to those assets in the event of, for example, a claim against an indemnity, warranty or guarantee provided as part of a seller business contract.

Another crucial strategy is quarantining your assets so that you can enjoy the benefits of controlling your assets without the risk of ownership. This involves building an ownership structure where you own nothing but still easily access the assets and the income they generate. One way to do this is by transferring the assets to someone who has a lower risk of being sued and who is isolated from your business. Commonly this is the business owner's spouse.

Gearing against your assets is an effective way to limit your ownership and therefore risk. So rather than paying off your mortgage on the sale of your business, you maintain some debt and free up equity to invest in other assets through structures that make investments for your benefit, in another name.

Trusts are one of the most flexible yet misunderstood and under-utilised structures available. The primary difference between a trust and a company is that trusts don't pay tax on their income, but all income must be distributed to the beneficiaries, who will pay tax on the earnings. Trusts offer excellent asset protection because assets are held for the benefit of the beneficiaries, without real ownership of the asset. Self-managed superannuation funds are also a form of trust and offer some excellent asset protection and tax advantages for retirement income. A testamentary trust can also be established to take ownership of your assets in the event of your death.

One final way of protecting your assets is through your will. In many cases a strategic direction can be established and then given to your accountants and lawyers to implement and manage on your behalf.

Please refer to our "Protect It" book and our website www.successionplus.com.au for further insight into how to protect your assets.

## 20.2 Case Study

Post-exit, John and Jane's asset composition had changed, so we conducted a review as at 1 July 2021, with Wes. We concluded that everything was largely in order.

Mr John & Jane Smith's personal balance sheets:

- Owner occupied home — jointly owned, value $1 million, no debt. John and Jane aim to downsize in a couple of years
- Investment property — value $500,000, debt of $200,000
- Share portfolio — 250,000 (no margin loan facility)
- Superannuation — $1.25 million, balance investment option, binding death benefit nominations in place
- Collectible and personal effects — $100,000
- Total net assets: $2.9 million.

Insurances:

- Life cover of $1 million each through superannuation — primary purpose is for establishing an inheritance for the children
- Private health cover through NIB
- No income to protect
- TPD and Trauma not utilised due to expensiveness of premiums.

# ESTATE PLANNING

## 21.1 Key issues with Estate Planning

When I talk to most business owners the two key outcomes they are looking for from an exit strategy are:

- Firstly, that the business continues successfully after they leave, and
- Secondly, that somehow the exit strategy can provide a financial mechanism not only to fund their retirement but to provide for their children and, in many cases, grandchildren.

It is very common for business owners to have goals like paying for the grandchildren's private school education, or to fund a daughter or son into their first investment property.

One of the key issues with estate planning becomes the ownership of assets given the tax advantages of self managed superannuation funds previously described. It may be that we can use a self managed superannuation fund as a family wealth vehicle, providing benefits in terms of asset protection, simplicity and efficiency of operation as well as estate planning aspects where the underlying ownership of the assets can provide benefits to family members and subsequent generations.

We also commonly see business owners purchase related assets, for example the commercial premises the business operates from, in a property trust, family trust or self- managed super fund. Again, that asset can be left for the benefit of family members into the future, long after the business exit has been completed.

This area is often ignored by many business owners who may have had a will drawn up when they owned the business but haven't changed it once their position has changed. After the exit the mix of assets and the risk profile is substantially different, and this needs to be taken into account, as well as personal and financial goals for the family.

## 21.2 Case Study

For the same reason as in Step 20, we also conducted an Estate Planning review, with help from Wes Anderson, and the family lawyer, Bill Travis.

### Family Governance

Both John and Jane have Wills in place with Testamentary Trusts, Powers of Attorney and Guardianship:

- in the first instance, the surviving spouse will receive control of all assets via a Testamentary Trust, with Grace and Chloe, their two non-dependent children to join as primary beneficiaries
- if both pass, the assets pass to a single Testamentary Trust — to be controlled by Grace
- Powers of Attorney and Guardianship are both enduring and both transfer decision making power to each other in the first instance
- if both were to lose capacity, then Grace and Chloe become Attorneys and Guardians jointly.

# WHAT IF IT'S TOO LATE?

It's never too late
Succession planning is a process

While we recommend a full succession plan that progresses over several years, we also see a lot of clients who are close to retirement age or have hit poor health who may not have time to follow the ideal plan. It's not too late to take steps to maximise the investment you've made in your business and achieve a positive outcome whatever your circumstances.

## It's never too late

Think of it like trying to sell your house quickly — there are simple things you can do to increase the value of your house which don't require you to spend a lot of time or money, for example clearing out clutter, cleaning up the yard, a quick coat of paint. Likewise there are some things you can do to improve the value of your business in the short term. They won't have the same impact as a strategic succession plan, but they will improve the buyer's perception of your business.

Buyers use information as a means of assessing the value of your business, for example ensuring that your financial, operational and marketing information is well-organised, presented and up to date. Poorly managed information can raise doubt or fear in a potential buyer's mind. Key areas a potential buyer will look at are:

- Your accounts, financial statements, tax and GST returns
- Management accounting and financial information that the buyer can verify
- Contracts in place with suppliers
- Details of key client arrangements. Where no formal contracts are in place a document outlining the strength and length of key relationships will help
- Current staff employment agreements and assurances that staff will stay with the business
- Website and other marketing and promotional materials are current
- Documented business systems, processes, policies and procedures, including operating manuals.

You may also be able to identify intangible assets that add to your business value, for example customer database, proprietary software, a unique staff incentive that attracts and retains employees, or documented intellectual property.

If you don't have all of this information in place or up to date, outsourcing is a way of tidying up the business quickly and efficiently. With the help of professional advisers you can develop quality information in a short period of time to set you up for success.

## Succession planning is a process

Succession or exit planning is not an event. It's not a transaction. It's not something that happens quickly. In 99.9% of our clients, it's a process, and it takes a considerable amount of time and so, often, I talk about a multi-year process. I say to clients when they ask me, "How soon should I start this process?" The first part of my answer is "as soon as possible." The second part of my answer is that you need at least three to five years. The reason we need three to five years is not technical or practical. We could, for example, implement an employee share plan or sell a business on the market in three to six months, no problems at all for either of those two things to happen from a technical and practical point of view. But have we got the owner buy-in? Have we got the owner engaged in the process and involved? Have we prepared them adequately for retirement? Have we looked at those three frameworks, the business, the money and the individual to make sure we've got all of that sorted out?

The definition of successful succession or exit is getting those three things right, get:

1 the business right
2 the financial side right for the owner and their family, and
3 the individual right.

How are they going to gradually extract themselves from this business that they have been working in for so long? What are they going to do when they retire?

An interesting book to refer to is by Bo Burlingham called "Finish Big: How Great Entrepreneurs Exit Their Companies on Top." He talks about the process, as well as the exploratory phase — Stage

1 in our 21-Step process. This conversation with owners about what they would like to do, their role identity, their ongoing process for succession, how are we going to transition them, the business, their wealth, etc., as part of that overall process. That's a very significant step for business owners. We need to know all of this before we can design an exit strategy.

Before we can go and implement a strategy, we need to know what is the goal and outcome of the owner? What are the facts? What does the business look like? What does their wealth look like? What is their financial position? What are the risks that they're facing etc.? So, we can actually design the plan from there?

The most critical step in both the M3 Framework and in our 21-Step Process is that first step, starting, begin with the end in mind, and getting this background right before we go down the road to anything further.

In conclusion, the key thing to really understand is that psychology is a big piece of the jigsaw and it's a piece that you ignore at your peril. If we ignore that issue, you will never get the right relationship and level of engagement with clients. I know it works because we've got several clients that we've worked with at Succession Plus for many years.

Refer to our website www.successionplus.com.au for a number of insightful articles, blogs, videos and webinars.

# NOTES